Good
Food
from a
Small
Kitchen

Good Food
from a
Small
Kitchen

Moira Hodgson

Prentice Hall Press

New York   London   Toronto   Sydney   Tokyo

Prentice Hall Press
Gulf+Western Building
One Gulf+Western Plaza
New York, New York   10023

Copyright © 1985 by Moira Hodgson

Library of Congress Cataloging-in-Publication Data

Hodgson, Moira.
    Good food from a small kitchen / Moira Hodgson.
        p.   cm.
    Previously published: New York : Times Books, c1985.
    Bibliography: p.
    Includes index.
    ISBN 0-13-360306-7
    1. Cookery.   I. Title.
    TX652.H577   1989   641.5—dc20   89-3926
                                                   CIP

Designed by Doris Borowsky

Manufactured in the United States of America

10   9   8   7   6   5   4   3   2   1

First Prentice Hall Press Edition

for Michael

ACKNOWLEDGMENTS

Thanks go to John Cage, Nicola Civetta, Penelope Casas, Ray Dinardo, Mark David, Pascal Dirringer, Michel Fitoussi, Raeford Liles, Gianni Minali, Madeleine van Bruegel, Wolfgang Puck, Colette Rossant, Stephen Spector, and David Waltuck for ideas or recipes and to John Montuori of Jefferson Market.

CONTENTS

Introduction *1*

ONE. Hors d'Oeuvres and Salads *7*

TWO. Pasta, Pizza, Eggs, and Cheese *30*

THREE. Fish *59*

FOUR. Shellfish *83*

FIVE. Poultry and Game *100*

SIX. Meat *127*

SEVEN. Soups, Stews, and Curries *158*

EIGHT. Vegetables *190*

NINE. Rice, Legumes, and Grains *228*

TEN. Desserts *257*

ELEVEN. Basic Sauces and Stocks *278*

Bibliography *287*

Index *289*

Introduction

Landlords and architects think that people who live in small apartments hate cooking. This is why the typical city kitchen is an airless hole where the cook must work alone.

My kitchen is an afterthought, secreted in a disused closet off the hall. It measures 4½ by 6½ feet. Its layout may sound familiar: The refrigerator is set directly alongside the stove, which is in turn jammed against the sink. When the oven heats up, the side of the refrigerator buckles. If space is needed for anything more complicated than chopping onions, the dish drainer has to go into the hall. If I fry, I have to open the front door.

I've cooked here for more than fifteen years. In this exasperating cubicle I've done the research for cookbooks and food columns and prepared meals to serve as many as forty people at a time. I'm so used to its limitations that I'd probably be lost in one of those sleek professional kitchens featured in glossy magazines. I no longer envy those querulous and exacting cooks blessed with every kitchen gadget.

When you work in such a small space, you sometimes feel that your movements have been choreographed by Jacques Tati. At one ill-fated dinner party, coming from the kitchen with a roast leg of lamb in hand, I tripped over the cat. The roast made a pirouette and landed on the fur coat a guest had carelessly flung over a chair in the hallway. Bully (the cat) and I lunged for the meat while the carving knife, which lay on the plate I held, slid down into my thumb. I reached for a paper towel and the entire roll unraveled. I found a space for the dish, mopped up the blood, wrapped my thumb and was trying to wash the gravy from the coat when its owner called, "Anything I can do to help?" One of the first lessons a small kitchen teaches you is to keep calm, and I was able to reply without a quaver, "No, no, everything's fine."

You also learn not to be overambitious. Another event I'd hate to repeat was my attempt to roast a suckling pig one Christmas. It had to be soaked overnight, so I put it in the bathtub. A Julia Child recipe instructed me to remove its eyes with grape scissors but I had only an ordinary knife and used it to an effect that would have gone down well in a Brian de Palma film. When the pig was stuffed and ready for cooking, I discovered it was too big to go in the oven. So I had to cut it in half and serve it with a belly band of flowers.

Over the years I have tried every kind of recipe in this kitchen, from French to Mexican to Japanese. But it was a while before I finally learned that I couldn't produce lavish meals and also entertain my guests. I used to invite people to dinner and spend the entire evening alone in the kitchen.

All would have been fine had a I possessed one of these old-fashioned kitchens with Aga stoves, copper pans, and a long wooden table at which friends could sit and chat while I worked. But I was far away at the other end of a narrow hall listening to the hum of voices and laughter as they enjoyed themselves without me. After dinner I would be exhausted and my overfed friends would leave.

When your kitchen is too small to allow another person in to help, it's self-defeating to make complicated meals. Now I generally serve only a main course, usually a dish that can be prepared in advance or something that doesn't require constant attention. I follow it with green salad, French-peasant style—on the same plate—unless we've had fish. With the salad there is cheese and hot French bread. After the cheese and salad I offer perhaps a light homemade dessert.

I serve food as often as possible in the dish it was cooked in. Over the years I've collected casseroles that can go on top of the stove and in the oven. I have a wok, a cast-iron frying pan, a couscousière, a vegetable steamer, and a Moroccan *tagin* (an earthenware pot with a conical lid used for stews). Because most of the shelves are beyond reach, I've learned to think ahead so that I don't have to climb on a chair to forage in the top of a cupboard while a sauce curdles on the stove. Pots and pans I hang on the wall.

I have a twenty-five-year-old two-speed blender, a coffee and spice grinder, many sharp knives, wooden spoons, and two wooden chopping boards. On my four-burner gas stove I keep two iron trivets instead of lung-destroying asbestos mats. In the summer I grow basil, parsley, coriander, rosemary, thyme, and tarragon on the fire escape.

Three years ago I acquired a food processor. But I live without a sorbet machine, a pasta machine, a marble slab for pastry making, a freezer (except the top of the refrigerator), or canning equipment. I don't have a Garland stove, a Kitchen Aid® mixer or matching sets of copper pans.

For dinner parties I make stews the day before because this improves their flavor and leaves little kitchen work after the guests have arrived. Roasts are convenient. Once you know your oven, it's simply a question of timing, and they can be left to cook with only occasional basting.

I also like to bake a large fish, such as striped bass or red snapper, marinated first in orange, lemon, or lime juices, with herbs, spices, or garlic. I often cook chops, because they are easy. Like many neighborhoods these days, mine offers excellent fresh pasta. When I'm going to steam vegetables or stir-fry them (with the front door open, of course), I chop the ingredients in advance and store them in the refrigerator in plastic bags.

Although I've become philosophical about my kitchen, I still hate it. I'd like to meet the person who made the conversion. Did he think that the tenant of this lovely old Greenwich Village apartment, with its high ceilings, huge living room, and marble fireplace, would not wish to share its pleasures with friends? Or perhaps he thought that anyone who lived here was probably Bohemian enough to do most of the cooking in the fireplace.

I've only once appreciated my kitchen. It was on my return from a summer of cooking in the back of a Volkswagen bus. For six weeks, two of us had traveled through Lapland, drinking strange liqueurs and eating fresh salmon and reindeer meat. Our ideas of happy cookouts had been bruised by the first onslaught of mosquitoes, which descended like locusts. So we took our meals in the back of the bus where the furnishings consisted of two air mattresses and a Coleman stove.

It gives me perverse pleasure sometimes to dip into Escoffier and read about dishes that require two tablespoons of duxelles, a vol-au-vent crust, a julienne of truffles with perhaps a garnish of quenelles de brochet and shrimp tails and the exhortation to *serve instantly*. But Escoffier, in his most depressed moments, couldn't have conceived of a kitchen like mine.

So I decided to write a book of simple recipes for a small kitchen. Many of them can be put together easily after you get home from work. They are planned to use the least amount of dishes possible, and if they do require the space of a whole counter (while rolling out pastry, for example), they can be made ahead of time. They are eclectic, because I love all kinds of food. Food shops have become much more adventurous in the things they stock, so I have included recipes for some esoteric items, such as fava beans, monkfish, baby artichokes, shad, and quail. But the main thing is that the recipes in this book are simple and designed so that people with small kitchens can enjoy cooking without going mad.

ONE

Hors d'Oeuvres and Salads

For obvious reasons, salads are a boon for the cook with a small kitchen, especially in the summer, when the prospect of spending any time at all in the kitchen is less than alluring.

Ad-libbing a salad is one of the things I like to do most; I enjoy making up a meal from a mixture of raw and cooked things, composed according to what is at hand, and dressed with a good oil. It can be the main course, eaten with French or Italian bread, or served as a first course to be followed by something light, such as pasta.

Ingredients for a salade composée might consist of leftover roast beef or steak, veal, fish, roast chicken, or game. Boiled potatoes, cooked rice, or beans can be added. And there is a wide choice of vegetables: peas, young spinach leaves, or tiny beets, cooked and sliced, whole baby zucchini, sliced raw mushrooms or red peppers, charred and skinned, red onions, cauliflower or broccoli, broken into flowerets and blanched. Hard-boiled eggs, quartered and sprinkled with fresh herbs or decorated with tiny pieces of pimiento, or black olives always make the salad look pretty when arranged on top. Then there are canned foods that can be added, such as tuna or sardines, or those items that are expensive when bought in quantity, such as shellfish or lobster tails.

When you are putting salads together, cut the ingredients into similar-sized pieces. Do not chop them too small, mix together too many ingredients, or toss them into a mushy heap. For example, if you are adding tuna to a potato or white bean salad, place chunks of tuna on top of the salad rather than mixing it in and serve it on individual plates. Otherwise the salad will lose both flavor and texture.

When you're making a dressing for composed salads, it is sometimes a good idea to make two. A simple vinaigrette can be used to coat the vegetables, and then, if you are serving pieces of chicken or fish in the salad, you might make a thick, creamy sauce, such as mayonnaise, to pass separately at the table. A second sauce makes the whole thing more elegant.

When red currants are in season, apart from being made into jellies and desserts, they make a particularly lush salad dressing when puréed with oil and lemon juice. The sauce is a bright luminous pink, slightly tart, and it looks very attractive served on slices of ripe avocado.

To go with cold meat or broiled chicken, a delicious salad consists of very young haricot beans, just picked, blanched and tossed while hot in olive oil and raspberry vinegar. The slightly sweet-sour taste of raspberry vinegar also goes well with Kirby cucumbers.

Cultivated mushrooms don't have much character, but when you can find really fresh white ones, they can be sliced raw and sprinkled with lemon juice and fresh marjoram or summer savory. They go nicely with broiled chicken.

The secret to a good salad lies in the dressing. Here are some tips:

Use only the best olive oils, such as extra virgin oils available in specialty stores. They are made from the first cold pressing of the finest olives and have not been extracted by chemicals or heat. I particularly like the dark green fruity Tuscan olive oils and the clear, amber oils from France. If you can't get the extra virgin oils, Goya brand, widely sold in supermarkets, has a good strong flavor.

Walnut or hazelnut oil make excellent dressings. They should be bought in small cans and refrigerated, because they go rancid quickly.

Do not overdo the vinegar. Too much makes a salad watery and acid. The best vinegars are wine vinegars. They can be red or white and are sometimes flavored with tarragon. Balsamic vinegars from Italy are excellent, so rich and dark you need no help from mustard or garlic in a dressing.

Do not slavishly follow quantities given for salad dressings. Taste as you make it; the strength of vinegar varies.

When adding garlic to a salad dressing, pound it to a purée with salt and pepper (with a mortar and pestle) before adding it.

Do not add tomatoes to a green salad; their juice makes the lettuce leaves soggy.

Dressings for cooked vegetables, such as potatoes, beans, or cauliflower, should be added while the vegetables are warm. They will absorb the dressing more easily and, if allowed to sit for an hour or two before being served, will develop a powerful fragrance.

Fresh herbs, such as tarragon, chervil, or chives, should be snipped and added at the last moment.

Basil leaves should be torn or snipped with sharp scissors, not chopped, otherwise the edges will turn brown.

Avoid using dried herbs, except for oregano, in salad dressings.

When making mayonnaise, use good-quality oil. The oil and eggs must be at room temperature. If the mayonnaise curdles, it can be saved by beating in an extra egg yolk. For a light dressing, salad and olive oil can be combined.

To begin a meal, you might serve a small dish of antipasto—a perfect hors d'oeuvre with minimum fuss. It might consist of anchovies with sliced raw mushrooms, a piece of aged Parmesan with fennel, Genoa salami, black olives, or prosciutto with melon or figs (figs, incidentally, are also wonderful at the end of a meal, with goat cheese and a sweet white wine). Another delicious hors d'oeuvre or lunchtime salad can be made with seasonal vegetables whole and raw or peeled, sliced or chopped, served with *aïoli* or *aillade Toulousaine,* an *aïoli* made with pounded walnuts, olive oil, and garlic. This sauce, which is from the Languedoc, is also good with cold meat or chicken.

AVOCADO SALAD WITH RED CURRANT VINAIGRETTE

½ cup peanut or safflower oil
  Lemon juice to taste
¼ cup fresh red currants
  Sugar to taste
  Coarse salt and freshly ground pepper to taste
2 ripe avocados
2 tablespoons chopped chives

1. Combine the oil, lemon juice, and red currants in a blender. Blend until smooth. Season with sugar, salt, and pepper.

2. Spoon some of the sauce onto 4 small individual plates. Peel and slice the avocados and arrange the slices on top of the sauce. Spoon the remaining sauce on top of the avocado slices. Sprinkle with chives and serve immediately.

Yield: 4 servings.

AÏOLI

Much has been written about this sauce, which is basically a garlic mayonnaise. It is the classic accompaniment to Bourride (page 168), the fish stew, and also goes well with cold fish or meat and raw or cooked vegetables. It should be very thick and garlicky. Use a mortar and pestle or a food processor to make it.

```
4  garlic cloves
   Coarse salt
2  egg yolks at room temperature
   About 1 cup extra virgin olive oil
   Juice of 1 lemon
```

1. Peel the garlic and place the cloves in a mortar or a food processor. Add a little salt and pound or process them into a paste.

2. Add the egg yolks and beat thoroughly, until they are a pale creamy yellow. Very gradually add the olive oil, beating constantly until the sauce is extremely thick.

3. Add the lemon juice and a teaspoon of warm water and continue beating, adding more oil to thicken, or water to thin, until the sauce is the right consistency.

Yield: About 1 cup.

AILLADE TOULOUSAINE

¼ pound walnuts, shelled
3 garlic cloves
Coarse salt
½ to ¾ cup extra virgin olive oil
Freshly ground pepper (white, if possible)

1. Using a mortar and pestle, pound the walnuts and the garlic and salt to a paste.

2. Add the oil drop by drop to start with, then little by little, beating well until you have a smooth sauce. Season with salt and pepper.

Yield: About 1 cup.

SALADE AUX HARICOTS VERTS

1½ pounds haricots verts
½ cup extra virgin olive oil
2 to 3 tablespoons raspberry vinegar, or to taste
3 shallots, minced
Coarse salt and freshly ground black pepper to taste
1 tablespoon chopped chervil or flat-leafed parsley leaves

1. Cook the haricots verts in boiling water until tender but still crisp. Drain.

2. Combine the oil, vinegar, shallots, salt, and pepper. Pour the mixture over the beans and toss. Sprinkle with chervil and serve at room temperature.

Yield: 4 servings.

FAVA BEANS NIÇOISE

*When fresh fava beans are in season, this salad is a delightful varia-
tion on the traditional Salade Niçoise, which contains haricots verts.
Use only red ripe tomatoes in season.*

2 pounds fava beans in their shells
2 medium-sized ripe tomatoes
1 small red onion
4 tablespoons extra virgin olive oil
1 tablespoon red wine vinegar, or to taste
   Dash of Dijon mustard
   Coarse salt and freshly ground pepper to taste
1 can imported tuna fish
4 hard-boiled eggs
4 anchovy fillets
3 tablespoons snipped fresh basil or tarragon leaves
¼ pound black olives (Gaeta or Niçoise)

1. Shell the fava beans and simmer the beans in water to cover for 5
minutes, or until they are cooked. Drain.

2. Chop the tomatoes and onion and put them in a salad bowl with
the beans.

3. Make a dressing with the oil, vinegar, mustard, salt, and pepper.
Add to the salad and toss thoroughly.

4. Place chunks of tuna on top of the salad and garnish with the
eggs, quartered and arranged around the edge of the bowl to form a
border. Place a piece of anchovy on each. Sprinkle with basil and
garnish with the olives.

Yield: 4 servings.

WHITE BEAN SALAD

This can be served in mounds on a plate and topped with a wedge of good imported Italian tuna fish. Or, for a more robust flavor, you can use red wine vinegar, anchovies, and garlic, mashed to a paste, in the dressing. If you use canned beans, drain them thoroughly and rinse off the canning liquid.

White beans are also good cooked and puréed and mixed with olive oil and fresh mint leaves.

1½ cups white beans
2 carrots, scraped and cut into 2-inch pieces
1 onion, quartered
  Bouquet garni (thyme and parsley sprigs and bay leaf tied in a cheesecloth bag)

FOR THE DRESSING

½ cup extra virgin olive oil (preferably green Tuscan)
2 tablespoons fresh lemon juice
3 scallions, including green part, chopped
  Coarse salt and freshly ground black pepper to taste
  Parsley, tarragon, or summer savory for garnish

1. Soak the beans overnight in water to cover. Bring them to a boil with the carrot, onion, and bouquet garni. Simmer for 1 to 1½ hours. The beans should be tender but not mushy.

2. Meanwhile, prepare the dressing: Combine the oil, lemon juice, scallions, salt, and pepper. Taste as you go along.

3. Drain the beans and put them in a bowl. Add the dressing and toss. Marinate for 1 or 2 hours at room temperature before serving. Then taste again and add more salt, pepper, or lemon juice, if needed. Garnish with herbs and serve at room temperature.

Yield: 4 servings.

BEET SALAD MIMOSA

This delicate salad goes well with cold roast duck or chicken.

2 pounds beets
4 hard-boiled eggs
4 tablespoons extra virgin olive oil
2 garlic cloves
2 tablespoons red wine vinegar
  Coarse salt and freshly ground pepper to taste
  Chopped fresh chives for garnish

1. Simmer the beets in their skins in water to cover for 45 minutes.

2. Drain the beets and put them in a roasting pan. Bake for 20 minutes. Cool.

3. Meanwhile, peel and chop the eggs.

4. Heat the oil in a skillet and fry the garlic until it is golden. Remove from the heat. Remove the garlic and combine the oil with the vinegar, salt, and pepper. Peel and slice the beets while they are still warm and add them to the mixture. Toss thoroughly and arrange on a serving dish. Sprinkle with the chopped eggs and chives.

Yield: 4 servings.

CELERIAC VINAIGRETTE

Serve this as a first course or with cold turkey, ham, pork, tongue, or chicken.

1 head celeriac (about 1 pound)
1 cup chicken stock (page 285)
6 whole black peppercorns
¼ cup extra virgin olive oil
2 teaspoons red wine vinegar, or to taste
1 teaspoon Dijon mustard
  Coarse salt and freshly ground pepper to taste
3 scallions, minced
2 tablespoons chopped parsley leaves

1. Peel the celeriac and cut it into 1-inch cubes. Bring the chicken stock to a boil and add the celeriac, plus water if needed. Add the peppercorns. Cover and simmer until the celeriac is tender, about 20 minutes. Drain.

2. Combine the oil, vinegar, mustard, salt, and pepper. Slice the cooked celeriac and put it in a serving bowl. Add the dressing, scallions, and parsley. Toss and serve at room temperature.

Yield: 4 servings.

CELERIAC WITH MUSHROOMS AND PARMESAN

Serve as a first course.

1 head celeriac (about 1 pound)
1 pound very fresh white mushrooms
2 ounces good-quality aged Parmesan, cut into small pieces
  Juice of 1 lemon, or to taste
¼ cup extra virgin olive oil
2 tablespoons chopped parsley leaves
  Coarse salt and freshly ground pepper to taste

1. Peel the celeriac and cut it into matchstick-sized pieces. Put in a bowl of cold water to prevent from discoloring.

2. Wash the mushrooms, dry them thoroughly, and slice them thinly. Pat the celeriac dry with paper towels and combine it in a salad bowl with the mushrooms and Parmesan. In a separate bowl mix together the lemon juice, oil, parsley, salt, and pepper. Pour the mixture over the vegetables and toss. Correct the seasoning, if necessary.

Yield: 4 servings.

CHARRED RED OR YELLOW PEPPERS

These will keep for a week in a tightly closed jar in the refrigerator.

8 sweet red or yellow peppers
½ cup extra virgin olive oil
2 tablespoons balsamic vinegar
1 garlic clove, minced
   Coarse salt and freshly ground pepper to taste
2 tablespoons chopped parsley leaves
2 tablespoons chopped fresh mint leaves

1. Char the peppers by turning them over a gas flame with a fork or charring them on all sides under a hot broiler. Wrap them in paper towels and let them cool slightly. Then scrape off the skin, cut the peppers in quarters, and remove the seeds.

2. Combine the oil, vinegar, and garlic. Mix thoroughly and season with salt and pepper. Pour the mixture over the peppers and toss. Arrange the peppers on a serving dish and sprinkle them with the parsley and mint.

Yield: 4 servings.

TABBOULEH WITH FETA

Tabbouleh is a cracked wheat cereal. It makes a refreshing salad when it is flavored with feta, scallions, and mint. Serve this as a main course for lunch or to accompany cold meat or chicken.

1 cup cracked wheat (bulgur)
4 medium-sized ripe tomatoes
6 scallions
½ pound feta cheese, crumbled
4 tablespoons chopped mint leaves
2 tablespoons chopped parsley leaves
6 tablespoons extra virgin olive oil
Juice of 1 lemon, or to taste
Coarse salt and freshly ground pepper to taste

1. Put the cracked wheat in a bowl, cover it with cold water and allow it to sit for 20 minutes.

2. Drop the tomatoes into boiling water for a couple of minutes. Drain, peel, seed, and chop them. Slice the scallions.

3. Drain the cracked wheat and press out as much water as possible; then dry on paper towels. Put the cracked wheat in a serving bowl.

4. Stir in the tomatoes, scallions, feta, mint, and parsley. Add the olive oil, lemon juice, salt, and pepper. Toss, cover, chill until ready to serve.

Yield: 4 servings.

POTATO SALAD

Use yellow waxy or red-skinned potatoes. They should be coated with the mayonnaise—which is homemade—while they are still warm. This salad is also good in antipasto, arranged on a serving dish along with slices of pimiento, chopped cucumber, white beans tossed in olive oil, halved hard-boiled eggs, tomatoes, and chopped onion. It can be garnished with pitted Gaeta or Calamata olives and anchovies or served on individual plates, topped with chunks of good-quality imported tuna, sprinkled with capers.

6 medium-sized yellow or waxy or red-skinned potatoes
1 egg yolk
1 teaspoon red wine vinegar, or to taste
1 teaspoon Dijon mustard
   About ½ cup extra virgin olive oil
   About ½ cup safflower or peanut oil
   Coarse salt and freshly ground pepper to taste
1 small red onion, chopped
   Chopped fresh parsley leaves for garnish

1. Boil the potatoes in their skins in salted water to cover until cooked but firm. Meanwhile, make the mayonnaise. Beat the egg yolks in a small bowl with a fork until the yolk is thick and sticky. Mix in the vinegar and the mustard. Gradually add the oils, beating them in little by little until you have a thick mayonnaise. (If the mayonnaise curdles, beat in another egg yolk.) Season with salt and pepper.

2. When the potatoes are cooked, slice or quarter them while they are still warm. (They can be peeled if you prefer.) Toss them gently in the mayonnaise with the onion and the parsley. Serve at room temperature.

Yield: 4 servings.

FETA CHEESE AND SALAMI SALAD

Feta, a crumbly white salty cheese, is excellent in salads, with to-matoes, cucumbers, and black olives coated with a rich green extra virgin olive oil. It also makes a delicious hors d'oeuvre when served with stuffed vine leaves and flat Arabian bread.

Salads that include feta are substantial enough to be served as main courses. This cheese is very good crumbled into potato salad with Genoa salami and flavored with fennel seeds.

Feta was originally made from ewe's milk by shepherds in the mountains near Athens. The demand for it is now so great that it is often made with goat's milk or a combination of goat's milk and cow's milk, sometimes skimmed or partly skimmed. It is also made in the United States and Italy. The best feta is sold "pickled" in brine, often stored in large wooden kegs.

The cheese should not be allowed to dry out. If it is not used right away, it can be stored in milky water. Mature feta is sharper and saltier than young feta and loses some of its saltiness, while remain-ing moist, if stored in milk.

A mixture of red and yellow peppers looks especially attractive in this salad. A dry white wine or a chilled Beaujolais are good to drink with it.

 2 pounds new potatoes
 ¼ cup extra virgin olive oil
 2 tablespoons red wine vinegar
 1 teaspoon Dijon mustard
    Coarse salt and freshly ground pepper to taste
 4 sweet red peppers
 1 medium-sized red onion
 ½ pound Genoa salami, sliced
 2 teaspoons fennel seeds
 ¼ pound pitted Gaeta olives
 ½ pound feta cheese
 2 tablespoons chopped parsley leaves

1. Boil the potatoes in salted water to cover until they are cooked. Peel and slice them and put them in a bowl.

2. Combine the oil, vinegar, and mustard. Season with salt and pepper. Add to the potatoes and toss thoroughly.

3. Char the peppers over a gas flame or under a broiler and scrape off the skin. Remove the seeds and slice the peppers into strips. Add them to the potatoes. Slice and add the onion.

4. Cut the salami slices into quarters. Add to the potatoes. Add the fennel seeds and the olives.

5. Crumble the feta cheese and add it to the salad. Sprinkle with the parsley and serve.

Yield: 4 to 6 servings.

RAW MUSHROOM SALAD

Good for those tasteless cultivated mushrooms, although they must be very fresh.

½ pound mushrooms
½ cup extra virgin olive oil
    Juice of 1 lemon
    Coarse salt and freshly ground pepper to taste
 2 tablespoons chopped fresh marjoram or summer savory

1. Slice the mushrooms thinly, removing the tips of the stems.

2. Combine the oil, lemon juice, salt, and pepper. Mix thoroughly and pour over the mushrooms. Sprinkle with the herbs and serve at room temperature.

Yield: 2 to 3 servings.

Note: A minced small clove of garlic may also be added to the dressing.

CHICKEN SALAD WITH WALNUT VINAIGRETTE

An excellent summer salad, to be eaten with French bread and followed by cheese and fruit.

  2 whole cooked chicken breasts, skinned and boned
  4 scallions, chopped
  ½ cup finely chopped walnuts
     About 10 whole fresh basil leaves
  ¼ cup peanut or safflower oil
  ½ cup walnut oil
  ¼ cup raspberry vinegar, or to taste
     Coarse salt and freshly ground pepper to taste
     Salad greens (watercress, endive, red leaf lettuce, radicchio,
        arugola, Boston lettuce)
  2 tablespoons chopped chives

1. Cut the chicken breasts into slivers and place in a mixing bowl. Add the scallions, walnuts, and basil leaves, which have been torn into small pieces.

2. In a separate bowl, combine the oils and vinegar. Blend well and season with the salt and pepper.

3. Put the salad greens in a bowl and toss with enough of the dressing to coat the leaves lightly. Arrange the leaves on 4 individual plates.

4. Arrange the chicken pieces on the greens. Stir the chives into the remaining dressing and pour it over the chicken.

Yield: 4 servings.

COLD BEEF WITH TARRAGON VINAIGRETTE

Use roast beef or very rare steak. Potato Salad, page 19, and sliced ripe tomatoes, dressed with oil and vinegar, go well with this dish.

1½ pounds sliced rare beef
1 small red onion, sliced
1 bunch watercress
1 cup whole cornichons

FOR THE TARRAGON VINAIGRETTE

1 garlic clove
Coarse salt
½ cup extra virgin olive oil
About 2 tablespoons tarragon vinegar, or more or less to taste
1 tablespoon Dijon mustard
Freshly ground pepper to taste
2 tablespoons fresh tarragon leaves

1. Cut the beef in thin strips and put them in a large bowl.

2. Make the dressing. Using a mortar and pestle, pound the garlic into a purée with a little salt. Gradually add the oil, vinegar, and mustard. Season with the pepper and stir in the tarragon leaves.

3. Add the onion to the beef and pour on the dressing. Mix thoroughly.

4. Arrange the watercress around the edge of a serving dish. Mound the beef in the middle and decorate with the cornichons. Serve at room temperature.

Yield: 4 servings.

RICE SALAD WITH TONGUE AND EGGPLANT

Rice salads are easy to make and they are attractive. They can be put in an oiled mold for a few hours (or overnight), turned out onto a serving platter, and garnished with pimientos, orange or lemon slices, and fresh herbs, such as basil, mint, or tarragon. Oil the mold with safflower or peanut oil, then line it with a layer of plastic wrap. Carefully pat the salad down with the back of a spoon. To unmold, simply turn the bowl onto a serving dish or wooden platter and lift up, removing the plastic lining.

It is important not to overcook the rice. It should be al dente, slightly chewy, otherwise you will end up with a soggy salad.

You can also make delicious salads with cold fresh or smoked salmon, chicken, prosciutto, or leftover meat, fresh herbs and summer vegetables, such as tomatoes, peppers (skinned) and cooked eggplant. The recipe given below for eggplant and tongue salad is based on an idea from Elizabeth David's Italian Food. *The eggplant is peeled, cubed, and fried in olive oil and then combined with rice, pimiento, and tongue. The eggplant cubes should be salted and allowed to sit for an hour before being fried. This way the bitter juices are exuded—and the eggplant will not soak up the oil so greedily. The eggplant should be wiped dry before it is fried. Good-quality ham may be used instead of tongue.*

  2 cups long-grain rice
  2 eggplants
     Coarse salt
     Approximately ½ cup extra virgin olive oil
     Approximately ½ cup safflower or peanut oil
  2 garlic cloves, minced
  ¾ pound cooked tongue (or ham), sliced and diced
  ½ cup chopped Italian parsley leaves
  2 pimientos, chopped
     Freshly ground pepper to taste

24

1. Cook the rice until *al dente*. Drain, fluff with a fork, and spread out to dry on paper towels. Set aside.

2. Meanwhile, peel the eggplants and cut them into 1-inch cubes. Put the cubes in a colander, sprinkle with salt, and let sit for 1 hour. Pat dry with paper towels.

3. Heat half the oils in a frying pan. Brown the cubes on all sides, a few at a time. Add more oil as needed. Drain the cubes on paper towels. Add the garlic and cook until golden. Place eggplant cubes and garlic in a large bowl.

4. Add the tongue, parsley, pimientos, and rice. Toss and season to taste. Refrigerate until an hour before serving, placing the rice mixture in an oiled mold if you wish.

Yield: 4 servings.

RICE, CHEESE, AND HAM SALAD

Use good-quality ham, such as Smithfield or Kentucky (make sure that it is not too salty). For instructions on molding this salad, see the preceding recipe.

　2　cups long-grain rice
　2　sweet red peppers
　¼　pound pitted black olives (preferably Gaeta or Calamata)
　½　pound ham, diced
　½　pound imported Gruyère cheese, diced
　½　cup extra virgin olive oil
　　　Juice of ½ lemon
　1　teaspoon red wine vinegar, or more to taste
　1　teaspoon Dijon mustard
　　　Coarse salt and freshly ground pepper to taste
　2　firm ripe tomatoes, peeled, seeded, and diced
　1　bunch fresh basil leaves

1. Cook the rice until *al dente*. Drain, fluff with a fork, and spread out to dry on paper towels.

2. Char the peppers over a gas flame or under a broiler. Wrap in a paper towel, then scrape off the skin. Chop the peppers. Put them in a large bowl with the rice, olives, ham, and cheese.

3. Mix the oil, lemon juice, vinegar, and mustard in a small bowl. Add the salt and pepper and pour the mixture over the rice.

4. If serving immediately, add the tomatoes and snipped basil leaves. If not, reserve them until you are ready to serve the salad. If the salad is molded, arrange the tomatoes around the outside or in the center and garnish with the basil leaves.

Yield: 4 servings.

SMOKED SALMON TERRINE

This simple recipe comes from David Waltuck of the Chanterelle restaurant in New York. It is expensive but delicious and extremely useful for a special occasion, especially if you are giving a formal dinner party that involves a certain amount of preparation. It can be made the day before.

1½ pounds smoked Nova Scotia salmon
 ¼ pound unsalted butter, melted
     Juice of 1 lemon, or more to taste
  3 tablespoons chopped chives
     Freshly ground white pepper to taste
 ¼ pint heavy cream, whipped
  4 ounces American black caviar

1. In a blender, purée the salmon with the melted butter. Add the lemon juice, chives, pepper, and cream and mix thoroughly.

2. Place in a layer in a terrine, spread with the caviar, and cover with the remaining mixture. Refrigerate until ready to serve.

3. To serve, turn out on a plate and cut into slices. Serve with dark bread.

Yield: 8 servings.

SCALLOP SEVICHE

Serve this as a first course, accompanied by pieces of toasted French or Italian bread. The lemon and lime juice blanches and "cooks" the scallops.

 1 pound raw bay scallops (or sea scallops, halved)
   Juice of 1 lemon
   Juice of 1 lime
 2 shallots, minced
 2 fresh green chilies, seeded and minced
 ½ cup extra virgin olive oil
   Coarse salt and freshly ground pepper to taste
2½ tablespoons chopped fresh coriander leaves

1. Put the scallops into a large bowl. Combine the remaining ingredients, except the coriander, and pour the marinade over the scallops. Toss thoroughly, cover, and marinate in the refrigerator overnight.

2. Remove the scallops from the refrigerator ½ hour before serving. Sprinkle with the coriander, correct the seasoning, and serve.

Yield: 4 to 6 servings.

SCALLOPS WITH SAFFRON SAUCE ON
LAMB'S LETTUCE

Pinch of saffron threads
2 tablespoons dry white wine
2 cups lamb's lettuce
Extra virgin olive oil
Juice of ½ lemon
Coarse salt and freshly ground pepper to taste
2 tablespoons unsalted butter
2 shallots, minced
1 pound bay scallops
½ cup heavy cream

1. Combine the saffron threads and the white wine in a cup and set aside.

2. Wash the lamb's lettuce; then dry it and put it on four serving plates. Sprinkle with oil, lemon juice, salt, and pepper.

3. Melt the butter in a heavy skillet and gently sauté the shallots until they are soft. Add the scallops and cook for 2 minutes. Remove to a plate and keep warm.

4. Add the saffron-flavored wine through a strainer. Raise the heat and boil rapidly until the liquid has reduced to about ¼ cup. Add the cream and continue to boil until the sauce is thick. Season with salt and pepper.

5. Divide the scallops into four portions and arrange them on top of the lamb's lettuce. Pour on the sauce and serve.

Yield: 4 first-course servings.

TWO

Pasta, Pizza, Eggs, and Cheese

Pasta has everything. It is nutritious, high in carbohydrates that help produce energy, and low in fat. It is very inexpensive (unless you serve it with caviar or smoked salmon) and it is extremely simple to cook. You can buy fresh or dried pasta on the way home and have a meal on the table within an hour. For people with small kitchens, it is a boon both in summer and winter. A steaming bowl of fettuccine can be served as a main course, followed by a salad of fresh greens, and fruit for dessert. Or it might be a first course, served in small portions to be followed by broiled chicken or fish.

Pasta is now available in three different ways: dried, freshly made, and homemade. Dried pasta is a great standby since it keeps for weeks. Hollow shapes, like penne and shells, are good for meat sauces because they catch the sauce. Thin spaghetti is good for shellfish and light sauces.

One of the easiest meals can be made with bought, freshly made stuffed pasta, such as ravioli or tortellini. Filled with meat or spinach and ricotta cheese, these stuffed pastas need nothing more than butter and Parmesan cheese or perhaps a light cream or tomato sauce. (Note: This kind of pasta really does not freeze very well—it loses its consistency.)

Flat pasta for lasagne and cannelloni are better bought fresh. When dried they can be very heavy. Again, they can be frozen but won't be as good.

As for making fresh pasta yourself, the problems in a small kitchen begin with the question of where to put everything. Where do you store your hand-cranked machine or electric pasta maker, where do you hang the pasta to dry, and is there enough counter space to do all the rolling out and cranking? As far as I am concerned, much as I adore fresh homemade pasta, in a small kitchen it is not worth the effort.

In case I want to serve an impromptu meal or can't face going to the store, I keep on hand some cans of tomatoes, tomato purée, tuna fish, clams, anchovies, a jar of pimientos, a package of dried mushrooms, and a container of black oil-cured olives. A wide choice of pasta dishes is possible if there are also some onions, garlic, olive oil, eggs, butter or cream in the house. Chopped nuts can be used in a sauce, or frozen hamburger for a ragú. I have also found pastes made from olives or sun-dried tomatoes extremely useful for pasta sauces. Sun-dried tomatoes can be mixed with capers and olive oil or added to a tomato sauce. A paste of crushed black olives mixed with extra virgin oil and herbs called *caviale d'oliva* is also good on pasta (and on goat or mozzarella cheese or brushed on broiled fish).

To cook pasta, bring 4 quarts of cold, salted water to a rolling boil. Drop the pasta in a few at a time so that it doesn't stick. Dried pasta takes approximately 7 to 9 minutes to cook, freshly made pasta only 2 or 3 minutes. Every so often it should be tasted, because different shapes and thicknesses cook differently. Each strand should be separate and *al dente,* chewy, not mushy. Have ready a warmed serving bowl and put a little oil or a nob of butter into it to prevent the drained pasta from sticking. Toss and then toss again with the sauce immediately and serve at once. Parmesan cheese should be grated fresh just before the meal. Italians often serve it in a chunk at the table and grate it as they need it. They sell small silver-plated graters just for this purpose.

CONCHIGLIE WITH EGGPLANT AND ZUCCHINI

Conchiglie are hollowed shells of dried pasta. Fusilli, a spiral-shaped pasta, or penne, another kind that is a short, hollow tube, may also be used in this recipe.

The long, thin eggplants sold in Oriental stores are especially good in this dish, but if they are not available, ordinary eggplant will do perfectly well.

4   long, thin eggplants (or 1 regular eggplant)
2   zucchini
4   fresh shiitake mushrooms, or soaked dried shiitake
     mushrooms
2   tablespoons extra virgin olive oil
1   onion, finely chopped
2   garlic cloves, minced
2   cups canned Italian tomatoes, with their juice, or 1 pound
     fresh tomatoes, peeled
1   cup dry white wine
     Coarse salt and freshly ground pepper to taste
12 ounces conchiglie
     About 8 whole fresh mint or basil leaves

1. Slice the eggplants if using the small ones or cube the large one. Sprinkle with salt and drain in a colander for 1 hour.

2. Slice the zucchini and the mushrooms. Heat the oil in a frying pan and gently sauté the onion and the garlic until they are soft. Pat

the eggplant dry with paper towels and add to the zucchini and mushrooms. Sauté for 2 or 3 minutes; then add the tomatoes and the wine. Season with salt and pepper and simmer gently, covered, for 30 to 40 minutes, uncovering if the sauce is too liquid or adding a little water if it is too dry.

3. Meanwhile, bring 4 quarts of cold salted water to a rolling boil. Add the conchiglie and cook until *al dente*. Drain, place in a heated bowl, and top with the sauce. Garnish with the mint leaves and pass the cheese separately.

Yield: 3 to 4 servings.

FETTUCCINE WITH ASPARAGUS

A mixture of yellow and green fettuccine looks attractive in this spring dish. Peeled and chopped ripe tomatoes may be added to the cream sauce toward the end of the cooking.

1½ pounds asparagus
  3 tablespoons unsalted butter
  1 garlic clove, minced
  4 scallions, chopped
  1 cup heavy cream
    Coarse salt and freshly ground pepper to taste
 12 ounces fettuccine
    Freshly grated Parmesan cheese

1. Trim the tough ends of the stalks from the asparagus. With a vegetable peeler, pare away any tough skin from the lower half of the stalk. Rinse the asparagus in cold water.

2. Either cook the asparagus in a steamer or tie in a bundle standing in 2 inches of water. Cook until tender but firm. Drain and, when cool enough to handle, cut the stalks into ¾-inch pieces, Meanwhile, bring 4 quarts of water to a boil for the fettuccine.

3. Melt the butter in a large frying pan. Add the garlic and the scallions and sauté for 1 minute. Add the cream and bring to a simmer. Cook for several minutes, or until the sauce has thickened slightly. Season with salt and pepper. Add the asparagus and keep warm until the fettuccine is cooked.

4. Cook the fettuccine until *al dente,* drain, and transfer to a heated serving bowl. Add the sauce, toss, and serve. Pass the cheese separately.

Yield: 3 to 4 main-course servings

FETTUCCINE WITH BROCCOLI AND PORCINI MUSHROOMS

½ ounce dried porcini mushrooms
1 garlic clove
2 tablespoons unsalted butter
1 tablespoon chopped tarragon
1 tablespoon chopped Italian parsley leaves
1 cup broccoli, broken into tiny flowerets, blanched
  Coarse salt and freshly ground pepper to taste
12 ounces fettuccine
  Freshly grated Parmesan cheese

1. Soak the porcini in water to cover for 15 minutes.

2. Sauté the garlic in the butter in a large frying pan. Add the tarragon, parsley, broccoli, and mushrooms. Sauté for 10 minutes and season with salt and pepper.

3. Meanwhile, cook the fettuccine in 4 quarts of salted boiling water until *al dente.* Drain and transfer to a heated serving bowl with a nob of butter. Add the broccoli and mushrooms and toss. Pass the cheese separately.

Yield: 3 to 4 main-course servings

FETTUCCINE WITH BROCCOLI AND CHICKEN

This recipe comes from chef Mark David. Serve it as a main course.

½ cup sesame oil
1 cup diced chicken breast
2 teaspoons minced garlic
2 teaspoons slivered fresh ginger
3 cups packed broccoli flowerets
½ cup dry sherry
½ cup soy sauce
12 ounces fettuccine
3 tablespoons unsalted butter
½ cup freshly grated Parmesan cheese
½ cup toasted slivered almonds

1. Heat the oil in a wok until it is smoking. Stir-fry the chicken for 30 seconds. Add the garlic, ginger, and broccoli. Stir-fry for 1 minute. Add the sherry and soy sauce and simmer for 1 minute.

2. Meanwhile, cook the fettuccine in 4 quarts of salted boiling water until *al dente.*

3. When the fettuccine is cooked, drain it; then shock with 1 cup of cold water. Drain again.

4. Add the fettuccine and butter to the wok. Toss. Add the Parmesan and toss again.

5. Garnish with toasted almonds and serve with more cheese, handed separately.

Yield: 3 to 4 main-course servings.

FETTUCCINE WITH CHANTERELLES

½ pound chanterelles
2 tablespoons unsalted butter
1 tablespoon extra virgin olive oil
1 garlic clove, minced
12 ounces fettuccine
3 to 4 tablespoons crème fraîche (page 282)
2 tablespoons chopped chives
1 tablespoon chopped parsley
2 tablespoons chopped fresh tarragon leaves
Coarse salt and freshly ground pepper to taste
Freshly grated Parmesan cheese

1. Thoroughly rinse the chanterelles to remove all traces of grit. Wipe them dry with paper towels and slice them. Drain and set aside.

2. Heat the butter and the olive oil in a large frying pan. Gently fry the garlic until it is golden. Add the chanterelles and cook over low-to-medium heat for 15 minutes.

3. Meanwhile, cook the fettuccine in 4 quarts of salted boiling water until *al dente*. Drain and transfer to a heated serving bowl with a nob of butter.

4. Stir the crème fraîche into the chanterelles. Add the herbs, salt, and pepper. If more liquid is needed, add more crème fraîche. Add the mixture to the fettuccine, toss thoroughly, and serve. Pass the Parmesan separately.

Yield: 3 to 4 main-course servings.

FETTUCCINE WITH WHITE TRUFFLES

Fresh white truffles, imported from Italy, are in season from late fall to late winter. These odd brownish-gray nobs should be shared only with those who love them because they are very expensive. But a truffle weighing about one third of an ounce will be enough for two. This, thinly shaved over pasta that has been cooked and tossed with cream and butter and sprinkled with freshly grated well-aged Parmesan cheese, adds up to about the same price as a meal with veal chops or a prime steak. Followed by salad and fruit, it is enough for a complete meal.

White truffles grow near the roots of trees and are hunted by specially trained dogs in Tuscany, Romagna, and Piedmont. They are shipped in sawdust or rice to prevent spoilage. When you buy truffles, they are usually sold nestled in about a cupful of rice in a plastic container. The rice is permeated with the flavor of the truffle and should not be thrown away; use it to make a risotto. (Follow the instructions for Risotto alla Milanese on page 234, but omit the saffron.) Do not try to keep a truffle more than a day or two after you have bought it because it will spoil. There is no point in buying a truffle weighing less than a third of an ounce for two people because you will not taste it. Although there are special truffle slicers on the market, a cheese slicer will do the job perfectly well, provided you slice very carefully so that the truffle comes out in paper-thin slivers. Slice the truffle directly onto the pasta at the table on individual plates. Serve additional Parmesan at the table.

12 ounces fettuccine
 4 quarts cold water
    Coarse salt
 2 tablespoons unsalted butter
¼ cup heavy cream
    Freshly ground pepper to taste
 2 tablespoons freshly grated Parmesan cheese
 1 small white truffle (about ⅓ ounce)

1. Bring the salted water to a rolling boil and cook the fettuccine until *al dente*. Drain.

2. Meanwhile, put the butter and cream into a saucepan and heat through. Add the pasta and toss. Season with the salt, pepper and cheese.

3. Place the pasta on heated individual plates and grate some truffle on each serving. Pass more Parmesan cheese separately.

Yield: 3 to 4 main-course servings.

LINGUINE WITH FAVA BEANS AND BABY ARTICHOKES

Thawed frozen artichokes may be used in place of the fresh.

- 8 baby artichokes
- ½ lemon
- 3 tablespoons extra virgin olive oil
- 1 garlic clove, minced
- 2 cups canned Italian tomatoes, with their juice, or 1 pound fresh tomatoes, peeled
- 8 basil leaves, or 2 tablespoons fresh tarragon or mint leaves
- 1 pound fava beans, shelled
  Coarse salt and freshly ground pepper to taste
- 12 ounces linguine
  Freshly grated Parmesan cheese

1. Trim the outer leaves from the artichokes. Using a sharp knife, cut off the tops of the leaves remaining on the artichoke so that you are left with about 1½ inches on the bottom. Trim away the stalk and slice the artichokes into three pieces vertically. Place the slices in a bowl of cold water with the lemon half squeezed in, to prevent them from turning brown.

2. Heat the oil in a large frying pan and add the garlic and the artichokes. Sauté for 2 minutes; then add the tomatoes and basil leaves. Simmer, uncovered, for 8 minutes, or until the artichokes are almost tender.

3. Meanwhile, bring 4 quarts of cold salted water to a rolling boil for the linguine.

4. Add the fava beans to the artichokes and cook until tender, about 5 minutes. If the sauce needs to be reduced, raise the heat. If it is too thick, add a little water, stir and cover. Season with salt and pepper.

5. Cook the linguine until *al dente*, drain, and transfer to heated serving bowl. Add the sauce, toss and serve. Pass the Parmesan cheese separately.

Yield: 3 to 4 main-course servings.

PENNE WITH SAUSAGE AND RED PEPPERS

4 sweet red peppers
4 Italian sweet sausages
3 tablespoons extra virgin olive oil
2 garlic cloves, minced
   Coarse salt and freshly ground pepper to taste
1 pound penne
3 tablespoons chopped Italian parsley leaves
   Freshly grated Parmesan cheese

1. Skin the peppers by charring them under a broiler or over a gas flame and scraping off their skins. Remove the seeds and slice the peppers into ½-inch strips. Set aside.

2. Meanwhile, put the sausages into a small frying pan and cover with water. Cook, uncovered, turning occasionally, until the water has evaporated and the sausages have browned in their own fat.

3. Heat the oil in a frying pan and gently fry the garlic until it is golden. Add the peppers and heat through. Season with salt and pepper.

4. Meanwhile, bring 5 quarts of cold salted water to a boil and cook the penne until *al dente*. While it is cooking, slice the sausages and add them to the peppers. Keep warm while the pasta is cooking.

5. Put the pasta in a heated serving dish. Pour the sausage mixture on top, sprinkle with parsley and serve. Pass the Parmesan cheese separately.

Yield: 4 main-course servings.

PERCIATELLI MARINARA

Perciatelli (also called bucatini) is a thick spaghetti that goes espe-cially well with the spicy, robust flavor of this seafood sauce.

  2 tablespoons extra virgin olive oil
  1 medium-sized onion, finely chopped
  2 garlic cloves, minced
  2 pounds tomatoes, fresh, peeled, or canned
  3 sprigs parsley
     About 10 whole fresh basil leaves
  ½ teaspoon dried oregano
  ½ teaspoon hot red pepper flakes
     Coarse salt to taste
  ½ pound unshelled shrimp
  1 pound mussels
 12 clams
  1 pound perciatelli

1. Heat the oil in a casserole large enough to hold all the seafood comfortably. Add the onion and garlic and cook until soft.

2. Add the tomatoes (with their juice, if canned), parsley, basil leaves, oregano, red pepper flakes, and salt. Cover and simmer for 30 minutes, stirring occasionally

3. Meanwhile, rinse the shrimp. Beard and scrub the mussels and scrub the clams. Rinse well and set aside.

4. Bring 4 quarts cold salted water to boil and cook the perciatelli. Meanwhile, cook the clams and mussels in the tomato sauce for 5 minutes with the lid on. Add the shrimp and cook for 2 minutes longer.

5. Drain the perciatelli. Transfer it to a large heated serving bowl and pour the sauce and seafood on top. Serve immediately.

Yield: 4 servings.

SPAGHETTI WITH MUSHROOMS, TOMATOES, AND ROSEMARY

If you can get them, fresh shiitake or wild oak mushrooms are especially good here.

½ pound mushrooms
4 leeks
3 tablespoons extra virgin olive oil
1 garlic clove, minced
1½ teaspoons fresh rosemary, or ¾ teaspoon dried rosemary
    Coarse salt and freshly ground pepper to taste
3 large ripe tomatoes, peeled, seeded, and chopped
1 pound spaghetti
    Freshly grated Parmesan cheese to taste

1. Wash, dry, and slice the mushrooms. Slice the leeks in ½-inch pieces and rinse thoroughly under cold running water to remove all the grit. If the leeks are very gritty, soak them in cold water for 5 minutes, then rinse.

2. Heat the oil in a large frying pan and gently fry the leeks with the garlic until they are soft. Add the mushrooms, rosemary, salt, and pepper and cook over moderate heat for 10 minutes.

3. Add the tomatoes and cook for 10 minutes, stirring frequently. Meanwhile, cook the spaghetti until *al dente*.

4. When the spaghetti is cooked, drain and combine it in a heated serving bowl with the mushroom mixture. Toss thoroughly and serve. Serve the cheese separately.

Yield: 4 servings.

TAGLIATELLE WITH PROSCIUTTO AND TOMATOES

½ pound prosciutto end (see note)
1 tablespoon unsalted butter
1½ pounds fresh tomatoes
2 garlic cloves, minced
2 large sprigs fresh mint
   Coarse salt and freshly ground pepper to taste
12 ounces tagliatelle

1. Chop the prosciutto into small pieces and gently fry in the butter until golden. Meanwhile, peel the tomatoes, cut them in half, and squeeze to remove any excess juices. Press through a sieve.

2. Place the tomato purée in a small saucepan with the garlic, mint, salt, and pepper. Simmer for 5 minutes. Remove the mint.

3. Meanwhile, bring 4 quarts of salted water to a boil and cook the tagliatelle until *al dente*. Drain. Transfer to a heated serving bowl and pour on the tomato sauce and the sautéed prosciutto. Toss thoroughly and serve.

Yield: 2 to 3 main-course servings.

Note: Stores often sell prosciutto ends for considerably less than slices.

43

TAGLIATELLE WITH EGGPLANT SAUCE

Tagliatelle are long, narrow flat noodles, a little wider and thinner than fettuccine, and sold fresh. They are a Bolognese specialty and usually served with meat sauce.

    1   large or 3 small eggplants
        Coarse salt
        Flour for dredging
    1   to 1½ cups peanut or safflower oil
    1   onion, chopped
    2   garlic cloves, minced
    ½   pound ground beef
    ½   teaspoon dried oregano
    ½   teaspon ground cinnamon
        Coarse salt and freshly ground pepper to taste
 1½   pounds fresh or canned tomatoes, peeled, seeded, and
            chopped
    1   tablespoon tomato paste
    1   pound tagliatelle
    1   tablespoon unsalted butter
    2   tablespoons snipped fresh basil leaves
        Freshly grated Parmesan cheese

1. Cut the eggplant in slices ¼ inch thick. Put the slices in layers in a colander, salting as you go. Let stand for 1 hour. Wipe the eggplant dry with paper towels.

2. Dredge the slices lightly with flour. Heat the oil in a large frying pan and fry the eggplant a few slices at a time until golden on both sides. Remove and drain on paper towels.

3. Prepare the sauce: Using ¼ cup of the oil you have used for the eggplant, sauté the onion and garlic until soft. Add the meat. Cook until it loses its red color; then add the oregano, cinnamon, salt, pepper, tomatoes, and tomato paste. Mix well and cook for 1 hour, covered.

4. Cut the eggplant into strips.

5. Cook the tagliatelle in 5 quarts of salted boiling water until *al dente*. Drain. Toss the pasta with the butter.

6. Transfer the tagliatelle to a heated serving dish. Add the sauce and arrange the eggplant on top. Sprinkle with the basil and serve. Pass the Parmesan cheese separately.

Yield: 4 to 6 main-course servings.

TORTELLINI ALLA PANNA

These half-moons of pasta stuffed with meat make a fast last-minute meal when served in cream with Parmesan cheese. They are very filling and need nothing more than a salad to complete the meal.

  1 pound fresh tortellini
  2 tablespoons unsalted butter
  ¾ cup heavy cream
  ¼ pound freshly grated Parmesan cheese
      Coarse salt and freshly ground black pepper to taste

1. Bring 4 quarts of cold salted water to a rolling boil and add the tortellini. Cook for about 3 minutes, or until *al dente*.

2. Meanwhile, heat the butter and the cream in a large saucepan. Add the tortellini and grate in a little cheese. Season with salt and pepper and let stand for a couple of minutes to allow the pasta to absorb the sauce.

3. Serve in heated dishes, passing the rest of the Parmesan cheese separately.

Yield: 4 main-course servings.

TORTELLONI IN LIGHT TOMATO SAUCE

Tortelloni are large square dumplings, usually stuffed with spinach and ricotta or Swiss chard. They are delicious with the following tomato sauce. A combination of green and white tortelloni looks very pretty in the smooth, pale pink sauce.

2 tablespoons unsalted butter
1 garlic clove, minced
1 small onion, finely chopped
2 cups canned Italian tomatoes, with their juice, or 1 pound
    fresh tomatoes, peeled
1 cup crème fraîche (page 282)
½ cup snipped fresh basil leaves
    Coarse salt and freshly ground pepper to taste
1 pound tortelloni
    Freshly grated Parmesan cheese

1. Melt the butter in a frying pan and cook the garlic and onion until they are soft. Add the tomatoes, cover, and simmer for 20 minutes, adding a little water if the sauce is too dry. Meanwhile, bring 4 quarts of cold salted water to a boil.

2. Purée the tomato sauce in a blender and return it to the pan. Stir in the crème fraîche and the basil. Season with salt and pepper, cover, and simmer very gently while you cook the tortelloni.

3. Cook the tortelloni until *al dente* (about 2 to 3 minutes). Drain and transfer to a heated serving dish. Add the sauce and toss carefully. Pass the Parmesan cheese separately.

Yield: 4 main-course servings.

SCALLOPS WITH VERMICELLI

Bay scallops go beautifully with thin spaghetti. Cheese is not neces-sary with this dish.

- 1 pound bay scallops (or sea scallops, halved)
  Juice of 1 lemon
- 2 tablespoons chopped parsley leaves
- 1 onion, chopped
- 1 garlic clove, minced
- 2 tablespoons olive oil
- 2 tablespoons unsalted butter
- ¼ teaspoon dried oregano, or ½ teaspoon fresh oregano
- ¼ teaspoon dried thyme, or ½ teaspoon fresh thyme
- 2 tablespoons snipped fresh basil leaves
- 1½ cups canned Italian tomatoes
- 12 ounces vermicelli
- 2 tablespoons crème fraîche (page 282) or heavy cream
  Pinch of grated nutmeg
  Coarse salt and freshly ground pepper to taste

1. Rinse the scallops and marinate them in the lemon juice with the parsley while preparing the sauce.

2. In a heavy frying pan, cook the onion and the garlic in the olive oil and 1 tablespoon of the butter until they are soft. Add the oreg-ano, thyme, basil, and tomatoes. Cover and simmer, stirring occa-sionally, for 30 minutes.

3. Bring 4 quarts of salted water to a boil and cook the vermicelli.

4. Meanwhile, drain the scallops and fry them for 2 minutes in the remaining butter. Add the crème fraîche, nutmeg, and tomato sauce. Bring to a boil, stir well, and remove from the heat. Season with salt and pepper.

5. Drain the spaghetti. Add half the sauce to the pot; then add the spaghetti. Add the remaining sauce and mix thoroughly. Serve on heated plates.

Yield: 3 to 4 main-course servings.

PIZZA

Pizza is a quick and inexpensive meal that can easily be made at home. The variety of toppings is immense, among them ham, mushrooms, anchovies, olives, even clams or mussels. A brief consultation with the interior of the refrigerator almost always yields something that will be at home on a pizza. And instead of the traditional mozzarella and tomato, a more esoteric topping can be made with goat cheese and sundried tomatoes arranged on the dough, baked and sprinkled with fresh basil leaves. But the very simplest pizza consists of nothing more than the crusty dough sprinkled with coarse salt and extra virgin olive oil. Of course, all pizzas should be eaten with copious draughts of beer, chilled Beaujolais, or a robust red wine.

For those fortunate enough to own a food processor, making pizza dough will be no more troublesome than breaking an egg for an omelet. The kneading is done in the machine in seconds. But even for those without a machine, only a little kneading is required. The dough is then allowed to rise at room temperature for a couple of hours before being rolled out onto a pizza pan. In fact, the dough can be made the night before, allowed to rise, and then refrigerated. But once it has been rolled out onto the pizza pan, the dough should be allowed to rise at room temperature for about an hour before being baked. Small individual pizzas can be made by rolling out the dough and cutting it into rounds with a large glass or pastry cutter.

High-gluten flour is the best for a good pizza crust. Most flours are a blend of low- and high-gluten wheat. However, Hecker's, an unbleached flour, has a higher gluten content than most national brands. It produces a crust that is closer to the authentic Italian crust. The high-gluten flour handles easily after the dough has risen and rolls out without shrinking back. Semolina flour, which is often called pasta flour, made from hard durum wheat, takes longer to rise and may also be difficult to roll out. But the pizza crust it makes is excellent, hard and crunchy. A combination of flours works very well.

If you are making the following recipes when tomatoes are out of season, used drained canned Italian tomatoes.

PIZZA DOUGH

1 ¼-ounce package active dry yeast
¾ cup lukewarm water
1½ cups high-gluten flour
Pinch of salt
1½ tablespoons extra virgin olive oil

1. Combine the yeast with ¼ cup of the water. Cover and leave until doubled in volume. If the mixture does not rise, throw it away and use a fresh package of yeast.

2. If using a food processor, fit the bowl with a steel blade and put the flour, salt, olive oil, yeast mixture, and remaining water into the bowl. Process until the dough forms a ball, about 20 seconds. Place the dough on a smooth surface and knead for a couple of minutes, adding more flour if the dough is too sticky.

If using the hand method, combine the flour and salt and place the mixture on a smooth working surface. Make a well in the center and add the yeast mixture, olive oil, and remaining water. Gradually work the flour into the liquid, using a wooden spoon. When the dough is too stiff to work with the spoon, knead until smooth and shiny, about 8 to 10 minutes. Add more flour if the dough gets too sticky.

3. Put the dough in a large mixing bowl. Cover with a damp cloth or plastic wrap and let rise for 2 to 2½ hours in a warm place until tripled in size.

4. Punch down the dough, sprinkle it with flour, and knead for a minute. If not using until the next day, place in a bowl, cover, and refrigerate.

5. Grease a 12-inch pizza pan with oil. Roll out the dough with a floured rolling pin directly onto the pizza pan. Brush with olive oil. Let rise for 1 hour. The pizza is now ready for filling.

Yield: 1 12-inch pizza.

PIZZA WITH TUNA, BASIL, AND PINE NUTS

Pizza dough (see preceding recipe)
1½ pounds fresh tomatoes
3 tablespoons extra virgin olive oil
1 onion, thinly sliced
1 garlic clove, minced
2 6-ounce cans tuna fish, drained
Coarse salt and freshly ground pepper to taste
8 tablespoons pine nuts, lightly toasted
Fresh basil leaves for garnish

1. Make the pizza dough according to the recipe. Roll out on a pizza pan and leave to rise while preparing the filling.

2. Preheat the oven to 400 degrees.

3. Peel the tomatoes either by placing them in boiling water for a few minutes or by charring them over a gas flame or under a broiler. Slip off the skins while the tomatoes are still warm.

4. Heat 2 tablespoons of the oil in a large frying pan and soften the onion without browning it. Add the garlic and the tomatoes. Cook for about 20 minutes over medium heat, until the tomatoes are soft and the sauce has thickened. Add the tuna fish and mix thoroughly. Season with salt and pepper.

5. Spread the filling evenly over the pizza dough. Sprinkle with the pine nuts and the remaining oil. Bake for 25 to 30 minutes, or until done. Sprinkle with the basil and serve.

Yield: 4 servings.

GOAT CHEESE AND SUN-DRIED TOMATO PIZZA

    Pizza dough (see recipe page 49)
½ pound goat cheese
8 halves sun-dried tomatoes, cut into slivers
    Freshly ground pepper to taste
    Fresh basil leaves to garnish, in season, or ½ teaspoon dried
      oregano

1. Prepare the pizza dough according to the recipe. When the dough has risen, roll out onto a greased pizza pan. Set aside.

2. Preheat the oven to 400 degrees.

3. Slice the goat cheese thinly and arrange the slices in a concentric pattern on the pizza dough. Arrange the slivers of sun-dried tomato in spoke-like patterns on top. Sprinkle with the pepper.

4. Bake for 25 to 30 minutes. Sprinkle with the basil and serve.

Yield: 4 servings.

PIZZA WITH EGGPLANT AND MOZZARELLA

    Pizza dough (see recipe page 49)
 4 to 6 baby eggplants, or 1 large eggplant
1½ pounds ripe tomatoes
 ½ to ¾ cup safflower or peanut oil
    Flour for dredging
 3 tablespoons extra virgin olive oil
 1 medium-sized onion, chopped
 2 garlic cloves, minced
 ½ teaspoon dried oregano, or 1 teaspoon fresh oregano
 ¼ teaspoon dried thyme, or ½ teaspoon fresh thyme
    Coarse salt and freshly ground pepper to taste
 ¾ pound mozzarella, sliced

1. Prepare the pizza dough according to the recipe. When the dough has risen, roll out onto a greased pizza pan. Set aside in a warm place.

2. Slice the eggplant and sprinkle it with coarse salt. Allow to sit in a colander for at least ½ hour so that the juices exude.

3. Peel the tomatoes by putting them into boiling water for a few minutes or by charring them under a broiler or over a gas flame. Peel while still warm and set aside.

4. Preheat the oven to 400 degrees.

5. Pat the eggplant dry with paper towels. Heat the safflower or peanut oil in a heavy skillet. There should be about ⅛ inch of oil covering the bottom. Lightly dredge the eggplant with the flour. Shake off the excess and fry the eggplant over medium-high heat without crowding, a few slices at a time, until golden on both sides. Drain on paper towels.

6. Meanwhile, heat 2 tablespoons of the olive oil in a frying pan and cook the onion until it is soft but not brown. Add the tomatoes, garlic, oregano, and thyme. Season with salt and pepper and simmer gently for about 20 minutes.

7. Cool the tomato sauce. Spread it over the pizza dough. Arrange the eggplant slices on top, and then the mozzarella to form a circular flower pattern. Sprinkle with the remaining oil and bake for 25 to 30 minutes, or until done.

Yield: 4 servings.

EGG AND CHEESE DISHES

It is not hard to make a good omelet. First of all you need the proper sort of pan. It could be an omelet pan, a well-oiled cast-iron skillet, or a teflon frying pan. An omelet pan or cast-iron skillet should not be washed, but rather wiped with paper towels after being used. If something has stuck, scour it lightly and wipe it out with oil.

To make an omelet, put the eggs in a bowl and mix them well with a fork, seasoning them with salt and pepper. Melt butter in the pan. When it has almost started to brown, add the eggs. Leave them for a few seconds. With a fork or spatula, pull the eggs in from one side. Tilt the pan and let more egg run into their place. Do this all around the pan. When the omelet is slightly runny in the center, and set at the bottom, it is done. Hold a warm plate near the skillet and roll the omelet onto the plate. Another method is to fold the omelet in half while it is still in the pan. Run a spatula under one side to loosen it, then tilt the side of the pan up and flip the loosened half onto the bottom half.

Omelets are good for using small amounts of leftovers— but do not overstuff them. Creamed fish, chicken, or meat, heated or cooked separately, can be folded into the omelet just as it finishes cooking. Or you might sauté a chopped tomato in a tablespoon of butter and add it to the eggs just as they begin to set. Chopped mushrooms make a delicious filling when sautéed in a little butter with cream. If possible, get chanterelles, cèpes or morels. A spectacular filling can be made with fresh sorrel cooked in butter with cream. Or you might simply mix some fresh herbs, such as tarragon, chives, marjoram, or summer savory, into the eggs before you cook them.

SCRAMBLED EGGS

The secret of making good scrambled eggs is to cook the eggs over very low heat. They should be soft and very slightly runny, creamy rather than solid and congealed. Tarragon, chives, or other fresh herbs may be mixed into the eggs before they are cooked. You might also stir in some croutons or serve the eggs with creamed chanterelles or morels, fresh asparagus tips or cooked artichoke hearts. I happen to love scrambled eggs served quite plain on toast.

Crack the eggs into a bowl, season with salt and pepper, and beat them with a fork. Melt some butter in a heavy saucepan and cook the eggs over very low heat, stirring constantly. When the mixture starts to thicken, add a little cold butter, cut into small pieces. Add more as the eggs thicken. Remove the eggs from the heat before they are completely cooked. The heat of the pan will complete the cooking process.

PIPERADE

3 sweet red or green peppers
3 tablespoons extra virgin olive oil
1 medium-sized onion, chopped
1 garlic clove, minced
3 ripe tomatoes, peeled, seeded, and chopped
½ teaspoon fresh oregano, or ¼ teaspoon dried oregano
½ teaspoon fresh thyme, or ¼ teaspoon dried thyme
   Coarse salt and freshly ground pepper to taste
6 eggs
4 tablespoons unsalted butter
   Fresh basil leaves for garnish, if available

1. Preheat the broiler.

2. Cut the peppers in quarters. Remove the seeds and place the quarters skin side up on a rack covered with aluminum foil. Broil until the skins blister. Place the peppers in a paper bag or wrap in a dishcloth and leave for a couple of minutes. Peel the skin off the peppers and cut them into strips. Set aside.

3. Heat the oil in a heavy skillet and fry the onion and the garlic until soft. Add the tomatoes, oregano, thyme, salt, pepper, and peppers and cook over medium heat for 10 minutes, or until the vegetables are soft.

4. Meanwhile, lightly beat the eggs and season them with salt and pepper.

5. In a separate frying pan, melt the butter over low heat. Add the eggs, mixed with the vegetables, and cook gently until the eggs are soft but not fully set. Sprinkle with the basil, torn into strips, and serve.

Yield: 3 to 4 servings.

FRITTATA

This is the Italian way of cooking eggs, in an open-faced omelet that is lightly browned under the broiler before being turned out onto a serving dish. Diced peppers, zucchini, asparagus, artichokes, cheese, tomatoes, or fresh herbs may be added to the eggs. This version uses potatoes and onions. Served with a salad of ripe tomatoes, it makes a delightful lunch dish in the summer. The best pan to use is a well-oiled cast-iron skillet.

- 4 medium-sized potatoes
- 2 tablespoons vegetable oil
- 1 medium-sized onion, chopped
- 6 eggs
  Coarse salt and freshly ground pepper to taste
- 2 tablespoons unsalted butter
  Fresh herbs for garnish, if available

1. Peel and cut the potatoes into small dice. Heat the oil in a cast-iron skillet. Brown the potatoes on all sides. When they are cooked, remove them with a slotted spoon and drain them on paper towels.

2. Add the onion to the skillet and cook until it is golden brown. Remove with a slotted spoon.

3. If there is any food adhering to the pan, wipe it off with a paper towel or scrape it off with a knife. The pan must be clean or the eggs will stick.

4. Preheat the broiler to hot.

5. Break the eggs into a large bowl and beat them lightly with the salt and pepper. Mix in the potatoes and eggs.

6. Melt the butter in the skillet and, when it begins to turn brown, add the eggs. Tilt the pan so the eggs are spread out evenly. Cook the omelet over moderate heat and, after a couple of minutes, lift an edge and check whether it is browning underneath. If not, raise the heat.

7. Remove from the heat and quickly run under the broiler to brown the top lightly. Slide or turn out onto a heated platter and serve at once.

Yield: 4 servings.

SORREL OMELET

This recipe is adapted from New Classic Cuisine *by Michel and Albert Roux, owners of Le Gavroche restaurant in London.*

¼ pound sorrel, stalks trimmed
3 tablespoons unsalted butter
½ cup heavy cream
    Coarse salt and freshly ground pepper to taste
    Pinch of grated nutmeg
6 eggs
1 tablespoon grated Gruyère cheese

1. Cook the sorrel until wilted in 1 tablespoon butter. Set aside.

2. Lightly whip the cream and season it with salt, pepper, and nutmeg. Beat the eggs in a bowl with a fork and season to taste with salt and pepper.

3. Preheat the broiler.

4. Heat the remaining butter in an omelet pan. Add the eggs and when they are set but still runny in the center add the sorrel and spread over the middle. Fold the omelet and roll it onto a flame-proof dish. Pour on the cream and sprinkle over the grated Gruyère. Glaze quickly under the broiler—for 2 to 3 minutes, just long enough to turn the omelet a pale golden.

Yield: 2 servings.

GOAT CHEESE SOUFFLÉ

Use a soft, full-flavored cheese, such as Montrachet Bucheron. This simple soufflé can be cooked and on the table within an hour. Served with salad and followed by fruit, it makes a fine dish for lunch or dinner.

- 4 tablespoons unsalted butter
- 3 tablespoons all-purpose flour
- 1½ cups heavy cream
- ½ cup milk
- Bouquet garni (thyme and parsley sprigs and bay leaf tied in a cheesecloth bag)
- Coarse salt and freshly ground pepper to taste
- 6 ounces goat cheese, crumbled
- 4 egg yolks
- 6 egg whites
- 1 teaspoon dried thyme, or 2 teaspoons fresh thyme

1. Melt the butter in a saucepan and add the flour. Cook for 5 minutes, stirring. Do not allow it to brown. Meanwhile, scald the cream with the milk and add to the butter-flour mixture.

2. Add the bouquet garni, salt, and pepper. Put the mixture in the top of a double boiler and simmer gently for 30 minutes. Add the crumbled cheese and egg yolks and mix until smooth.

3. Preheat the oven to 400 degrees. Butter a soufflé dish. Whip the egg whites until they stand up in peaks. Fold the cheese mixture into the egg whites and pour into the soufflé dish. Sprinkle with the thyme.

4. Bake for 15 to 20 minutes, or until the soufflé has puffed up with a golden brown top.

Yield: 4 servings.

THREE

Fish

For those with small kitchens, fish is a godsend because it cooks quickly. In the past few years it has become easier to find all sorts of fresh fish in the market. Not long ago squid and monkfish were "trash" fish, avoided by most people who didn't know how to cook them and bought only fish fillets. Now everyone buys "calamari" or "lotte"—and the price has gone up, too.

When fish is really fresh it needs little embellishment. So it makes sense to choose the freshest you can find, and then decide how you want to cook it, instead of going out armed with a complicated recipe. To tell if fish is fresh, smell it. It should smell seaweedy. When you poke it, your finger should not leave an indentation. The skin should be shiny not dull, and the eyes should not be sunken and opaque.

BAKED WHOLE STRIPED BASS WITH ORANGES AND LEMONS

For very fresh striped bass. Serve with rice or new potatoes.

1 3- to 4-pound striped bass
1 orange
2 lemons
¼ cup chopped parsley leaves
   Coarse salt and freshly ground pepper to taste
1 tablespoon extra virgin olive oil
1 lime

1. Preheat the oven to 375 degrees. Wipe the fish dry with paper towels. Grate the zest from the orange and set it aside. Cut the orange in half and squeeze the juice of half the orange into the fish cavity and over the skin. Grate the zest of 1 lemon and add it to the orange zest. Squeeze the juice on the fish.

2. Put the parsley, salt, and pepper inside the cavity and place the fish in an oiled baking dish. Sprinkle with olive oil.

3. Cover the dish with foil and bake for 20 to 30 minutes or until the fish flakes when tested with a fork. Do not overcook.

4. To serve, garnish with sliced lemon, sliced lime, and the orange and lemon zest.

Yield: 4 servings.

STRIPED BASS WITH CORIANDER

Red snapper may also be used for this Moroccan dish. Serve with rice or Quick Couscous, page 256.

1   striped bass (about 4 pounds)
1   lemon
    Coarse salt and freshly ground pepper to taste
1   bunch fresh coriander
2   garlic cloves, crushed and peeled
2   medium-sized potatoes, peeled and thinly sliced
1   carrot, cut into thin strips
½   teaspoon Hungarian paprika
½   teaspoon ground cumin
2   tablespoons extra virgin olive oil
1   sweet green pepper, seeded and sliced
1   lime, sliced

1. Wipe the fish dry with paper towels. Squeeze the lemon juice on the skin and inside the fish cavity Sprinkle the cavity with salt and pepper. Chop the coriander leaves. Stuff the cavity with the garlic and a small handful of leaves. Set the remaining leaves aside. Marinate the fish at room temperature for an hour or so before baking.

2. Preheat the oven to 400 degrees. Place the potatoes and carrot on an oiled baking dish large enough to hold the fish. (If you do not have a dish large enough, place a big piece of foil, double thickness, on a baking sheet and sprinkle it with oil.) Place the potatoes and carrots in the center. Put the fish on top and sprinkle with the paprika, cumin, salt, pepper, some of the coriander, and olive oil. Arrange the pepper slices on top. Cover (or if using foil, wrap tightly) and bake for 30 minutes, or until the fish flakes when tested with a fork.

3. Decorate with lime slices and remaining coriander and serve.

Yield: 4 servings.

BRAISED HALIBUT STEAKS WITH ORANGES AND GREEN PEPPERCORNS

Serve with a green vegetable, such as Fava Beans with Summer Savory, page 197, or Puréed Spinach, page 224.

2 halibut steaks
2 oranges
  Peel of ½ orange
2 white turnips
2 tablespoons unsalted butter
2 shallots, minced
¾ cup dry white wine
¼ cup dry vermouth
  Coarse salt and freshly ground pepper to taste
1½ tablespoons green peppercorns
  Fresh basil or parsley leaves for garnish

1. Wipe the halibut steaks dry with paper towels. Squeeze the juice of 1 of the oranges over the steaks and marinate at room temperature for 1 hour.

2. Meanwhile, blanch the orange peel and cut it in julienne. Pare the turnips. Cut them in half; then cut the halves into thirds. Shape the thirds into ovals (they should be about the size of a pecan). Simmer in water to cover until barely tender. Drain and set aside. Peel the remaining orange and cut it into slices.

3. Melt 1 tablespoon of the butter in a large heavy skillet and cook the shallots until they are soft. Remove the halibut from the orange juice, pat it dry with paper towels, and brown the steaks lightly on both sides.

4. Add the wine, vermouth, and orange juice marinade. Season with salt and pepper, cover, and cook the steaks over moderately high heat for 5 minutes.

5. Remove the lid, turn the steaks over, and cook, uncovered, until done. If the sauce is too liquid, turn the heat up so that it boils down. Remove the steaks to a heated platter and keep warm.

6. Add the peppercorns, turnips, and orange slices. Heat through. Correct the seasoning and swirl in the remaining butter gradually until the sauce is thick and glossy.

7. Pour the sauce onto the steaks, with the orange slices arranged in the middle, and sprinkle with the basil.

Yield: 2 servings.

BROILED HALIBUT WITH GINGER-LIME BUTTER

Halibut is a fine fish for broiling. It is particularly good served with a flavored butter. Butter combined with lime juice and fresh ginger, oranges—preferably Seville—tarragon, or other fresh herbs may be used in butter. Once made, it can be kept in the refrigerator for a couple of weeks, so it is useful to double the recipe.

   6 tablespoons unsalted butter, softened
   2 tablespoons chopped chives
      Juice of 2 limes
   2 teaspoons grated lime rind
   1 teaspoon grated fresh ginger
   ½ teaspoon chopped fresh thyme leaves, or ¼ teaspoon dried
         thyme
      Coarse salt and freshly ground black pepper to taste
   4 halibut steaks
      Chopped parsley for garnish

1. First make the butter. Using an electric beater, if available, and a warm bowl, beat the butter for a couple of minutes to make it fluffy. Gradually add the chives, lime juice, lime rind, ginger, and thyme. Season with salt and pepper and mix well. Form the butter into a ball, wrap it in aluminum foil, and refrigerate. Use the freezer compartment if you are making the butter within 2 hours of serving the fish, so that the butter is not too soft.

2. Pat the fish steaks dry with paper towels. Season them with salt

and pepper and wrap them in buttered foil. Broil over hot coals or under high heat for 5 to 7 minutes on each side, depending on the thickness of the fish. Test for doneness by opening the foil and seeing if the fish flakes when prodded with a fork.

3. Arrange the fish on individual serving plates. Cut the butter in neat, even slices and place them on the fish steaks. Garnish with parsley and serve.

Yield: 4 servings.

MACKEREL WITH SORREL OR GOOSEBERRY SAUCE

Gooseberries have such an affinity for mackerel that in France they are known as groseilles au maquereau. *Their slightly acid taste is remarkably similar to that of sorrel. The gooseberries are stewed, sieved, and then mixed with cream and served separately with the fish. Sorrel, on the other hand, when stewed with a little butter, purées itself. It can simply be thinned with cream or a mixture of cream and fish stock.*

Serve this dish with boiled or baked potatoes.

 2 tablespoons unsalted butter
 ½ pound sorrel, or ¼ pound gooseberries
 ½ to ¾ cup heavy cream
    Coarse salt and freshly ground pepper to taste
 4 small mackerel

1. Melt the butter in a large saucepan and add the gooseberries or sorrel. Cook until a purée forms. If using gooseberries, strain through a sieve.

2. Add the cream to the purée and season with salt and pepper. Keep warm.

3. Make two or three slashes in the thickest part of the mackerel flesh. Broil the fish over hot coals or under high heat for 5 to 7 minutes on each side. The skin should be brown and crisp. Pass the sauce separately in a bowl.

Yield: 4 servings.

BROILED MONKFISH TAILS
HERBES DE PROVENCE

Monkfish has been called poor man's lobster because it has a lobster's texture, although not its delicate flavor. It is becoming increasingly popular. Serve this dish with rice or boiled new potatoes.

  4 monkfish tails
  ¼ cup extra virgin olive oil
      Juice of 1 lemon
  ½ cup mixed fresh herbs (dill, marjoram, oregano, basil, thyme)
  1 garlic clove, minced
      Freshly ground pepper to taste
      Coarse salt to taste
      Fresh chopped herbs for garnish

1. Remove the skin, if any, from the monkfish tails; then rinse and pat the tails dry. Combine the oil, lemon juice, herbs, garlic, and pepper. Put the tails in a shallow dish, coat with the mixture, and marinate for a couple of hours at room temperature or overnight in the refrigerator.

2. Heat the broiler. Place the fish on a broiling rack and grill on both sides, basting with the marinade mixture. The fish is cooked when it is snowy-white; the flesh should be firm and not dried out.

3. Place the fish on a serving dish and season with salt to taste. Sprinkle with herbs and serve.

Yield: 4 servings.

MONKFISH WITH SAFFRON SAUCE

Serve this delicate dish with rice.

       2 shallots, minced
       5 tablespoons unsalted butter
       2 ripe tomatoes, peeled, seeded, and chopped
       2 tablespoons chopped parsley leaves
     ½ teaspoon saffron threads, crumbled
     ½ cup dry white wine
       2 pounds monkfish fillets, cut into 1-inch pieces
       1 cup heavy cream
          Coarse salt and freshly ground pepper to taste

1. Cook the shallots in 2 tablespoons of the butter in a large frying pan. Add the tomatoes, parsley, saffron threads, and white wine. Simmer for 1 minute.

2. Add the monkfish and cook for 6 to 7 minutes. Remove with a slotted spoon and keep warm.

3. Add the cream to the pan and bring to a boil. Allow to thicken slightly, then remove from the heat and stir in the remaining butter, cut in pieces. Season with salt and pepper and pour the sauce over the fish.

Yield: 4 servings.

Fish

GRILLED SALMON STEAKS WITH HERB BUTTER

Make the herb butter in advance. Frozen, it can be kept for up to 2 weeks.

FOR THE HERB BUTTER

3 ounces unsalted butter at room temperature
2 tablespoons snipped basil leaves
1 tablespoon minced tarragon leaves
1 tablespoon minced chives
1 tablespoon fresh lemon juice
Coarse salt and freshly ground pepper to taste

FOR THE SALMON

3 tablespoons unsalted butter, melted
4 salmon steaks, about ¾ inch thick
1 tablespoon peanut or vegetable oil

1. Cream the 3 ounces of butter in a large bowl until it is smooth and soft. Add the basil, tarragon, and chives and mix thoroughly. Add the lemon juice, salt, and pepper and mix.

2. Shape the butter into a cylinder about 1 inch in diameter. Wrap in plastic wrap or aluminum foil and chill, either for 30 minutes in the freezer or for 1 or 2 hours in the main part of the refrigerator.

3. Heat the broiler. Melt the remaining butter in a small saucepan. Brush the salmon steaks with the butter and oil and grill about 6 inches from the heat, for about 6 minutes on the first side, 4 minutes on the other side. Baste while grilling.

4. When the fish is cooked, place on individual plates. Put a slice of herb butter on each steak.

Yield: 4 servings.

SALMON WITH WATERCRESS-SPINACH SAUCE

*Spring herbs and vegetables puréed into a deep green sauce go espe-
cially well with salmon. Serve new potatoes with this dish.*

1 bunch watercress
1 pound spinach
2 pounds salmon fillets
2 tablespoons clarified butter (page 283)
1 cup dry white wine or fish stock (page 284)
2 tablespoons chopped chives
2 tablespoons chopped tarragon leaves
   Coarse salt and freshly ground pepper to taste
½ cup crème fraîche (page 282)

1. Remove the stems from the watercress and spinach. Wash the
leaves and set them aside.

2. Sauté the salmon in the butter until it is just cooked. Remove to a
serving dish and keep warm. Add the wine and scrape up the cooking juices.

3. Add the watercress, spinach, chives, and tarragon. Season with
salt and pepper and cook for 2 minutes, or until wilted. Purée in a
blender.

4. Return the mixture to the pan, season and bring to a boil. Add
the crème fraîche, bring to a boil, stirring, and remove from the
heat. Pour the sauce over the salmon and serve.

Yield: 4 servings.

FILLETS OF SHAD STUFFED WITH SPINACH

Spring marks the arrival of shad and shad roe in the market. As the water gets warmer, the fish come to the rivers to spawn. At this point they are at their fattest and most succulent.

Shad has a delicate white flesh and a spectacular roe. Because the fish itself is very bony it is normally sold in fillets. Even then the flesh should be checked carefully for any lurking bones. These can be removed with tweezers. Fillets usually have the skin left on, and in order to get at the bones, fishmongers usually cut the flesh so that two convenient flaps are fashioned. These can be folded over a stuffing. Puréed fresh young spinach or sorrel is especially good stuffed inside the fillet which can then be broiled. If using sorrel, do not bother to purée it.

Serve this dish with new potatoes, boiled with a sprig of mint.

1 pound shad fillets
   Juice of ½ lemon
1 pound spinach
1 tablespoon unsalted buttter
1 shallot, minced
   Coarse salt and freshly ground pepper to taste
1 tablespoon peanut or vegetable oil
   Lemon quarters for garnish

1. Place the fillet of shad on a plate and squeeze the lemon juice over the flesh. Marinate at room temperature for 1 hour or so.

2. Remove the stems from the spinach and carefully wash the leaves in several changes of water. Drain.

3. Melt the butter in a frying pan and soften the shallot. Add the spinach and cook until it is barely wilted. Season with salt and pepper and purée.

4. Heat the broiler. Take a piece of foil twice the width of the shad fillet and place the shad skin side down on one side of the foil so that later you can turn the fillet over onto the other side of the foil.

Place the spinach purée in the middle of the fillet and close the overhanging flaps of flesh over it. Flip the fish over on the foil so that it is now skin side up. Sprinkle with oil.

5. Broil until the skin is crisp (about 5 minutes). Using the foil as a lever, turn the fish over. Broil until done, about 3 to 4 minutes, and serve.

Yield: 2 servings.

SHAD ROE WITH BACON

Shad roe is a perfect dish for one or two people. In England it is still sometimes eaten for breakfast, a tradition that dates back to Victorian times. In the following recipe, it is simply browned in butter and served with bacon.

1 pair shad roe
4 slices bacon
   Flour for dredging
2 tablespoons unsalted butter
   Coarse salt and freshly ground pepper to taste
2 lemon quarters
   Chopped parsley for garnish

1. Poach the roes in boiling water for 2 minutes. Drain and cool.

2. Meanwhile, fry the bacon until it is crisp. Drain and keep warm.

3. Dip the roes in the flour and dredge lightly, shaking off all excess. Melt the butter in a frying pan and fry the roes until they are golden on both sides. Handle carefully to prevent from splitting.

4. Place the roes on individual heated plates, season with salt and pepper, and garnish with the bacon, lemon quarters, and parsley. Serve with boiled or mashed potatoes.

Yield: 2 servings.

BROILED RED SNAPPER WITH THYME

In the Mediterranean, tiny red mullet are a favorite fish, marinated and broiled over sprigs of thyme or fennel stalks. Small red snapper can be successfully cooked this way and makes a spectacular dish when marinated in red wine, olive oil, and fresh thyme. They are then placed over sprigs of thyme on aluminum foil and broiled. Black olives and slices of lemon make an attractive garnish.

- 4 small or 2 medium-sized red snappers
- 1 cup dry red wine
- ½ cup extra virgin olive oil
- 2 tablespoons chopped fresh thyme leaves
  Coarse salt and freshly ground pepper to taste
  About 8 sprigs fresh thyme
- 1 cup pitted Gaeta or Niçoise olives
- 8 lemon slices

1. Score the fish twice in the thickest part of the flesh on each side. Combine the wine, oil, thyme, salt, and pepper in a large flat dish with a rim. Marinate the snapper in the mixture for 1 or 2 hours at room temperature.

2. If cooking under a broiler, place a sheet of aluminum foil on a rack on the broiling pan. Oil the foil with olive oil and strew it with the sprigs of thyme. Place the fish on top and broil for 5 minutes on each side, depending on the size of the fish. Baste with the marinade.

3. Arrange the fish on a serving dish and garnish with the olives and lemon slices.

Yield: 4 servings.

GRILLED FISH YUCATÁN STYLE

Mexicans often grill fish over an open fire or on small charcoal braziers called comales, *in a style that has not changed since the Aztec and Mayan civilizations. The following recipe can be cooked on an outdoor grill or inside under a broiler. It is good with rice. The chilies can be bought at Spanish specialty stores. Fresh green chilies can be substituted if the dried ones are not available.*

1	4-pound red snapper, cleaned, with head and tail intact
4	limes
4	chilies *ancho*
4	chilies *pequín*
3	garlic cloves
	Coarse salt and freshly ground black pepper to taste
⅓ to ½	cup red or white wine vinegar
3	tablespoons peanut or sesame oil

1. Wipe the fish dry with paper towels and squeeze the juice from 2 of the limes on the skin and inside the cavity of the fish. Leave to marinate.

2. Soak the chilies *ancho* and *pequín* in boiling water to cover for 30 minutes. Put them in a blender with the garlic, salt, pepper, vinegar, and oil. Blend to a purée.

3. Coat the fish with the chili paste. Broil over hot coals or under high heat, basting occasionally with additional oil. Turn once. Serve with the remaining limes cut into wedges.

Yield: 6 to 8 servings.

STEAMED FISH WITH SEAWEED

Squares of nori, *Japanese seaweed that is sold in health food stores, are wrapped around the fish which is then steamed. The seaweed gives the fish a wonderful flavor of the sea. Use firm, white-fleshed whole small fish, such as red snapper or bass, cleaned and scaled but with their heads on, or fish fillets. If using fillets, cook for less time, depending on the thickness of the fillets. Serve this with rice and Stir-Fried Cabbage with Shiitake Mushrooms, page 204.*

  4 small whole white-fleshed fish or fillets
  8 squares seaweed
  2 tablespoons minced fresh ginger
  4 teaspoons soy sauce
     Juice of ½ lemon
     Freshly ground pepper to taste

1. Rinse the fish under cold water. Moisten each square of seaweed as you use it so that it softens and wraps easily around the fish. Place a fish on a piece of seaweed, put some ginger in the cavity, and sprinkle the cavity, with soy sauce, lemon juice, and pepper. Wrap the seaweed around the fish and cover any gaps with a second layer of seaweed.

2. Place the wrapped fish side by side in the top half of a steamer. Steam for 15 to 20 minutes, or until the fish is cooked and flakes easily when tested with a fork.

Yield: 4 servings.

SOLE MEUNIÈRE WITH LIMES

Serve with rice or mashed potatoes.

4 tablespoons unsalted butter at room temperature
   Coarse salt and freshly ground pepper to taste
2 limes
2 tablespoons chopped chives
½ teaspoon grated fresh ginger
4 sole fillets or other white fish fillets
   Flour for dredging
3 to 4 tablespoons clarified butter (see page 283)

1. Mash the unsalted butter with the salt and pepper in a small bowl. Work in the juice of 1 of the limes. Grate a teaspoon of the rind and add with the chives and grated ginger. Mix thoroughly, shape into a roll about 1 inch in diameter, wrap in foil, and place in the freezer.

2. Pat the fish fillets dry with paper towels. Dredge them lightly with flour. Heat the clarified butter and fry the fillets, turning once, until they are golden brown.

3. Arrange the fish on a heated serving dish and garnish with the remaining lime, cut into quarters, and slices of the lime butter, placed on top of the fillets.

Yield: 4 servings.

SOLE WITH SAFFRON SAUCE

Any firm white-fleshed fish fillet can be used on this recipe. I first made it with yellowtail in Nantucket one winter. The sauce, which should be strained, is a burnished gold color. Serve the fish with rice or mashed potatoes.

To expand this recipe to feed four, use 2 pounds of fillets and add an extra peeled tomato and ½ cup of white wine or water to the sauce. If necessary, add more liquid.

2 tablespoons unsalted butter
2 shallots, minced
1 ripe tomato, peeled
1 teaspoon tomato purée
   Pinch of saffron threads
1 cup dry white wine
   Sprig of thyme
   Sprig of rosemary
1 pound sole or other white-fleshed fish fillets
   Coarse salt and freshly ground pepper to taste

1. Melt 1 tablespoon of the butter in a frying pan and sauté the shallots until soft but not brown. Add the tomato, tomato purée, saffron, wine, thyme, and rosemary. Bring to a boil, cover, lower the heat, and cook for 10 minutes.

2. Strain the sauce into a bowl. Melt the remaining butter in the frying pan and add the fillets. Cook for 2 minutes; then turn the fillets over. Add the sauce, cover, and simmer for 5 minutes, or until the fish is cooked. If the sauce is too liquid (the fillets will yield some juice), remove the fish and keep it warm. Reduce the sauce over high heat, correct the seasoning, and pour it over the fish.

Yield: 2 servings.

SOLE WITH ZUCCHINI

Use the smallest, most tender zucchini you can find. Zucchini blossoms are exquisite added toward the end of the cooking. Their delicate but intense flavor—almost like "essence" of zucchini—goes beautifully with sole. In this recipe, which is very quick and simple, the fish and vegetables are cooked separately and served in one dish.

FOR THE ZUCCHINI

- 1 pound small zucchini
- 1 tablespoon extra virgin olive oil
- 1 shallot, minced
- 1 garlic clove, minced
- Zucchini blossoms, if available (about 1 cup)
- Coarse salt and freshly ground pepper to taste
- Fresh basil or tarragon leaves for garnish

FOR THE SOLE

- 4 sole fillets
- 1 egg, beaten
- Coarse salt and freshly ground pepper to taste
- 1 cup dry bread crumbs
- 3 to 4 tablespoons clarified butter (page 283)
- 1 lemon, quartered

1. Preheat the oven to 350 degrees. Slice the zucchini in 1-inch pieces. Heat the oil in a large frying pan and brown the zucchini with the shallot and the garlic. Cook until tender. Add the zucchini blossoms and fry, stirring, for 3 to 5 minutes. Season with salt and pepper and sprinkle with the basil. Keep warm in a slow oven while you cook the fish.

2. Wipe the fillets with paper towels and dip them into the beaten egg seasoned with salt and pepper and then coat with the bread crumbs. Shake off any excess.

3. Heat the clarified butter in a large frying pan and fry the sole,

one or two at a time, until golden on each side. Be careful not to overcook or the sole will disintegrate. Put the cooked sole in the center of a serving dish and keep warm while you finish cooking the remaining fillets.

4. Garnish the sole with the lemon quarters and arrange the zucchini around the edge of the dish.

Yield: 4 servings.

VENETIAN SOLE

4 small sole fillets
4 tablespoons chopped fresh mint leaves
4 tablespoons chopped parsley leaves
1 garlic clove, minced
4 tablespoons unsalted butter
Coarse salt and freshly ground pepper to taste
1 lemon, quartered

1. Wipe the sole dry with paper towels. Score twice against the grain on each side with a knife.

2. Combine the mint, parsley, garlic, and butter. Mix well with a fork and season with salt and pepper.

3. Place the sole on a broiling pan that has been covered with aluminum foil. Press half the herb butter over each sole. Turn the fish over and repeat on the other side. Set aside until ready to broil.

4. Heat the broiler to high. Broil the sole for 2 to 3 minutes on one side. Carefully turn over with a spatula. Broil on the other side until the sole starts to flake when tested with a fork, about 3 to 4 minutes. Do not overcook.

5. Arrange the sole on a platter or individual plates. Pour on the juices remaining in the pan. Garnish with lemon quarters.

Yield: 4 servings.

SWORDFISH AU BEURRE BLANC

This recipe comes from chef Pascal Dirringer. Serve it with fresh leaf spinach, new potatoes, and chilled Muscadet.

FOR THE BEURRE BLANC

- 1 cup finely chopped shallots
- 1 cup dry white wine
- 1 cup white wine vinegar
- 12 ounces unsalted butter, softened
   Coarse salt and freshly ground white pepper to taste

FOR THE SWORDFISH

- 1 shallot, chopped
- 1 bay leaf
- 2 sprigs parsley, chopped
- 6 small swordfish steaks or large ones, halved (about 3 pounds total weight)
   Coarse salt and freshly ground pepper to taste
- 1 cup dry white wine

1. Prepare the beurre blanc. Combine the shallots, wine, and vinegar in a casserole over medium heat. Allow to reduce almost completely.

2. Fold the butter slowly into the shallots. Place the butter sauce in the top of a double boiler to keep it warm but not hot or it will separate. Season with the salt and pepper. The sauce should be ivory in color and velvety in texture.

3. Prepare the swordfish. Line the bottom of a casserole with the chopped shallot, bay leaf, and parsley. Arrange the swordfish in the casserole and add the salt, pepper, and wine. Cover the contents with water and cook over medium heat for 10 minutes.

4. Remove the swordfish to a warm serving dish and spoon the beurre blanc over the steaks.

Yield: 6 servings.

SWORDFISH STEAKS WITH OLIVE AND TOMATO SAUCE

FOR THE SAUCE

- 1 tablespoon safflower oil
- 2 shallots, minced
- 1 garlic clove, minced
- 4 tomatoes, peeled, seeded, and chopped, or 1½ cups canned tomatoes
   Grated rind of ½ lemon
- ½ cup chopped Greek or Italian olives
   Coarse salt and freshly ground pepper to taste
   Cayenne pepper to taste
- 1 tablespoon dry vermouth
- ½ cup dry white wine

FOR THE FISH

- 2 swordfish steaks, about 1 pound each
- 3 to 4 tablespoons crème fraîche (page 282)
- 1 tablespoon chopped chives
- 2 tablespoons chopped Italian flat-leafed parsley

1. Heat the oil in a frying pan and add the shallots and garlic. Cook gently without browning until they are soft. Add the tomatoes (with their juice), the lemon rind, olives, salt, pepper, cayenne, vermouth, and wine. Cover and simmer for 15 to 20 minutes over low heat. If the sauce is too thick, thin it with a little wine or water.

2. Meanwhile, heat the broiler. Brush the steaks with the crème fraîche and broil about 2 inches from the heat for 5 to 7 minutes on each side, turning once and basting with more crème fraîche if they are drying out. Remove to a heated platter.

3. Taste the sauce for seasoning and pour it over the fish. Sprinkle with the chives and parsley and serve.

Yield: 4 servings.

BAKED TROUT WITH FENNEL

Good for bland commercial trout. Serve with boiled new potatoes.

2 tablespoons unsalted butter
1 garlic clove, minced
1 slice prosciutto, minced
1 head fennel, finely chopped
4 trout
   Coarse salt and freshly ground pepper to taste
   Juice of 1 lemon
   Fennel leaves for garnish
1 lemon, quartered

1. Preheat the oven to 375 degrees.

2. Melt the butter in a frying pan and sauté the garlic, prosciutto, and fennel until the fennel begins to soften.

3. Butter a fireproof dish. Sprinkle the cavities of the trout with salt, pepper, and lemon juice. Arrange the prosciutto-fennel mixture inside the cavities and around the fish. Bake for 10 to 15 minutes, or until the trout flakes when pierced with a fork.

4. Garnish with the fennel leaves and lemon quarters.

Yield: 4 servings.

GRILLED TROUT

Serve with boiled new potatoes and a green vegetable or salad.

  4 trout
    Coarse salt and freshly ground pepper to taste
  ½ cup unsalted butter
  3 lemons

1. Using a sharp knife, make 2 or 3 diagonal cuts in the sides of the trout. Sprinkle them inside and out with salt and pepper.

2. Preheat the broiler to hot.

3. Meanwhile, melt the butter and add to it the juice of 1 of the lemons. Keep warm.

4. Place a piece of aluminum foil on the broiling rack and heat the pan. When it is hot, brush the fish with melted butter and lay them on the pan. Broil for 5 minutes, close to the heat, basting with the butter. Then move the trout further away from the heat and broil for another 2 to 4 minutes. Turn the fish over and broil on the other side. The skin should be browned and the flesh tender but not dry.

5. Place the trout on a heated serving dish and pour over the basting juices. Garnish with the remaining lemons, cut into quarters.

Yield: 4 servings.

GRILLED TUNA WITH TOMATO SAUCE

Tuna is a rich, fatty fish so in this recipe it is coated with crème fraîche to seal in its juices while it cooks. It is served with a light tomato sauce that contains no oil or butter, but is seasoned with a touch of balsamic vinegar. It is a lovely dish for the summer when it can be made with fresh tomatoes and basil. Serve with baked or mashed potatoes and Puréed Spinach, page 224.

1 tuna steak (about 1 pound)
1 tablespoon crème fraîche (page 282)
2 medium-sized ripe tomatoes, peeled
½ cup chicken stock (page 285)
1 tablespoon balsamic vinegar, or to taste
   Coarse salt and freshly ground pepper to taste
   Chopped fresh basil leaves for garnish

1. Spread the crème fraîche thinly over the surface of the tuna and set it aside.

2. Place the tomatoes, chicken stock, and vinegar in a blender and purée. Place the purée in a small pan and season with salt and pepper. Bring to boil and simmer gently until the sauce has thickened. If necessary, add more chicken stock. Correct the seasoning, adding more vinegar, if necessary.

3. Preheat the broiler and broil the tuna for about 5 to 7 minutes on each side. It should be pink in the middle.

4. Arrange the tuna on a serving dish, pour the sauce over the top, and garnish with the basil leaves.

Yield: 2 servings.

FOUR

Shellfish

Nothing is as redolent of the sea as fresh shellfish in its natural state. And since the quality and availability of seafood in our markets has improved immeasurably in the last few years, it is now possible to cook the sort of meals that once seemed possible only at the seaside. For people with small kitchens, shellfish offers a variety of dishes that are easy to prepare—and usually inexpensive. Chowders or bowls of steamed mussels or clams, served with French bread and salad, make a complete one-dish meal with little fuss. (Mussels are a certain amount of trouble to clean—they must be scrubbed and their "beards" removed—but they are one of the cheapest foods and contain high quantities of iron and calcium.)

Shrimp fetch higher prices, but they, too, are quick to cook. The large ones are good broiled or steamed in their shells and served with homemade mayonnaise. I also like to cook smaller shrimp in their shells in white wine and shallots, just enough to turn them pink, and then turn them into a bowl and serve them immediately with homemade mayonnaise. (Be careful not to overcook shrimp or they will become dry.)

Scallops are a real convenience food—they require very little cooking and can be broiled or sautéed and served in a sauce, accompanied by rice. Squid is also easy to prepare, whether it is stir-fried with garlic and ginger, or stuffed with ricotta cheese and spinach, or Parmesan and ham, flavored with saffron and baked.

CLAM CHOWDER

This easy and filling chowder makes a complete meal when followed by cheese and salad. The combination of salt pork and clams is rather salty, so do not add any more salt to the chowder. If the chowder seems too salty, add more milk or another potato.

- 1 dozen quahog or 2 dozen cherrystone clams
- ¼ pound salt pork, diced
- 1 medium-sized onion, chopped
- 1 sweet green pepper, chopped
- 3 large potatoes, peeled and diced
- 2 cups milk
  Freshly ground pepper to taste
  Paprika to taste

1. Open the clams and strain their juice through a double layer of cheesecloth or a paper towel placed in a colander over a bowl. Set the clams and juice aside.

2. Simmer the salt pork in water to cover for 5 minutes. Drain. In a large stock pot, sauté the salt pork until it is golden. Add the onion and green pepper and cook until they are soft.

3. Strain off the fat and add the clam juice and potatoes. If there is not enough liquid, add water to cover the potatoes. Bring to boil, lower the heat, and simmer until the potatoes are tender.

4. Chop the clams coarsely. Add the milk, pepper, and paprika to the pot. Bring to boil and taste for seasoning. Add the clams. Cook for 3 minutes and serve.

Yield: 4 servings.

SOFT SHELL CRABS WITH LIME SAUCE

This recipe is adapted from Colette Rossant's Slim Cuisine. *The crabs are steamed and served with an egg-based lime and basil sauce. It is a delicious and different way to serve soft shell crabs.*

 2 limes
 3 eggs
 ¼ cup snipped fresh basil leaves
    Coarse salt and freshly ground pepper to taste
 1 2-inch piece fresh ginger
 8 ready-to-cook soft shell crabs
    Basil leaves for garnish

1. Grate the zest of the limes and set it aside.

2. Squeeze the juice of the limes into a bowl. Beat together the lime juice and the eggs. Cook the egg mixture in the top of a double boiler over simmering water, whisking all the time, until it thickens into a sauce. Remove from the heat and add the basil, grated lime zest, salt, and pepper. Keep warm over the hot water.

3. Grate the ginger. Place the crabs side by side in a steamer, place some grated ginger on top of each crab. Steam, covered, for 8 minutes. Serve on individual plates. Garnish with basil leaves and pour some sauce on the side.

Yield: 4 servings.

MOULES MARINIÈRE

It is now possible to find mussels that have been grown on wooden frames or stakes and shipped in 2-pound bags from Maine. Their black and silver shells are so smooth they even appear already washed. They are at their best in September through May and can be especially low priced toward the end of the season. A couple of pounds of mussels can make an exceedingly inexpensive dinner for two.

Moules Marinière are a popular dish in French restaurants, but, curiously, few people bother to make them at home. It is remarkably easy. A court bouillon is made from white wine, onion, and herbs and the mussels are then steamed in the broth for 5 minutes. With French bread and a green salad to follow, you have a complete meal. If the broth seems at all sandy, strain it through cheesecloth before serving it with the mussels.

Scrub the mussels with a stiff brush under cool running water. They have a little "beard" on one side of their shells and this should be pulled off. The shells should be closed. If they are open, run them under cold water. If they remain open, the mussel is probably dead and should be thrown away. Discard any mussels that are heavy for their size—they may be filled with sand or pebbles—or any that have broken shells.

In Belgium, plump orange mussels are sold from street carts, along with French fries. They are as popular as hot dogs in the United States.

1 onion, chopped
3 sprigs parsley plus 2 tablespoons chopped parsley leaves
¼ teaspoon dried thyme
2 pieces lemon peel
1 teaspoon whole peppercorns
1 cup dry white wine
1 cup water
2 pounds mussels
2 tablespoons unsalted butter

1. Combine the onion, parsley sprigs, thyme, lemon peel, peppercorns, wine, and water in a casserole large enough to hold the mussels. Bring to a boil, lower the heat, and simmer, covered, for 10 minutes.

2. Meanwhile, pull off the beards from the mussels. Scrub the shells and rinse them thoroughly in cool water. Discard any that feel unusually heavy (they may be filled with sand) or that are open.

3. Bring the court bouillon to a boil and add the butter. When it has melted, add the mussels. Cover and shake the casserole a couple of times so the mussels are distributed evenly. Boil for 5 minutes, or until the mussels have opened.

4. Remove the mussels with a slotted spoon. Stir the remaining parsley into the sauce and pour the sauce over the mussels.

Yield: 2 main-course servings, or 4 first-course servings.

Note: If the broth is at all sandy, strain it through cheesecloth before adding the parsley. Then pour it over the mussels.

SCALLOPS

One winter I went scalloping in Nantucket—a place that at that time of year probably has as much appeal for many people as a visit to Miami Beach in August. In fact, it is a remarkable time to go: There are few tourists and the beaches are empty except for gulls foraging in the surf and sandpipers that run along the shore so fast their legs are a blur. The weather changes in seconds from fog to sunshine.

The morning after I arrived, I dressed in several layers of wool and head-to-foot in oilskins and went out on the bay in a small wooden boat. Piled on a board in front of me was an enormous heap of eel grass, rocks, monkfish (with snapping teeth), baby flounder, crabs, and conch shells. My job was to sort through this for the scallops. It was raining.

I had expected to rise before dawn, so on a day such as this I was glad that scalloping is forbidden before 6:30 A.M. (It's also forbidden if the water is colder than 28 degrees.) On the shore we had felt awkward and ridiculous in our enormous boots, heavy hooded slickers, and giant orange oilskin pants held up by suspenders, like babies' rompers. Out on the water all this felt barely sufficient.

We brought the scallops up in dredges made of metal frames interwoven with string and iron rings that scrape along the bay floor, dragging up the scallops and whatever else happens to be down there. As we sorted through them, the rain fell gently on our faces, misting up our glasses and forming salt on our noses.

Underwater, the scallop flits like a bird through the eel grass where it lives and hops along by snapping together its two shells like a castanet, squirting water through the membrane between the fluted edges of the shells. The water is propelled by a single muscle that connects the shells and opens and closes them. The muscle is the part that we eat. In the United States and Canada, the rest of the creature is almost always thrown out, even though it is edible. The shells are light and fluted and come in the most glorious colors: yellow, purple, rose, brown, black, and white, and often have the most curious things stuck to them.

The scallop shell is familiar to many as the essential component of coquilles St. Jacques. It is also called a Pilgrim's Badge, since, during the Middle Ages, the shells were used as cups or spoons and were worn around the necks of the devout on the annual pilgrimage to Santiago de Compostella in Spain. There are many versions of the legend of St. James. In the story preferred by the late Waverley Root, a nobleman was riding in his wedding procession when his horse bolted and plunged into the sea. With its rider clinging to its back, the horse swam toward an approaching boat, which happened to be carrying the body of St. James, the apostle of Christ who had been beheaded by King Herod in Jerusalem. Horse and rider, covered with scallop shells, returned to land with the body of the saint. The nobleman was at once converted to Christianity though the horse, says Root, "we may safely assume was already in a state of grace."

When we had sorted two bushels of scallops, we returned to shore. Normally the scallops would be shucked for the market in the harbor by shuckers who are paid by the pound, but we took our haul to a shack behind our friends' house.

Shucking scallops can be a disconcerting experience once you learn that each one has about thirty eyes. You imagine them staring at you as you open the shells. Although these eyes are the size of pinheads, they can distinguish light and movement, they have a cornea, lens, and an optic nerve— and they are bright blue.

You open the scallops by inserting the blade of a knife along one side of the shell and prying it open. If you don't hold the knife at the correct angle, you'll cut the scallop (the adductor muscle that holds the two halves of the shell together) in half. When you open the shell properly, inside you find what looks like a clam sitting on top of a scallop (the "clam" part is actually the innards and the roe). Occasionally we'd find a baby crab inside, too.

There are many ways to cook scallops: in chowder; with garlic and herbs; with other seafood, such as lobster, clams or fish; and as a sauce for pasta. Sea and bay scallops can be used interchangeably, but the flavor of sea scallops is not as delicate as that of the bay scallops, and they are much larger. All scallops excude a lot of juice when they are cooked and they should be cooked as little as possible, or they will become tough.

That night I returned home with our catch. We ate half the

scallops raw, with lemon juice. The rest I sautéed with shallots and white wine. Those scallops, caught by us in the bay hours earlier, were like nothing I had ever eaten before. For me the experience was comparable with eating the best caviar, the freshest farm egg, or the most perfect foie gras. It was a simple meal, and I had gone out and caught it myself.

BROILED SCALLOPS WITH RED PEPPER

These scallops can be broiled in scallop shells or in the heavy frying pan in which the garlic has been cooked, placed under the boiler. Serve them with a green vegetable and rice or baked potatoes.

- 2 pounds bay or sea scallops
  Juice of 2 lemons
  Juice of 2 limes
- 2 tablespoons extra virgin olive oil
- 2 garlic cloves, minced
- 1 teaspoon hot red pepper flakes, or more, according to taste
- ¾ cup toasted fine dry bread crumbs, preferably homemade
- 4 tablespoons finely chopped parsley leaves
  Coarse salt and freshly ground pepper to taste
- 2 tablespoons unsalted butter, cut into small pieces

1. Marinate the scallops for 1 hour in the lemon and lime juice.

2. Preheat the broiler.

3. In a heavy skillet, heat the oil and gently sauté the garlic until it is soft. Add the hot pepper flakes and mix thoroughly. Remove from the heat.

4. Add the scallops to the pan with half the bread crumbs and the parsley. Season with salt and pepper and mix well.

5. Put the scallop mixture into four scallop shells. Top with the remaining bread crumbs and the pieces of butter. Broil for 2 to 3 minutes, just enough to brown the top without overcooking the scallops or they will become tough.

Yield: 4 servings.

SCALLOPS WITH SHALLOTS AND WINE

This simple recipe is good for scallops that are very fresh. There will probably be quite a lot of juice, so barely cook the scallops and keep them warm while you boil down the juices with the wine for the sauce. Be very careful not to overcook the scallops or they will be tough.

3 tablespoons unsalted butter
2 shallots, minced
2 pounds bay scallops
½ cup dry white wine
   Coarse salt and freshly ground pepper to taste
1 lemon, cut into quarters
   Chopped fresh parsley for garnish

1. Melt 2 tablespoons of the butter in a heavy skillet and cook the shallots until they are soft but not brown. Add the scallops and cook for 2 minutes. (You may need to sauté them in two batches.) Remove with a slotted spoon and keep them warm.

2. Add the wine to the skillet and bring to a boil. Reduce the sauce to about ¾ cup. Correct the seasoning.

3. Remove the skillet from the heat and beat in the remaining butter. Pour the sauce over the scallops, garnish with the lemon and parsley, and serve.

Yield: 4 to 6 servings.

SCALLOPS WITH CREAM AND TOMATO SAUCE

This goes with rice. Be careful not to overcook the scallops or to have too high a heat when you are thickening the sauce with the egg yolks.

- 2 pounds bay scallops
  Juice of 1 lemon
- 2 tablespoons unsalted butter
- 2 shallots, minced
- ½ cup dry white wine
- 2 cups ripe tomatoes, peeled, seeded, and cubed, or use canned tomatoes
- 1 cup heavy cream
- 2 egg yolks
  Coarse salt and freshly ground pepper to taste

1. Marinate the scallops in the lemon juice for 1 hour.

2. Melt the butter in a large frying pan and gently fry the shallots without browning them. Add the scallops and cook for 2 minutes. Remove with a slotted spoon and keep them warm.

3. Add the wine and the tomatoes and cook for 10 minutes. Add the cream and any juice that has accumulated around the scallops in the bowl.

4. Beat the egg yolks and spoon ½ cup of the hot sauce into the yolks. Mix thoroughly. Add the mixture to the sauce, stirring, and cook over medium-low heat until the sauce has thickened. Season with salt and pepper.

5. Return the scallops to the sauce and heat through.

Yield: 4 to 6 servings.

STIR-FRIED SCALLOPS WITH SESAME SEEDS

Serve this Oriental dish with steamed rice.

1 pound scallops
Juice of 1 orange
Juice of ½ lemon
2 tablespoons peanut or safflower oil
3 scallions, finely chopped
1 teaspoon minced fresh ginger
1 small fresh green chili, seeded and finely chopped
2 tablespoons toasted sesame seeds
Soy sauce to taste
2 tablespoons chopped fresh coriander leaves
1 teaspoon cornstarch mixed with 1 teaspoon dry sherry or
water

1. Marinate the scallops for 1 hour in the orange and lemon juice.

2. Heat the oil in a wok or large frying pan. Stir-fry the scallions with the ginger and chili for 1 minute. Add the scallops with their juice and stir-fry for 2 to 3 minutes. Remove with a slotted spoon and keep warm. Add the cornstarch mixture and bring to a boil.

3. Add soy sauce to taste, stir in the coriander and sesame seeds, pour over the scallops, and serve.

Yield: 3 to 4 servings.

SHRIMP WITH TOMATO AND FETA CHEESE SAUCE

This Greek dish is especially good during the summer. Follow it with a mixed green salad and fruit. If you wish to make it more substantial, accompany it with rice. Use an ovenproof dish that goes both on top of the stove and in the oven. A cast-iron skillet works very well here.

1   medium-sized onion, chopped
3   tablespoons extra virgin olive oil
2   garlic cloves, minced
1½ pounds very ripe tomatoes, peeled, seeded, and chopped, or
        3 cups canned tomatoes
½   dry red or white wine
½   cup chopped parsley leaves
     Coarse salt and freshly ground pepper to taste
     Cayenne pepper to taste
2   pounds unshelled shrimp
½   pound feta cheese, crumbled

1. Preheat the oven to 400 degrees.

2. Cook the onion in the olive oil over medium-to-low heat until it is soft. Add the garlic, tomatoes, wine, parsley, salt, pepper, and cayenne.

3. Meanwhile, peel the shrimp. Add the cheese to the tomato sauce and stir in the shrimp. Bake for 15 minutes, or until the shrimp are cooked. Be careful not to overcook the shrimp or they will be dry.

Yield: 4 servings.

Note: In the summer, fresh basil leaves may be sprinkled on top of this dish just before it is served.

BROILED SHRIMP WITH DILL MARINADE

If you have a food processor you can save time by mincing the garlic cloves (you don't have to peel them) with the dill leaves, using the blade attachment.

- 1 pound unshelled large shrimp
- 4 cloves garlic, minced
- ¾ cup minced fresh dill
- 1 tablespoon hot red pepper flakes
- 3 tablespoons extra virgin olive oil
  Juice of 1 lemon
  Freshly ground pepper to taste
  Coarse salt to taste

1. Rinse and drain the shrimp. Combine the remaining ingredients, except the salt. Coat the shrimp thoroughly with this mixture and marinate for 1 hour at room temperature.

2. Preheat the broiler to hot and broil the shrimp, basting with the marinade mixture. They will take only a minute or two on each side, depending on how big they are. Be careful not to overcook them or the shrimp will taste floury. Season with salt before serving.

Yield: 2 servings.

SQUID

Squid is the least alluring of the mollusks. Even though it is inexpensive and readily available, Americans are put off by its peculiar shape and its resemblance in miniature to a Hollywood monster of the deep. But they are missing a treat. Squid is much beloved in the Mediterranean, where it goes under the prettier names of calamari, kalamari, or calmar. It can be made into the most fragrant of stews and has the most perfect shape for stuffing of any food. It also has the added advantage of being low in fat and calories and high in protein. Squid is inexpensive, with little waste in cleaning.

When cooked properly, the flesh becomes very light and tender. Spinach, ham, rice, or cheese make fine stuffings. Squid can also be stewed with tomatoes and white wine, flavored with rosemary, oregano, or basil. Chopped anchovies and a liberal dose of hot red pepper flakes are also good in the sauce. Saffron goes well with squid, too, and produces a deep orange sauce. One of the best seafood dishes one finds in Venice is squid cooked in its own ink, which makes a rich black gravy; it is served with slices of toasted polenta. The Spanish and Cubans also cook squid in its own ink—with rice. Pieces of chopped squid are also delicious in fish soup and paella.

The most important thing to remember about squid is that it must be cooked either for a very short or a very long time. Anything in between will make it rubbery. Frying should take a minute. If you are steaming squid, 5 minutes is ample—just enough to turn the flesh opaque. When squid is simmered, cook it for at least 40 to 45 minutes and test with a toothpick to make sure the flesh is tender.

When buying squid, choose those that are milky white with pale pink overtones underneath the outer mottled, grayish-purple skin. Squid that is not fresh may have darkened right through.

To prepare squid for cooking, hold it with one hand and with the other reach inside the body and pull away the head and tentacles. Peel away the dark skin. Inside the body is a transparent cartilage that looks as though it is made of plastic. Pull this out and discard it.

Cut the tentacles from the head above the eyes. If there is an ink sac, remove it. If you are using it for a sauce, set it aside; otherwise, discard it. Throw away the remains of the head. Rinse the body and tentacles under cool running water. Make sure that you have cleaned the cavity thoroughly so that it does not taste sandy when it is stuffed. If you are slicing the squid, it can be rinsed again after you have sliced it.

SQUID STUFFED WITH RICOTTA AND SPINACH

Do not overstuff the squid or they may split while they cook. Rice and braised fennel go well with this dish.

8 large squid (about 2 pounds)
1 medium-sized onion, minced
1 garlic clove, minced
2 tablespoons olive oil
1 tablespoon unsalted butter
½ pound fresh spinach, trimmed of stems and washed, or ½
    package frozen, thawed
⅔ pound ricotta
1 egg
1 tablespoon chopped Italian parsley leaves
  Coarse salt and freshly ground pepper to taste
  Hot red pepper flakes to taste
½ cup dry white wine
2 cups canned Italian tomatoes
1 lemon, quartered

1. Preheat the oven to 375 degrees. Clean the squid and chop the tentacles finely. Set them aside.

2. Sauté the onion and the garlic in 1 tablespoon of the olive oil and the butter until the onion is soft. Add the tentacles and cook for 2 minutes. Add the spinach and sauté, stirring, until it has wilted. Drain off any extra liquid and cool the spinach.

3. In a mixing bowl, combine the ricotta, egg, parsley, and the cooled spinach mixture. Mix thoroughly and season with salt, pepper, and hot pepper flakes.

4. Stuff the mixture loosely into the squid and close the openings securely with a toothpick.

5. Use the remaining tablespoon of olive oil to grease a rectangular baking dish large enough to hold the squid comfortably in one layer. Arrange the squid in the dish and add the wine and tomatoes. Season with salt, pepper, and more hot pepper flakes, if you wish.

6. Bake for 40 to 45 minutes, or until the squid is tender and the sauce has thickened. If there is too much sauce, raise the oven temperature and allow the liquid to reduce. If there is too little, add more white wine. Serve the squid with lemon quarters.

Yield: 4 servings.

SQUID WITH SAFFRON SAUCE

Rice and a green vegetable go with this dish.

8 large squid (about 2 pounds)
1 tablespoon extra virgin olive oil
1 small onion, chopped
1 garlic clove, minced
2 egg yolks
½ cup freshly grated Parmesan cheese
¼ pound smoked ham, diced
½ cup fresh white bread crumbs
   Coarse salt and freshly ground pepper to taste
2 tablespoons chopped parsley leaves

FOR THE SAFFRON SAUCE

- 1 tablespoon olive oil
- 1 small onion, chopped
- 1 garlic clove, minced
- 1 cup chopped, peeled tomatoes, canned Italian or fresh in season
- 1 cup dry white wine
- 1 teaspoon crumbled saffron threads
- 1 bay leaf
- 1 teaspoon dried thyme
- ½ teaspoon dried oregano
  Coarse salt and freshly ground pepper to taste
- 2 tablespoons chopped Italian parsley leaves

1. Clean the squid and chop the tentacles. Heat the oil in a large frying pan and cook the onion and garlic until soft but not brown. Add the tentacles and cook for 5 minutes.

2. In a mixing bowl, combine the egg yolks, Parmesan, ham, bread crumbs, salt, pepper, and parsley. Add the tentacles and mix thoroughly.

3. Stuff the squid with the mixture and close the openings securely with a toothpick.

4. Make the sauce. Heat the oil in a heavy fireproof casserole or frying pan that will hold the squid comfortably in one layer. Sauté the onion and garlic until they are soft. Add the stuffed squid and the remaining ingredients, except the parsley. Simmer, covered, for 20 minutes, basting the squid with the sauce, if necessary.

5. Uncover the squid and cook for 35 minutes longer. Correct the seasoning and baste frequently. Remove the bay leaf, sprinkle the squid with the parsley, and serve.

Yield: 4 servings.

FIVE

Poultry and Game

Factory farming has brought us cheaper birds at the expense of taste. When it comes to chicken, unless you can get a farm-raised free-range bird, you have to think of it as a vehicle for many different flavors. Chicken can be flavored with tarragon, mustard, or saffron, marinated in yogurt and grilled until tender and juicy, or roasted with whole cloves of garlic.

There are many braised dishes in this chapter. They are very simple to make—the ingredients can be chopped and put in the pan and left to cook, which makes them ideal for preparing at the end of the day after work. They also save on washing up—most of them can be served in the pan they have cooked in, whether it is a cast-iron skillet or a casserole.

ROAST CHICKEN WITH GARLIC

In this recipe, the chicken is roasted with a whole head of garlic divided into cloves and cooked in their skins. It may sound like an awful lot of garlic, but, when cooked this way, the cloves are sweet and fragrant and do not develop a strong or harsh flavor. Use only plump, fresh heads of garlic. When the cloves have been roasted with the chicken they can be peeled at the table and the soft insides spread on the chicken or on slices of bread, like butter.

Let the chicken rest before serving it so that the juices do not flow when you carve it. It can sit for up to an hour at room temperature and will be far moister than it is when eaten straight from the oven.

Accompany the chicken with a green or tomato salad. Followed by homemade Strawberry Ice Cream (page 277) or fresh fruit, this makes an especially pleasant spring or summer meal. The chicken is also good cold.

1   3- to 4-pound roasting chicken
1   lemon, cut in half
1   head garlic, separated into cloves
½   cup water
2   tablespoons extra virgin olive oil

1. Preheat the oven to 400 degrees. Wipe the chicken dry with paper towels. Remove the loose fat from inside the cavity. Squeeze the lemon juice on the skin and inside the chicken cavity.

2. Arrange the chicken in a roasting pan. Place the garlic around the chicken and pour in the water. Sprinkle the chicken with the oil.

3.   Roast for 45 minutes to 1 hour, or until the chicken is cooked, basting frequently. The garlic should roast without burning once the water has evaporated. Should the garlic brown too fast, add a little more water.

4. To serve, arrange the chicken surrounded by garlic on a platter.

Yield: 4 servings.

ROAST CHICKEN STUFFED WITH APRICOTS
AND CRACKED WHEAT

Baked potatoes and a green vegetable, such as Puréed Spinach, page 224, or Zucchini with Summer Herbs, page 227, go well with this dish. The stuffing can also be used with Cornish hens.

1	3- to 4-pound roasting chicken
1	lemon
¾	cup cracked wheat (bulgur)
1½	cups water
½	cup dried apricots
	Port to cover (about ¾ cup)
2	tablespoons unsalted butter
1	small onion, chopped
1	garlic clove, minced
2	celery stalks, chopped
	Coarse salt and freshly ground pepper to taste
¼	teaspoon dried thyme

1. Wipe the chicken inside and out with paper towels. Remove the loose fat from inside the cavity. Squeeze the juice of the lemon on the skin and inside the chicken cavity. Set the chicken aside.

2. Put the cracked wheat in a small bowl and add the cold water. Put the apricots in a small saucepan and cover with the port. Let stand for 1 hour.

3. Bring the apricots to a boil, cover, and simmer gently over low heat for 30 minutes, or until tender.

4. Preheat the oven to 350 degrees. Drain the water from the cracked wheat. Melt the butter in a frying pan and gently soften the onion with the garlic and celery. Add the cracked wheat, salt, pepper, and thyme. Mix well and cook for 5 minutes. Add the apricots, whole or chopped, with their juice. Mix thoroughly and cook for another 5 minutes.

5. Stuff the mixture into the chicken and truss, closing the cavity with small skewers or a needle and thread.

6. Roast the chicken for 40 minutes to 1 hour. Let rest at room temperature before serving.

Yield: 4 servings.

CHICKEN WITH ASPARAGUS AND ALMONDS

Serve this with rice.

- 1 3- to 3½-pound chicken, cut up
- 1 tablespoon extra virgin olive oil
- 3 tablespoons unsalted butter
- 2 shallots, minced
- ½ to 1 cup dry white wine
- 1½ pounds asparagus, trimmed to 3-inch pieces
   Coarse salt and freshly ground pepper to taste
- 4 tablespoons sliced toasted almonds
- 2 tablespoons chopped parsley leaves for garnish

1. Wipe the chicken pieces dry with paper towels. In a large casserole, heat the oil and 1 tablespoon of the butter. Brown the chicken pieces a few at a time and set them aside.

2. Add the shallots to the casserole and cook until they are soft. Return the chicken to the pan with ½ cup of white wine. Cover and cook over low heat for 30 minutes.

3. Add the asparagus, salt, and pepper and more wine, if necessary. Cover and cook until the asparagus are tender.

4. Remove from the heat, swirl in the remaining butter, and sprinkle with the almonds and parsley.

Yield: 4 servings.

CHICKEN PROVENÇAL

This is an uncomplicated dish that is full of the flavor of Provence. It goes with Potatoes with Sage or Rosemary, page 222 (in which case omit the basil), or rice. If you are making this in the winter when tomatoes are out of season, use canned tomatoes and substitute flat-leafed parsley for the basil.

- 1 3- to 3½-pound chicken, cut up
- 3 to 4 tablespoons extra virgin olive oil
- 1 medium-sized onion, chopped
- 2 garlic cloves, minced
- 1 leek, well washed and sliced
- 6 ripe tomatoes, peeled
- 1 cup dry white wine
- 20 black Niçoise olives, pitted
- Coarse salt and freshly ground pepper to taste
- Fresh basil leaves for garnish

1. Pat the chicken pieces dry with paper towels. In a heavy casserole, heat the olive oil. Sauté the chicken pieces a few at a time, until they are golden. Set them aside.

2. Add the onion, garlic, and leek to the casserole and sauté until they are soft.

3. Return the chicken to the casserole and add the tomatoes, wine, and olives. Season with salt and pepper. Simmer, covered, for 20 minutes. Remove the cover, turn the chicken pieces in the sauce, and continue cooking, uncovered, for 30 to 40 minutes, turning occasionally. (If the sauce becomes too dry, cover the casserole.) Test for doneness with a skewer or a fork.

4. To serve, sprinkle with the basil leaves torn into medium-sized pieces. (Chopping basil with a knife turns the edges of the leaves brown.)

Yield: 4 servings.

Note: Sprigs of fresh rosemary or ¼ teaspoon of dried rosemary may be used instead of basil. Add when the tomatoes are added.

CHICKEN IN WHITE WINE WITH PARSNIPS

The combination of mushrooms, coriander, and orange peel is a French-Mediterranean one and it goes very well with the comparatively delicate flavors of chicken and parsnips. Steamed string beans or spinach are a good accompaniment.

1	3- to 4-pound chicken, cut up
1	tablespoon unsalted butter
1	tablespoon extra virgin olive oil
1	medium-sized onion, chopped
1	garlic clove, minced
4	large mushrooms (preferably shiitake)
1	carrot, cut into 1-inch pieces
4	parsnips, cut into 1½-inch pieces
1	tablespoon all-purpose flour
1	tablespoon tomato purée
20	coriander seeds, coarsely ground
	Sprig of thyme
2	strips orange peel
2	strips lemon peel
1	cup dry white wine
	Coarse salt and freshly ground pepper to taste

1. Pat the chicken pieces dry with paper towels. Heat the butter and the oil in a casserole and gently brown the chicken pieces. Remove them and add the onion and garlic. Sauté gently until soft but not brown.

2. Slice the mushrooms and add them to the pan with the carrot and parsnips. Sauté briefly and sprinkle with the flour. Cook for another 2 minutes, stirring.

3. Return the chicken pieces to the pan. Add the tomato purée, coriander, thyme, orange and lemon peels, and the white wine. Cover and simmer for 30 to 40 minutes. If necessary, add a little water during cooking. Correct the seasoning and serve.

Yield: 4 servings.

CHICKEN WITH CHILI AND WALNUT SAUCE

This chicken dish is based on a Peruvian Indian recipe. The chicken is cut up and cooked in a rich, thick sauce made with ground walnuts, peanuts, and chilies. It is a one-dish meal that looks extremely attractive served in a pretty casserole and sprinkled with coriander leaves, sesame seeds, and strips of sweet red pepper. It needs no accompanying vegetable, but can be followed by a green salad.

1 3- to 4-pound chicken, cut up
   Water to cover
5 fresh green chilies
2 tablespoons peanut or vegetable oil
4 ounces shelled walnuts
4 ounces shelled peanuts
2 slices bread, crusts removed
2 medium-sized onions, sliced
2 garlic cloves, peeled
2 thick slices fresh ginger, peeled
½ teaspoon ground mace
½ teaspoon ground cinnamon
2 whole cloves
   Coarse salt and freshly ground pepper to taste
   Toasted sesame seeds for garnish
   Coriander or parsley leaves for garnish
1 sweet red pepper, cut into strips

1. Simmer the chicken pieces in 3 cups of water (or more to cover) until almost cooked. Drain and cool, reserving the liquid.

2. Toast the chilies, using a fork, over a gas flame. Wrap in paper towels and set aside.

3. Heat the oil in a large frying pan and fry the walnuts, peanuts, and the bread until lightly browned. Meanwhile, peel and seed the chilies. Combine in a blender with the nut-bread mixture, onions, garlic, ginger, spices, salt, and pepper. Add 1½ cups of the chicken liquid and purée.

4. Thin the mixture with 1 to 2 cups of the chicken liquid until you have a smooth purée. Return to the pan and bring to a boil. Add the chicken and simmer for about 20 minutes, uncovered, until the sauce is thick.

5. Sprinkle with the sesame seeds and coriander leaves. Garnish with the red pepper strips.

Yield: 4 servings.

BROILED CHICKEN IN LEMON-GARLIC MARINADE

Marinate the chicken for a couple of hours or overnight. Serve with grilled sweet corn or rice.

- 2 fresh green chilies, seeded
- 3 garlic cloves, peeled
  Juice of 1 lemon
- 2 tablespoons extra virgin olive oil
- 2 tablespoons chopped parsley leaves
  Freshly ground pepper to taste
- 1 3- to 4-pound chicken, cut up

1. Combine all the ingredients, except the chicken, in a blender and purée. Coat the chicken pieces with the purée and marinate for several hours or overnight.

2. Broil the chicken pieces 7 inches from the broiler flame for 10 minutes on each side, or until done.

Yield: 4 servings.

TANDOORI MARINATED CHICKEN

Serve on lettuce leaves with saffron rice and Indian breads. A salad of tomatoes and onions with chopped coriander or cucumbers with garlic in yogurt also goes well.

½ cup safflower oil
1 cup plain yogurt
1 1-inch piece fresh ginger, minced
½ teaspoon ground cumin
½ teaspoon coriander seeds
½ teaspoon ground turmeric
Juice of 1 lemon
2 small fresh green chilies, minced
2 3-pound chickens, cut up
Chopped fresh coriander leaves for garnish

1. Mix the safflower oil with the yogurt. Put the ginger, cumin seeds, coriander seeds, and turmeric in a spice grinder or mortar. Pulverize. Add the lemon juice. Mix thoroughly and add to the yogurt mixture with the chilies.

2. Skin the chicken pieces and toss them in the marinade. Cover and refrigerate overnight.

3. Preheat the broiler to hot and grill the chicken for about 10 minutes on each side for white meat, 15 for dark, depending on the speed with which the pieces cook. Baste frequently with the marinade. Sprinkle with the coriander and serve.

Yield: 6 servings.

BRAISED CHICKEN WITH PROSCIUTTO
AND PORCINI

Serve this with rice or potatoes.

- 1 ounce porcini mushrooms
- 1 3- to 3½-pound chicken, cut up
- 1 tablespoon vegetable oil
- 1 tablespoon unsalted butter
- 1 small onion, sliced
- 1 garlic clove, minced
- 1 bay leaf
- ½ teaspoon rosemary leaves (preferably fresh)
  Pinch of grated nutmeg
- ¼ cup dry vermouth
- 3 slices prosciutto, julienned
  Coarse salt and freshly ground pepper to taste

1. Soak the mushrooms in warm water to cover for 15 minutes.

2. Heat the oil in a large casserole and brown the chicken pieces. Drain the fat from the casserole.

3. Melt the butter and add the onion and garlic. Cook until soft. Add the chicken and the remaining ingredients. Cover and cook for 30 to 40 minutes, or until the chicken is done.

Yield: 4 servings.

CHICKEN BREASTS STEAMED WITH FENNEL

This low-fat recipe goes well with plain rice.

2 whole chicken breasts, skinned and boned
  Coarse salt and freshly ground black pepper to taste
2 tablespoons minced fresh tarragon leaves or chives, if
    tarragon is not available
1 cup water
1 cup dry white wine
1 carrot, coarsely chopped
1 onion, quartered
2 heads fennel
⅓ cup crème fraîche (page 282)
  Juice of ½ lemon

1. Trim the chicken breasts and cut them in half. Season with salt and pepper and a tablespoon of the tarragon. Set aside.

2. Bring the water, wine, carrot, and onion to a boil in the bottom of a steamer. Slice the bulb ends of the fennel and reserve them. Coarsely chop the stalk and leaves and add them to the stock.

3. Place the chicken breasts in alternating layers with the fennel slices in the top of the steamer. Cover and steam for about 12 minutes, or until the chicken is cooked but still slightly pink and juicy in the center. Remove to a heated plate, cover loosely with aluminum foil, and keep warm.

4. Strain the steaming liquid and reduce it over high heat to 1 cup. Add the crème fraîche and reduce the liquid to 1 cup. Correct the seasoning and add the lemon juice. Pour the sauce over the chicken breasts and fennel and sprinkle with the remaining tarragon.

Yield: 4 servings.

CHICKEN TARRAGON WITH CRÈME FRAÎCHE

When tarragon is in season, this is a particularly easy and appealing dish. It goes with new potatoes or rice. If you like, put some tarragon leaves under the skin of the chicken breasts before cooking them. Heavy cream, with a squeeze of lemon juice may be used in place of crème fraîche. However, do not boil it or the sauce may curdle.

  4 whole chicken breasts, boned
  2 tablespoons unsalted butter
      Coarse salt and freshly ground pepper to taste
  1 small bunch tarragon
  ½ to ¾ cup crème fraîche (page 282)

1. Preheat the oven to 375 degrees. Trim the chicken breasts and cut them in half. In a fireproof pan, melt the butter and lightly brown the chicken. Season with salt and pepper and sprinkle with half the tarragon leaves. Cover and bake for 10 to 15 minutes, or until the breasts are cooked.

2. Remove the pan from the oven and stir in the crème fraîche. Heat through and sprinkle with the remaining tarragon leaves. Correct the seasoning and serve.

Yield: 4 servings.

SMALL BIRDS

Small birds, such as Cornish game hens, pigeons, or young pheasants, make convenient meals for one or two. They are also luxurious and attractive dinner-party dishes, especially appropriate in winter because they go with chestnuts, celery, brussels sprouts, turnips, or red cabbage.

They can also be used interchangeably in the recipes given on the following pages.

CORNISH GAME HENS WITH ROSEMARY AND TURNIPS

Fresh Cornish game hens have been appearing in the markets with increasing frequency in the past few years. The quality is markedly better than it was; the birds have more flesh and their flavor has improved. They are also inexpensive. Whenever possible buy fresh Cornish game hens instead of frozen ones, which have little taste.

1   lemon
2   Cornish game hens
2   sprigs rosemary plus 1 tablespoon rosemary leaves
4   slices thick-cut bacon, diced
1   tablespoon unsalted butter
1   onion, sliced
2   carrots, sliced
1   pound white turnips, cut into 1-inch cubes
1   teaspoon sugar
⅓   cup Cognac
2   tablespoons chopped parsley leaves
     Coarse salt and freshly ground pepper to taste

1. Squeeze the lemon juice over the skin and inside the cavity of the Cornish game hens. Place a sprig of rosemary inside the cavity of each hen. Set the hens aside.

2. In a heavy casserole, brown the bacon; then drain it on paper towels. Brown the hens in the bacon fat and set them aside.

3. Pour off the bacon fat. Melt the butter and add the onion, carrots, and turnips. Sprinkle with the sugar. Sauté until glazed and lightly browned.

4. Return the hens to the casserole breast up. Add the Cognac and light it. When the flames die, turn the hens breast down, cover, and simmer for 15 minutes. Turn the hens breast up and cook for 10 minutes longer, or until the juices run yellowish-pink. Sprinkle with

the bacon, the remaining rosemary leaves, and the parsley. Season with salt and pepper and serve.

Yield: 2 servings.

Note: To serve four, double the recipe and cook in two separate casseroles.

PHEASANT WITH CELERY AND APPLE RINGS

Game birds, such as small pheasants, pigeons, partridges, and quails, have become more available. They are raised on farms in a semi-wild condition and are allowed to wander about outside in pens. Although they don't have the flavor of wild game, they have considerably more than chicken.

All game birds, however, tend to be tough and if roasted are best wrapped in bacon or pork fat so that they will not dry out. But, to be completely safe, braise them. The liquid in the casserole will seal in the juices.

Pheasant develops flavor and becomes more tender as it is aged. Leave it unwrapped on a shelf in the refrigerator for a couple of days. The cool air will circulate around it and the skin will dry so that when it is roasted it will become taut and crisp. The same method can be used for Cornish game hen, chicken (overnight is long enough), partridge, or pigeon.

- 2   pheasants
- 4   slices bacon, chopped
- 3   tablespoons unsalted butter
- 1   onion, sliced
- 8   celery stalks, sliced
- ⅓ cup Calvados
- 2   Rome apples, peeled, cored, and cut in ½-inch-thick slices
      Coarse salt and freshly ground pepper to taste
- 3   tablespoon chopped parsley leaves

1. Wipe the pheasants dry with paper towels. In a heavy casserole, brown the bacon. Remove with a slotted spoon and drain it on paper towels. Brown the pheasants on all sides and set them aside. Pour off the fat from the pan. Add 1 tablespoon of the butter and the onion and celery. Cover and cook gently for 5 minutes.

2. Add the birds, pour on the Calvados, and light it. When the flames die, turn the birds breast down, cover, and simmer for 35 to 40 minutes, or until the birds are tender.

3. Meanwhile, fry the apple rings in the remaining butter.

4. Add the pheasant livers, if available, to the pheasants and cook for 5 minutes, mashing the livers into the cooking juices.

5. Arrange the pheasants on a platter. Season with salt and pepper, sprinkle with the parsley and bacon, and serve, surrounded by the apple rings.

Yield: 4 servings.

PIGEON STUFFED WITH COUSCOUS

Pigeon stuffed with couscous, raisins, and almonds in a honey-glazed sauce is a popular Moroccan dish, a treat that is generally served at birthdays and weddings. The pigeons are braised in a saffron-flavored stock that imparts a beautiful golden color to their skins. Although Moroccans use couscous that requires a couple of steamings before being stuffed in the pigeons, Quick Couscous (page 256) does the job perfectly well with much less fuss. Boiling stock is poured onto the grains, which are fluffed up with a fork and mixed with butter.

  2 pigeons
     Juice of 1 lemon
¼ cup raisins
½ cup chicken stock (page 285)
½ cup couscous

   4 tablespoons unsalted butter
 ½ cup almonds, toasted
   2 pinches saffron threads, pulverized
      Coarse salt and freshly ground pepper to taste
 ⅛ teaspoon ground cinnamon
 ⅛ teaspoon paprika
 ⅛ teaspoon ground cumin
   1 teaspoon honey
   3 leeks, washed well and sliced
   3 tablespoons chopped fresh coriander leaves

1. Wipe the pigeons dry and squeeze on the lemon juice. Set the pigeons aside. Soak the raisins in hot water to cover for 20 minutes.

2. Bring the chicken stock to boil and pour it over the couscous in a bowl. Mix and let it sit for 2 to 3 minutes. Stir in 1 tablespoon of the butter.

3. Drain the raisins and add them to the couscous with half the almonds, and 1 pinch of saffron, the coarse salt and freshly ground pepper, cinnamon, paprika, and cumin. Add the honey. Mix thoroughly and stuff into the pigeon cavities. Sew up the cavities with a needle and thread or close with skewers.

4. Melt the remaining butter in a casserole. Add the leeks and cook until barely soft. Add 1 cup of water, the remaining saffron, and the pigeons breast down. Simmer for 20 minutes, basting frequently. Turn the pigeons over and cook for 10 minutes more, or until they are done.

5. Sprinkle the pigeons with the coriander and the remaining almonds and serve.

Yield: 2 servings.

PIGEONS BAKED IN A SALT CRUST

This is a remarkable method of cooking small birds. A salt crust is made of equal amounts of salt and flour and the bird is wrapped in the crust and baked. It comes out with a tender flesh. Any herbs that have been put in while the bird is baking will give it a very strong flavor. When you crack open the salt crust, the bird will be moist inside. No extra fat is used; the bird roasts in its own juices which are drawn out by the salt crust. The crust does not make the bird taste salty.

Any small birds can be used with this method. Cornish game hens can have fresh tarragon leaves tucked under their skin and in the cavity. Rosemary (not too much or the effect will be overpowering), fresh marjoram, or oregano can also be used.

    4 cups all-purpose flour
    4 cups salt
    1 to 1½ cups water
    2 pigeons
    2 sprigs fresh rosemary
       Freshly ground pepper to taste

1. In a large mixing bowl, combine the flour and salt. Add the water and knead together until you have a dough like a normal pastry dough. Cover and let stand for 30 minutes.

2. Preheat the oven to 375 degrees.

3. Wipe the birds dry and place the rosemary in the cavity. Sprinkle the birds with pepper.

4. Cut the dough in half. Roll out each half on a floured board until you have a big enough layer to wrap each bird. Wrap the pigeons in the dough and make sure that there are no holes through which the juices can escape.

5. Place the pigeons on a flat roasting rack over a pan. Bake for 25 minutes.

Yield: 2 servings.

116

QUAIL PRIMAVERA

This is Nicola Civetta's Quaglie Giardiniere (Quail Gardener's Style) from Primavera restaurant in Manhattan.

Quail must be carefully cooked because they can toughen and dry out quickly. Frozen quail tend to be dry. To restore moisture, defrost them in water.

Serve with toasted Polenta, page 251, and a dry red wine.

8 quail
Coarse salt and freshly ground pepper to taste
½ cup extra virgin olive oil
1 carrot, chopped
½ pound fresh peas, shelled
1 zucchini, chopped
6 mushrooms, chopped
2 shallots, minced
4 tablespoons unsalted butter
½ cup dry red wine
1 cup chicken stock (page 285)
2 slices foie gras

1. Season the quail inside and out with salt and pepper and truss them.

2. In a large frying pan, lightly sauté the birds in the oil until they are golden brown, turning them to be sure they are done on all sides. Remove and keep warm.

3. Add the carrots and peas and cook for 5 to 10 minutes. Add the zucchini and mushrooms and cook for 5 minutes longer.

4. Sauté the shallots in the butter in a separate pan. Add the wine and the chicken stock and reduce it to 1 cup. Add the vegetables and quail. Simmer, uncovered, for 10 minutes. Stir in the foie gras and mix well.

Yield: 4 servings.

DUCK

These days one of the hardest things to cook correctly is roast duck. It was only a few years ago that rare duck breast began to appear on the menus of chic French restaurants in the United States. Recreating this at home, however, is another thing entirely. If the breast is properly pink, the legs are underdone. If the legs are cooked through, then the breast is dried out and gray. At the same time, there is all that fat to contend with. Unless it is cooked so that the skin becomes crisp, the duck will be greasy.

A solution is to make two meals out of one bird. Thus, the breast can be served one day and the legs can be broiled a day or two later. Duck does not have much meat—the enormous breast is largely bone—so one bird will feed only two people.

In the following recipes, the duck is roasted at a high temperature for a short period of time. While it is cooking, a stock is made from the heart, liver, and gizzards. It becomes the basis for a sauce flavored with brandy and green peppercorns. When the duck has cooled slightly, the breast is carved in long slices that are arranged on a serving dish and coated with the sauce. The rest of the duck is refrigerated for another day. The duck fat should be saved; there is nothing better for frying or roasting potatoes.

One way to get the duck's skin close to the lacquered quality of Peking duck is to prick it all over with a fork, salt it, and dry it for 10 minutes with a hand-held hair dryer. The hot air opens up the pores and the fat runs out. Even more fat will come out if the duck is first plunged into boiling water and simmered for a few minutes.

The duck carcass makes an excellent stock that can be used for cooking black-eyed peas, navy beans, or lentils. Elizabeth David in *French Provincial Cooking* suggests using the stock as a basis for soup flavored with funghi porcini and tomatoes, and sprinkled with Parmesan cheese. She also suggests cooking beets in the stock. When the fat has been strained off, the result is a beautiful dark red consommé, which can be served hot or cold with sour cream.

Cauliflower Purée, page 206, goes especially well with duck. The cauliflower is steamed in a little milk, puréed in a blender and a beurre noisette is stirred in just before the purée is served. Roast or scalloped potatoes cooked with duck fat (see Pommes Boulangère, page 221) also go well with both duck breast and broiled duck legs. A handful of crushed juniper berries sprinkled on the legs gives them a delicious flavor.

DUCK BREAST WITH GREEN PEPPERCORNS

1 4-pound duck with heart, liver, and gizzards
  Coarse salt and freshly ground pepper
2 shallots, minced
1 tablespoon unsalted butter
1 cup dry red wine
¼ cup brandy
¼ cup water
4 tablespoons green peppercorns
½ cup heavy cream
1 teaspoon cornstarch

1. Preheat the oven to 450 degrees. Prick the duck all over with a fork to allow the fat to escape while it is cooking. Sprinkle salt and pepper inside the cavity and on the skin. Place in a roasting pan and cook for 30 minutes. Meanwhile, prepare the sauce.

2. In a small saucepan, cook the shallots in the butter until they are soft. Add the heart, gizzards, and liver. Sauté for a couple of minutes and then add the wine, brandy, and water. Bring to a boil, cover, lower the heat, and simmer for 25 minutes.

3. Crush the peppercorns lightly, using a mortar and pestle. Set them aside.

4. Skim the fat from the gizzard stock. Strain the stock into another saucepan and add the peppercorns. Mix a tablespoon of the cream with the cornstarch until it is smooth. Add to the sauce with the cream.

5. Bring the sauce to a boil and simmer for a few minutes, until the sauce has thickened. Correct the seasoning.

6. Slice the duck breast into long, fairly thin pieces. Arrange on a heated serving platter and pour the sauce on top. Serve immediately.

Yield: 2 servings.

BROILED DUCK LEGS

2 duck legs (see recipe above)
 Coarse salt and freshly ground pepper
1 teaspoon crushed juniper berries

1. Preheat the broiler. Put the duck legs on a rack 5 inches from the heat. Sprinkle with the salt, pepper, and juniper berries.

2. Broil the legs until they are crisp and browned. Serve hot.

Yield: 2 servings.

DUCK WITH SAUCE PIQUANTE

1 4- to 5-pound duck
 Coarse salt and freshly ground pepper to taste
½ cup wild rice
 Baked rice (page 229)

FOR THE SAUCE

- 2 tablespoons minced shallots
- 1 tablespoon olive oil
- 2 tablespoons sugar
- ½ cup red wine vinegar
- 3 cups chicken or meat stock (page 285)
- 1 teaspoon cornstarch mixed with 1 teaspoon water
- 1 tablespoon drained capers
- 2 tablespoon chopped oil-cured black olives
- 2 tablespoons chopped parsley leaves

1. Preheat the oven to 450 degrees. Wipe the duck with paper towels, season the cavity and skin with salt and pepper. Prick the skin all over with a fork to allow fat to escape while cooking. Roast the duck for 1 hour and 10 to 20 minutes. Cool and set aside.

2. While the duck is cooking, prepare the sauce, the wild rice, and the rice for baking. Put the wild rice on to boil in 4 cups of water. Cook for 45 minutes, or until done. Start the on-top-of-the-stove cooking of the baked rice (see recipe page 229).

3. For the sauce, cook the shallots in the olive oil until they are soft. Add the sugar and vinegar and bring to a boil. Simmer, stirring, until it begins to caramelize. Be careful not to burn it. Add the stock and bring to a boil. Lower the heat and reduce the sauce to 2 cups.

4. Add the cornstarch mixture, capers, and olives. Bring to a boil, lower the heat, and simmer gently until smooth and thickened. Season to taste.

5. To assemble, carve the duck in thin slices. Mix the wild rice with the baked rice. Arrange in a mound on a serving dish. Place the duck slices all around. Pour the sauce on the duck slices and sprinkle with the parsley.

Yield: 4 servings.

ROAST DUCK WITH JUNIPER BERRIES

Serve with potatoes roasted alongside the duck or with Pommes Boulangère, page 221.

1 3-pound duck
1 orange
  Coarse salt and freshly ground pepper
1 small onion, sliced
1 teaspoon fresh rosemary or sage leaves, or ½ teaspoon dried rosemary or sage
  Pinch of dried thyme
1 tablespoon crushed juniper berries

FOR THE SAUCE

  Duck neck, gizzards, and liver
1 small onion, unpeeled and quartered
1 carrot, sliced
1 celery stalk, sliced
  Parsley stems
1 teaspoon cornstarch
½ cup dry red wine
½ cup gin
1 teaspoon crushed juniper berries
  Coarse salt and freshly ground black pepper to taste
2 teaspoons julienned orange peel, blanched
2 teaspoons chopped fresh parsley leaves

1. Preheat the broiler. Wipe the duck dry inside and out with paper towels. Slice the orange and reserve the peel.

2. Season the cavity of the duck with salt and pepper. Place the onion, orange slices, rosemary, thyme, and crushed juniper berries in the cavity. Close securely with a small skewer.

3. Salt the skin of the duck on all sides (this will help to draw off the fat). Prick the skin all over with the prongs of a fork. Place the duck

under the broiler and broil until golden on all sides. Remove and pour off the fat.

4. If the broiler is in the oven, turn the oven temperature to 375 degrees and wait until it is hot. If the broiler is separate from the oven, preheat the oven while browning the duck.

5. Roast the duck for 30 to 40 minutes, or until done. The breast should be pinkish. If it is rare, the legs will not be cooked.

6. While the duck is cooking, simmer the neck and gizzards (reserving the liver for step 7) in water to cover with the onion, carrot, celery, and parsley stems. Strain the stock and set it aside.

7. When the duck is done, remove it to a serving dish and keep it warm. Drain off all the fat from the pan in which the duck was roasted. Slice the duck liver and add it to the pan. Sauté for 1 to 2 minutes. Scrape up the cooking juices and sprinkle with the cornstarch. Bring to a boil over high heat; then add the wine, gin, and a little stock. Stir well, add the juniper berries, and simmer for 2 to 3 minutes, adding more stock, if necessary. Season to taste with salt and pepper. Stir in the orange peel, sprinkle with the parsley, and serve in a heated sauceboat.

Yield: 2 to 3 servings.

RABBIT

Many Americans are beginning to discover rabbit, a meat widely eaten in Europe and now becoming more readily available here. One weekend in Montana, where the rabbit on the prairie is in anything but short supply, there were 20 guests for dinner, eight rabbits and eight cooks. A competition was held and we sat down to eight different rabbit dishes. These three were the winners.

RABBIT IN RED WINE

Do not be daunted by the square of plain chocolate used in this recipe. It is frequently added to many French, Spanish, Italian, and Mexican dishes. The chocolate helps to produce a thick dark sauce, but its flavor is so subtle that it is hard to identify.

Serve this with boiled potatoes.

2 tablespoons unsalted butter
1 tablespoon extra virgin olive oil
1 medium-sized onion, chopped
1 garlic clove, minced
2 slices bacon, chopped
1 rabbit, cut up
  Flour for dredging
1 square (½ ounce) bitter chocolate, chopped
1 cup chicken stock (page 285)
1 cup dry red wine, or more, to cover
  Bouquet garni (thyme and parsley sprigs and bay leaf tied in a
    cheesecloth bag)
  Coarse salt and freshly ground pepper to taste

1. Heat the butter and olive oil in a large heavy casserole. Gently fry the onion with the garlic and bacon until they are golden. Remove with a slotted spoon and set them aside.

2. Wipe the pieces of rabbit dry with paper towels and dredge with the flour. Brown them lightly in the oil and butter.

3. Return the onion, garlic, and bacon to the casserole and add the chopped chocolate, stock, and wine, pouring in more wine if necessary to cover. Add the bouquet garni, season with salt and pepper, and simmer, covered, for 20 to 30 minutes, or until the rabbit is cooked. Correct the seasoning and serve.

Yield: 3 to 4 servings.

RABBIT WITH LEMONS

Serve with rice.

1 rabbit, cut up
   Flour for dredging
1 tablespoon extra virgin olive oil
1 tablespoon unsalted butter
8 white baby onions, peeled
3 lemons, sliced
   Coarse salt and freshly ground pepper to taste
2 cups chicken stock (page 285)
   Bouquet garni (thyme and parsley sprigs and bay leaf tied in a
      cheesecloth bag)
   Chopped fresh parsley leaves for garnish

1. Wipe the rabbit pieces dry with paper towels. Dredge with flour.

2. Heat the oil and butter in a heavy casserole and lightly brown the rabbit pieces. Remove and set aside.

3. Brown the onions in the butter and oil and remove.

4. Arrange a layer of lemon slices on the bottom of the pan. Add the rabbit pieces and onions. Season and cover with the remaining lemon slices.

5. Pour in enough stock barely to cover. Add the bouquet garni, cover, and simmer for 20 to 30 minutes, or until the rabbit is cooked. If the sauce seems too liquid, uncover toward the end of cooking so that it will evaporate. If it seems too thick, add more chicken stock. Garnish with the parsley and serve with rice.

Yield: 3 to 4 servings.

LAPIN À LA MOUTARDE

This is a classic French bistro dish. The rabbit is served in a cream and mustard sauce. Care must be taken to ensure that the rabbit is not allowed to dry out while cooking and that there is always plenty of sauce. Serve with rice and a light dry red wine.

1 rabbit, cut up
2 tablespoons Dijon mustard
2 tablespoons unsalted butter at room temperature
1 tablespoon extra virgin olive oil
1 cup dry white wine
   Coarse salt and freshly ground pepper to taste
1 cup heavy cream
3 tablespoons chopped fresh parsley leaves for garnish

1. Wipe the rabbit pieces dry with paper towels. Coat them with a mixture of mustard, butter, and oil. Preheat the oven to 400 degrees.

2. Arrange the rabbit in a greased baking dish and pour in the wine. Cook, covered, for 45 minutes, basting frequently. Season with salt and pepper and remove the rabbit pieces from the casserole.

3. Pour in the cream and scrape up the cooking juices with a wooden spoon over low heat on top of the stove. Correct the seasoning. Return the rabbit to the dish and coat thoroughly with the sauce. Serve sprinkled with the parsley.

Yield: 3 to 4 servings.

SIX

Meat

The dishes in this chapter can either be made in a short time, such as steaks and chops, or assembled quickly and left to cook.

Many of them are marinated overnight, which improves their flavor. I've come across some unusual and spicy dishes from Mexico and Morocco, where I lived, and an exotic Italian method of cooking by braising beef or pork in milk. I was skeptical of this last dish at first, until I ate it in Italy; I was quickly won over.

I love to use fresh herbs and have managed to keep pots of them growing almost year-round on my windowsill. But if fresh herbs are not available, I recommend using any dried ones except basil.

I also like to broil kebabs. In the Middle East, there are wonderful lamb dishes that are served with salads of chopped herbs and cracked wheat, yogurt and cucumber, and pita bread. In winter, I love a good pork chop and, once in a while, a steak broiled and served with the marrow from beef bones mashed with shallots and unsalted butter. The bones are wrapped in foil and baked in the oven. The butcher gives them away for nothing.

STEAK AUX DEUX POIVRES

- 2 pounds beefsteak (filet mignon, sirloin, etc.)
  Whole black peppercorns, well crushed
- 2 tablespoons peanut or safflower oil
- ¼ cup Cognac
- 1 cup heavy cream
- 3 tablespoons green peppercorns
  Coarse salt to taste

1. Trim the steaks and pat them dry with paper towels. Work the peppercorns into the flesh on both sides.

2. Heat the oil in a large frying pan. Sauté the steaks on both sides in the oil. Remove and keep them warm in a slow oven.

3. Pour off the fat, add the Cognac, and bring to a boil. Add the cream and reduce the sauce until it has thickened. Season with the green peppercorns and salt.

4. Remove the steaks from the oven. Add any juices that have accumulated around the steaks to the sauce. Mix the juices into the sauce. Pour the sauce over the steaks and serve.

Yield: 4 servings.

KOFTA KEBABS WITH YOGURT AND DILL SAUCE

These marinated kebabs can also be made with ground lamb. Serve them with rice.

FOR THE KOFTA

1½ pounds ground beef
½ teaspoon ground cumin
¼ teaspoon paprika
½ teaspoon ground coriander
   Pinch of ground cinnamon
   Pinch of ground cloves
   Freshly ground pepper to taste

FOR THE YOGURT-DILL SAUCE

1½ cups plain yogurt
¾ cup minced fresh dill
2 fresh chilies, minced
3 garlic cloves, peeled and minced
   Juice of ½ lemon
   Coarse salt and freshly ground black pepper to taste

1. Put the beef in a large mixing bowl and combine it with all the spices and the pepper. Cover and refrigerate overnight or marinate for 1 hour at room temperature.

2. Meanwhile, make the sauce. Combine all the sauce ingredients and mix thoroughly. Set aside.

3. Make the koftas. Take about 2 tablespoons of the beef mixture, enough to make an oval about 1 inch in diameter, and shape it around skewers in ovals, using about four to a long skewer. Be sure that they are thoroughly mashed down. Otherwise bits of beef will flake off while cooking.

4. Heat the broiler and grill the koftas for a couple of minutes on each side. Serve with the yogurt-dill sauce.

Yield: 3 to 4 servings.

BEEF BRAISED IN MILK

The idea of cooking meat in milk is not as unusual as it sounds. In Tuscany it has been a common practice for years. Even chicken can be cooked this way. The flesh becomes extraordinarily tender and the milk combines with the cooking juices to form a sauce which has a subtle, caramelized flavor.

The procedure is easy. First the meat is browned in a casserole and the fat is poured out. Milk is heated in a separate pan and added to the meat. As it simmers with the meat, the milk forms a protective coating that seals in the juices. The sauce can then be poured into a blender and puréed until smooth, or simply put through a strainer. The result is a light, creamy sauce, flavored with onions or leeks that have cooked with the meat. Both the meat and the sauce are good cold.

When the meat is ready it is sliced and arranged in a row on a serving dish and the sauce is poured down the middle of the slices. The platter may be garnished with pieces of braised fennel or celery.

The only trick is not to overcook the meat. Beef fillet is best rare. If there is any doubt how long it needs, take its temperature. A 2-pound fillet should take about 40 minutes. If the fillet is overcooked it will be tough.

Puréed celery root and potatoes or mashed potatoes go with this dish.

2   pounds beef fillet
1   tablespoon olive oil
3   leeks, well washed and chopped
1   garlic clove, peeled
1   cup milk
1   cup heavy cream
3   tablespoons red wine vinegar
1   sprig rosemary
    Freshly ground pepper
    Coarse salt to taste
    Chopped parsley leaves for garnish

1. Brown the beef in a casserole that is just large enough to hold it. Remove the beef and pour off the fat. Add the olive oil and cook the leeks with the garlic until the leeks are soft.

2. Return the beef to the casserole. Heat the milk and cream in a small saucepan and add it to the beef. Stir, scraping up any pieces of leek that may be adhering to the bottom of the pan. Add the vinegar, rosemary, pepper, and salt and mix well. Cook for about 40 minutes. The beef should be rare, otherwise it will be tough.

3. Remove the beef from the casserole and transfer it to a heated serving dish. Keep warm.

4. Remove the rosemary sprig from the sauce. Purée the sauce in a blender or strain it through a sieve.

5. Slice the beef and place the slices in a row on a heated serving platter. Sprinkle with salt, if you wish. Pour the sauce down the middle of the slices. Any extra sauce can be poured into a heated sauceboat and handed around separately. Garnish the beef with parsley and, if available, a few leaves of fresh rosemary.

Yield: 4 servings.

LAMB CHOPS WITH SORREL AND MINT SAUCE

The best lamb to use for this recipe comes from a rack of lamb. Very small tender spring lamb chops will also do. They are cooked very quickly and the juices are deglazed with white wine and made into a sauce with cream and sorrel. The combination is inspired by a recipe of Albert and Michel Roux, owners of Le Gavroche in London and the Waterside Inn at Bray.

8   small lamb chops
1   pound sorrel
3   tablespoons unsalted butter
1   cup dry white wine
1   cup heavy cream
    Coarse salt and freshly ground pepper to taste
    Shredded fresh mint leaves for garnish

1. Trim the fat from the chops and set the chops aside. Remove the stems from the sorrel.

2. Melt 2 tablespoons of the butter in a large frying pan. Cook the chops on both sides until they are browned on the outside and pink in the middle. Transfer to a serving dish and keep warm

3. Pour off the fat from the frying pan. Add the sorrel and cook for a couple of minutes. Add the wine and cook over high heat for 3 minutes. Add the cream and remaining butter. Season to taste with salt and pepper.

4. Pour the sauce over the lamb chops and sprinkle with the mint. Serve immediately.

Yield: 4 servings.

LAMB CHOPS WITH TOMATO-BASIL SAUCE

This sauce can only be made in the summer when tomatoes and basil are in season. It is also very good with fish steaks and chicken. The flavor improves if it is made a few hours in advance and then warmed over low heat so that the flavors become more pronounced.

Leftover sauce can be used in salad dressings or as a filling for an omelet.

2 medium-sized ripe tomatoes
1 garlic clove, minced
1 tablespoon coriander seeds, crushed
8 basil leaves, snipped
  Juice of 1 lemon
½ cup extra virgin olive oil
  Coarse salt and freshly ground pepper to taste
8 thick-cut loin lamb chops

1. Peel the tomatoes by dropping them into boiling water for a few minutes or charring them under a broiler or over a gas flame. While warm, remove the skins and discard the seeds. Chop the flesh and put it in a small, heavy saucepan (preferably enameled).

2. Add the remaining ingredients, except the chops, and mix thoroughly. Let sit for a few hours.

3. When you are ready to broil the chops, heat the sauce over very low heat—just enough to bring out the flavor. Do not boil.

4. Broil the chops and pass the sauce separately.

Yield: 4 servings.

FRIED BREADED LAMB CHOPS

When coated with bread crumbs and fried, lamb chops come out with a golden brown skin and are juicy and tender inside. They are spread with a garlic purée, dipped in egg yolk and bread crumbs, and fried in oil until crisp. With them serve a tomato, onion, and basil salad, or a mixed green salad with avocado. A full-bodied red wine or a chilled Beaujolais goes well with this dish.

Two cloves of garlic may seem a lot for only four chops, but the cloves are first boiled in their skins until soft and mashed into a paste which is spread on the chops The result is a delicate purée which is not in the least overpowering or harsh.

Use dried homemade bread crumbs for the coating. They are infinitely preferable to store-bought and can be made by grinding stale pieces of bread in a blender. The crumbs keep indefinitely in a tightly closed jar.

A large cast-iron skillet is the best pan for this recipe. Quantities are given for two. For four, double the ingredients and use two pans or cook the chops in two batches.

```
4   rib lamb chops
2   garlic cloves
1   egg yolk
¼   teaspoon dried thyme
½   cup fine dry bread crumbs
1   tablespoon olive oil
1   to 2 tablespoons peanut or safflower oil
    Coarse salt and freshly ground pepper to taste
2   tablespoons chopped parsley leaves for garnish
```

1. Trim all but a very thin layer of fat from the chops.

2. Simmer the cloves of garlic in their skins in water to cover for 20 minutes; then mash the garlic. Spread it on one side of each chop.

3. Put the egg yolk in a shallow bowl and beat in the thyme. Put the bread crumbs in another shallow bowl. Meanwhile, heat the oils in

a skillet over moderately high heat, but do not allow them to smoke. The oil must be hot, however, or the chops will not fry properly.

4. Dip the chops first in the egg and then in the bread crumbs to coat them thoroughly. Shake off any excess crumbs and place the chops in the skillet. Fry for about 4 to 5 minutes on each side, turning the heat down if the chops get too brown. They should be pink in the middle. If you prefer them more done, cook longer, taking care not to burn the coating.

5. Drain on paper towels. Season with salt and pepper and garnish with parsley and serve.

Yield: 2 servings.

ROAST LEG OF LAMB WITH CHINESE MUSTARD

1 5- to 6-pound leg of lamb
2 garlic cloves, cut into slivers
2 tablespoons soy sauce
2 tablespoons Chinese mustard
8 anchovy fillets, cut in half lengthwise
   Coarse salt and freshly ground pepper to taste

1. Wipe the lamb dry with paper towels and scrape off any blue markings. With a sharp knife make incisions in the flesh and insert the slivers of garlic.

2. Mix the soy sauce and mustard to a paste with ¼ cup of water. Coat the lamb with the paste and arrange the anchovies in lines over the top. Cover and marinate overnight in the refrigerator or for a few hours at room temperature.

3. Preheat the oven to 350 degrees. Roast the lamb for 1¼ to 1½ hours, or until it registers 125 to 130 degrees on a meat thermometer.

Yield: 6 to 8 servings.

EGGPLANT AND LAMB KEBABS WITH YOGURT-BASIL SAUCE

Eggplant goes especially well with lamb, garlic, fresh basil, and olive oil—the quintessential flavors of the Mediterranean. It is excellent broiled and served with a sauce made with yogurt, garlic, lemon, and basil.

In addition to the more common large purple eggplant, it is possible to find long, thin pale mauve ones or round white ones with thin, tender skins. The bigger eggplant sometimes have rather tough skins, so when using them for kebabs be sure to peel them.

FOR THE SAUCE

  1 cup plain yogurt
  ½ cup fresh whole basil leaves
  1 garlic clove, minced
     Juice of ½ lemon
     Coarse salt and freshly ground pepper to taste

FOR THE KEBABS

  1 large eggplant peeled, or 2 small eggplants
     Coarse salt
1½ pounds boneless lamb from the leg, cut into 1-inch pieces
  2 small young onions, cut into wedges
  8 ripe cherry tomatoes
  3 tablespoons extra virgin olive oil
     Freshly ground pepper to taste

1. Combine all the ingredients for the sauce in a small bowl and set it aside until the kebabs are cooked.

2. Cut the eggplant into 1-inch cubes and sprinkle them with salt. Drain for 1 hour in a colander.

3. Pat the eggplant cubes dry with a paper towel. Thread onto a skewer with the lamb, the onion wedges, and the tomatoes, in alternating pieces. Brush with the olive oil.

4. Preheat the broiler until it is hot. Grill the kebabs for 15 to 20 minutes, turning frequently, or until the eggplant is cooked and the lamb is dark and crisp on the outside and pink in the middle. Season with salt and pepper and serve with the yogurt and basil sauce.

Yield: 4 servings.

MARINATED LAMB AND PEPPER KEBABS

These kebabs make an appealing spring dish, when lamb is especially tender. They can be marinated overnight or for an hour before being broiled. Serve with rice or baked potatoes and Leeks with Mustard Sauce, page 216.

If fresh herbs are not available, dried herbs can be substituted but the flavor will not be as subtle.

  2 pounds boneless lamb from the leg, cut into 1½-inch pieces, fat trimmed
  4 Italian frying peppers
  3 tablespoons extra virgin olive oil
  3 garlic cloves, minced
  1 teaspoon fresh rosemary leaves or ½ teaspoon dried rosemary
 ½ teaspoon fresh oregano, or ¼ teaspoon dried oregano
 ½ teaspoon fresh marjoram, or ¼ teaspoon dried marjoram
    Coarse salt and ground pepper to taste
    Juice of ½ lemon

1. Wipe the pieces of lamb dry with paper towels. Cut the peppers in half, remove the seeds and ribs, and cut the peppers into quarters.

2. Combine the remaining ingredients in a large bowl and toss the lamb thoroughly in this mixture. Marinate for 2 hours or overnight.

3. Thread the lamb and peppers on skewers. Broil the skewers over (or under) high heat so that the lamb is brown and crisp on the outside and pink in the middle. Brush with the marinade as it broils.

Yield: 4 servings.

RACK OF LAMB WITH HERB-GARLIC BUTTER

Rack of lamb is useful for people with small kitchens because it is so easy to cook. It should be roasted at a high temperature and served rare. A rack usually contains about 6 to 7 small chops—enough for two people. A crown roast is made from two or three racks sewn together to make a crown. A purée of potatoes, or potatoes and celery root, or cracked wheat with raisins and pine nuts can be put in the middle of the rack of the lamb when it is served. Baked Plum Tomatoes with Rosemary, page 226, are a nice accompaniment.

FOR THE HERB-GARLIC BUTTER

1 garlic clove, peeled
  Coarse salt
4 tablespoons unsalted butter
  Freshly ground pepper to taste
  Fresh herbs in season (tarragon, chives, thyme, or rosemary)
2 tablespoons chopped Italian parsley leaves

FOR THE LAMB

1 rack of lamb (about 6 to 7 chops), trimmed
1 garlic clove, crushed and peeled
  Coarse salt and freshly ground pepper to taste

1. Mash the garlic for the butter into a purée with a little salt in a mortar and pestle. Work in the butter until smooth. Add the pepper,

fresh herbs in season, and parsley. (If using the herbs, reduce or omit the parsley.) Shape the butter into a cylinder and wrap in aluminum foil. Put in the freezer.

2. Preheat the oven to 450 degrees. Rub the rack of lamb with the garlic, salt, and pepper. Cover the bone ends with twists of aluminum foil to prevent them from burning.

3. Roast for 15 minutes fat side down on a rack in a roasting pan. Turn bone side down and roast another 5 minutes. For rare lamb, it should take 15 to 20 minutes.

4. Slice the lamb on a heated platter and pass the butter, cut into slices, on a separate small plate.

Yield: 2 servings.

BRAISED MARINATED PORK CHOPS

There are few things as comforting as a pork chop, cooked simply and served with boiled new or mashed potatoes and young fresh peas, carrots, or cauliflower. For one or two, it makes a quick, economical meal. But the humble pork chop can be one of the biggest stumbling blocks in the kitchen. When broiled it can toughen and dry out so that eating it is like chewing shoe leather. The best way to cook a pork chop is to braise it in a skillet. First sauté it on both sides so that it is browned and then cook it, covered, until it is done.

Pork takes well to marinades, the simplest of which consists of olive oil, garlic, freshly ground pepper, and thyme, spread over a chop which marinates in the mixture for an hour or two at room temperature before being cooked. Another good marinade is a mixture of soy sauce, vermouth, garlic, and scallions. When the chop is braised, toasted sesame seeds are sprinkled over it. This recipe is especially good with puréed potatoes and celery root.

When buying pork chops, choose those that are pearly pink with resilient fat. The chops are done when they are whitish-pink and juicy in the center. Trichinosis parasites are killed at an internal temperature of 150 degrees. The temperature given in many cookbooks is 185 degrees which results in dry, overcooked pork.

2 loin pork chops
3 tablespoons soy sauce
3 tablespoons dry vermouth
1 garlic clove, minced
3 scallions, chopped
   Freshly ground pepper to taste
1 tablespoon peanut or vegetable oil

140

½ cup dry white wine
    Coarse salt to taste
 2 tablespoons toasted sesame seeds

1. Marinate the chops in a mixture of the soy sauce, vermouth, garlic, scallions, and pepper for 2 hours or overnight, if possible.

2. Heat the oil in a skillet large enough to hold the chops comfortably. Remove the chops from the marinade, pat them dry with paper towels, and brown them on both sides. Add the marinade and the wine. Cover and simmer for about 30 minutes, turning once, or until the pork is whitish-pink in the center and tender. Be careful not to overcook the meat. Season with salt and pepper.

3. Place the chops on a heated platter. Reduce the juices in the pan and pour the sauce over the chops. Sprinkle with sesame seeds and serve.

Yield: 2 servings.

BONELESS PORK CHOPS BRAISED IN RED WINE WITH FENNEL SEEDS

This is a very easy dish to prepare. Serve it with puréed sweet potatoes and green peas. Be careful not to overcook the chops or they will become tough and dry. If the sauce seems too liquid, remove the chops with a slotted spoon and keep them warm while you reduce the sauce over high heat until it has thickened.

- 6 boned loin pork chops
- 2 tablespoons extra virgin olive oil
- 2 garlic cloves, peeled and minced
- 2 tablespoons chopped fresh parsley leaves
- ¼ teaspoon dried oregano, or ½ teaspoon chopped fresh oregano
- ¼ teaspoon dried thyme, or ½ teaspoon chopped fresh thyme
- 1 teaspoon fennel seeds
- 1 tablespoon tomato paste
- 1 cup dry red wine
  Freshly ground pepper to taste

1. Trim the fat from the chops and pat them dry with paper towels.

2. Heat the oil in a heavy skillet large enough to hold the chops in one layer (use cast-iron, if possible). Add the garlic, herbs, and fennel seeds. Place the chops on top and brown lightly. Turn over and brown the other side.

3. Add the tomato paste, wine, and pepper. Cover and simmer for 20 minutes, or until the chops are cooked but not dried out. Correct the seasoning and serve.

Yield: 4 to 6 servings.

PORK CHOPS WITH PORT AND PRUNES

Puréed Spinach, page 224, and mashed potatoes are good with this dish.

10 dried pitted prunes
½ cup port
½ orange
 2 leeks
 4 thick-cut pork chops
 1 tablespoon vegetable oil
 2 tablespoons unsalted butter
   Juice of ½ lemon
 2 cups chicken stock (page 285)
   Coarse salt and freshly ground pepper to taste

1. Put the prunes in a small saucepan with the port and just enough water to cover. Simmer for 15 minutes and set aside.

2. Peel the orange and cut the peel into julienne. Blanch and set aside. Cut the tough outer leaves and the roots from the leeks, rinse the leeks and slice them. Rinse them again thoroughly.

3. Trim any loose fat from the chops and pat them dry with paper towels. Heat the oil in a heavy skillet and brown the chops on both sides. Remove to a warm platter. Pour the fat from the pan.

4. Melt the butter in the pan and sauté the leeks until they are soft. Add the prunes with their liquid, the lemon juice, the chicken stock, and the orange peel. Return the chops to the pan, season with salt and pepper, and cook, covered, for about 20 minutes, or until done. If the sauce needs to be reduced, uncover the pan; if it is too dry add more water or chicken stock.

Yield: 4 servings.

GOOD FOOD FROM A SMALL KITCHEN

PORK CHOPS WITH MUSTARD SEEDS

Serve this with Leeks with Mustard Sauce, page 216, or Baby Carrots with Fennel, page 205.

4 thick-cut pork chops
4 tablespoons light mustard seeds
1 garlic clove, peeled and minced
2 tablespoons extra virgin olive oil
1 tablespoon fresh marjoram and oregano leaves, or ½
     tablespoon dried leaves
   Coarse salt and freshly ground pepper to taste

1. Trim all but a thin layer of fat from the chops and wipe them dry with paper towels. Combine the mustard seeds, garlic, olive oil, and herbs and marinate the chops in this mixture overnight or for a couple of hours.

2. Heat a cast-iron skillet and add the chops, with their marinade. Brown on both sides. Lower the heat and cook gently, covered, for 20 minutes. You should not need any liquid, but if the chops start to dry out, moisten them with a little water.

Yield: 4 servings.

MARINATED PORK RIBS WITH BARBECUE SAUCE

2 pounds pork ribs
1 garlic clove, minced
1 cup tomato ketchup
¼ cup red wine vinegar
1 teaspoon dry mustard
1 teaspoon hot red pepper flakes
1 teaspoon sugar
   Freshly ground pepper to taste

1. Place the ribs in a large bowl.

144

2. Combine the remaining ingredients and mix thoroughly. Coat the ribs well with the mixture. Cover and marinate in the refrigerator for 1 or 2 days.

3. Bring to room temperature before cooking. Broil until the meat is cooked but still juicy. Do not let it dry out. Baste with the sauce as the meat is cooking.

Yield: 2 servings.

MARINATED PORK RIBS WITH ORANGE AND ROSEMARY

These ribs can be marinated for a day or two before being broiled. They go with whole acorn squash baked and served with butter, nutmeg, and a pinch of ground cinnamon.

2 pounds pork ribs
1 orange
1 lemon
2 garlic cloves
2 tablespoons extra virgin olive oil
2 tablespoons fresh rosemary leaves, or 1 tablespoon dried
     rosemary
  Coarse salt and freshly ground pepper to taste

1. Trim away any fat from the ribs. Place them in a large bowl. Squeeze the juice from the orange and lemon and add to the ribs.

2. Mince the garlic and add it to the ribs with the olive oil, rosemary, salt, and pepper. Coat the ribs thoroughly with the mixture and marinate.

3. When ready to cook, broil the ribs under high heat until cooked through. They should be moist and tender inside, not dried out.

Yield: 2 servings.

PORK BRAISED IN MILK

This is a common Tuscan practice and it ensures that the flesh of the pork comes out extraordinarily tender. Milk is heated in a separate pan and added to the pork. As it simmers with the pork, it forms a protective coating that seals in the juices. The sauce is then puréed in a blender or put through a strainer.

Be careful not to overcook the meat. Trichinosis parasites in pork are killed at an internal temperature of 150 degrees but many cookbooks suggest a temperature of 185 degrees for pork at which it will be overcooked and dry. A boned 2-pound loin of pork should be done in about 1½ hours in a 350-degree oven or on top of the stove. If there is any doubt, take its temperature.

This dish goes with purée of celery root and potatoes, or Cauliflower Purée, page 206.

    2 pounds boneless pork loin
    1 tablespoon olive oil
    1 onion, finely chopped
    2 carrots, sliced
    1 teaspoon coriander seeds, crushed
    1 garlic clove, peeled
    2 cups milk
       Freshly ground pepper
       Coarse salt to taste
       Chopped fresh parsley leaves for garnish

1. Brown the pork in a casserole that is just large enough to hold it. Remove the pork and pour off the fat. Add the olive oil and sauté the onion and carrots until they are golden brown. Add the coriander and garlic. Return the pork to the casserole.

2. In a small saucepan heat the milk. Add to the pork with the pepper. Bring to a boil, lower the heat, and simmer, covered, for 1¼ to 1½ hours.

3. Remove the pork to a heated serving dish. Purée the sauce in a blender or strain through a sieve. Season with salt and pepper.

146

4. Slice the pork and arrange the slices on a serving dish. Season with salt and pepper if you wish. Spoon the sauce on top of the slices and serve any extra sauce separately in a heated sauceboat. Garnish the pork with the parsley and serve.

Yield: 4 servings.

SAUSAGES WITH PORCINI MUSHROOMS

A lovely winter meal when served with Polenta, page 251. While the sausages are cooking, you can make the polenta. The sausages have a thick, dark sauce, which also goes well with thick pasta, such as conchiglie or penne. This needs no cheese and can be followed by a green salad.

- 2 ounces dried porcini mushrooms
- 1 pound Italian sweet sausage
- 1 medium-sized onion, sliced
- 2 tablespoons extra virgin olive oil
- 1 tablespoon tomato paste
- 2 cups chicken or meat stock (page 285)
  Chopped fresh rosemary or oregano leaves
  Coarse salt and freshly ground pepper to taste

1. Put the mushrooms in a small bowl and soak them in hot water to cover for 15 minutes. Slice the sausages into 2-inch pieces.

2. Sauté the onion in the olive oil in a heavy skillet (preferably cast-iron) until soft. Add the sausages and brown them lightly.

3. Add the tomato paste, mushrooms with their water, stock, and herbs. Bring to a boil, lower the heat, and simmer gently for ½ hour. Season with salt and pepper. If the sauce gets too thick, add more stock.

4. Meanwhile, make the polenta (or heat water to cook pasta).

5. Serve the sausages with their sauce on top of the polenta or pasta.

Yield: 4 servings.

VEAL SCALLOPS WITH LEMONS

Scallops should never be overcooked or the meat will shrink and become tough. Pound the scallops before cooking them. Serve the scallops with Potatoes with Sage or Rosemary, page 222, or Puréed Spinach, page 224.

  4 veal scallops
  2 tablespoons unsalted butter
  1 tablespoon extra virgin olive oil
  1 bay leaf
  1 garlic clove, crushed and peeled
     Coarse salt and freshly ground pepper to taste
     Juice of 1 lemon

1. Pound the scallops until they are very thin.

2. Heat the butter with the oil in a heavy skillet. Add the bay leaf and garlic. Add half the meat and sauté quickly over high heat. Season with salt and pepper and remove to a heated platter.

3. Cook the remaining scallops and keep them warm. Remove the bay leaf and garlic. Squeeze the lemon juice into the pan, scrape up the cooking juices, and pour them over the scallops. Correct the seasoning and serve.

Yield: 2 servings.

VEAL SCALLOPS WITH MUSTARD AND CRÈME FRAÎCHE

Serve this with noodles. Be careful not to overcook the scallops or they will toughen.

 4 veal scallops
 2 tablespoons unsalted butter
 1 shallot minced
 ½ to ⅔ cup dry white wine
 1 teaspoon Dijon mustard
 1 teaspoon fresh thyme leaves, or ½ teaspoon dried thyme
 ⅓ cup crème fraîche (page 282)
   Coarse salt and freshly ground pepper to taste

1. Pat the veal dry with paper towels. Melt the butter in a frying pan and brown the scallops lightly on both sides. Remove them to a side dish.

2. Add the shallots and cook until they are softened. Add the wine, mustard, thyme, and crème fraîche. Mix thoroughly, bring to a boil, and return the scallops to the pan.

3. Season with salt and pepper and cook for 3 to 5 minutes, or until the scallops are done (they should be pinkish and juicy in the middle).

Yield: 2 servings.

WIENER SCHNITZEL

If possible, marinate the veal scallops in lemon juice overnight. Serve them with boiled or mashed potatoes.

- 3 lemons
- 8 veal scallops, pounded thin
- 1 egg
  Coarse salt and freshly ground pepper to taste
- 1 cup all-purpose flour
- 1 cup fine bread crumbs
  Approximately ¾ cup safflower oil
  Chopped parsley leaves for garnish

1. Squeeze the juice of one of the lemons over the scallops. Marinate for an hour or overnight.

2. Beat the egg and season it with salt and pepper. Pat each scallop dry with a paper towel and dip it into the flour. Dredge lightly, shaking off any excess. Dip the scallops into the egg and then into the bread crumbs. Refrigerate for 20 minutes.

3. Pour about ½ inch of oil into a large frying pan. When the oil is hot, fry the scallops, two at a time, on both sides, for 2 to 3 minutes. Drain on paper towels. Keep warm while cooking the remainder of the scallops. Cut the remaining lemons into quarters. Garnish the scallops with the parsley and lemon quarters and serve.

Yield: 4 servings.

VEAL CHOPS WITH BASIL

In this recipe the chops are cooked with mushrooms, basil, and prosciutto. You can save considerably by buying prosciutto ends instead of slices.

Serve this with noodles or rice.

- 4 veal chops
  Flour for dredging
- 2 tablespoons olive oil
- 1 medium-sized onion, sliced
- 1 garlic clove, minced
- 4 tablespoons chopped prosciutto
- ½ cup fresh whole basil leaves
- ¼ pound mushrooms, sliced or left whole if small
- ¼ to ½ cup dry white wine
  Coarse salt and freshly ground pepper to taste

1. Dredge the chops lightly in the flour. In a large frying pan, heat the oil and brown the chops. Remove them and set them aside. Add the onion, garlic, and prosciutto and cook until they are soft.

2. Return the chops to the skillet, overlapping them slightly if necessary. Add the basil (reserving some for garnish) and the mushrooms and cook for 15 to 20 minutes, or until the chops are cooked. They should be pink in the middle.

3. Remove the chops from the pan. Add the wine, salt, and pepper and bring to a boil. Cook for 2 to 3 minutes. Return the chops to the pan and heat through. Sprinkle with the reserved basil and serve.

Yield: 4 servings.

VEAL CHOPS WITH WATERCRESS

This recipe is based on a dish created by Jean and Pierre Troisgros. Serve it with mashed potatoes or potatoes puréed with celery root.

- 1 bunch watercress
- 2 veal chops
- 2 tablespoons unsalted butter
- 1 shallot, chopped
- ½ cup crème fraîche (page 282)
  - Juice of ½ lemon
  - Coarse salt and freshly ground pepper to taste

1. Trim the stems from the watercress and set a few leaves aside. Dry the veal chops with paper towels. Melt the butter in a frying pan large enough to hold the chops comfortably and brown them on both sides without burning. Remove and set them aside.

2. Soften the shallot in the butter and add a couple of tablespoons of water, the watercress, and the crème fraîche. Bring to a boil, scraping up the juices, and return the chops to the pan with the lemon juice. Cover and simmer gently until the chops are cooked (do not overcook them). Season them with salt and pepper.

3. Garnish with the remaining watercress leaves and serve.

Yield: 2 servings.

VEAL CHOPS WITH ORANGES AND LEMONS

A cast-iron skillet is the best pan for cooking these veal chops. They are seared and browned over high heat and then covered and cooked in their juices on top of the stove. The juices are scraped up with vermouth and flavored with orange and lemon. Serve this with noodles and Puréed Spinach, page 224, or Fava Beans with Summer Savory, page 197.

    2 thick-cut veal chops
    1 tablespoon vegetable oil
    1 orange
    1 lemon
    ½ cup dry vermouth
       Coarse salt and freshly ground pepper to taste

1. Wipe the veal chops dry with paper towels. Heat the oil in a heavy skillet (preferably cast-iron) and brown the chops on both sides. When thoroughly browned, lower the heat, cover, and simmer for 15 to 20 minutes, turning once, until they are cooked (pinkish in the middle and still juicy).

2. Meanwhile, peel the orange and lemon. Blanch half the peel in boiling water and cut it into julienne. Slice the peeled lemon and orange and set them aside.

3. Remove the chops to a heated serving dish and keep them warm.

4. Pour the vermouth into the skillet and scrape up the cooking juices. Bring to a boil and add the lemon and orange peels and slices. Season with salt and pepper.

5. When the sauce has thickened, pour it over the chops, placing the orange and lemon slices in the center of the chops.

Yield: 2 servings.

VEAL KIDNEYS IN MUSTARD SAUCE

The kidneys must be served pink, otherwise they will be as tough as bullets. Serve this dish with buttered noodles and spinach.

    2 veal kidneys
    2 tablespoons unsalted butter
    2 tablespoons brandy or Calvados
    2 shallots, minced
    ½ cup dry white wine
    1 tablespoon Dijon mustard
    ¼ cup heavy cream
       Coarse salt and freshly ground black pepper to taste

1. Trim the fat from the kidneys and cut them into ½-inch slices.

2. Melt 1 tablespoon of the butter in a heavy skillet and sauté the kidneys for 1 minute so that they are golden but still almost raw. Add the brandy and light it. Remove the kidneys immediately with a slotted spoon and keep them warm.

3. Add the remaining butter and the shallots and cook until they are soft. Add the wine and reduce it by half.

4. Add the mustard and cream and bring to a boil. Season with salt and pepper and return the kidneys with their juices to the pan. Bring to boil and immediately pour into a serving dish. Serve at once.

Yield: 2 servings.

VEAL KIDNEYS WITH CRANBERRY SAUCE

The tart taste of cranberries goes very well with the richness of veal kidneys. This dish is good with mashed potatoes or buttered noodles.

1 orange
2 lemons
4 tablespoons port
2 tablespoons sugar
¼ pound fresh cranberries
2 tablespoons white wine vinegar
2 cups veal or chicken stock (page 285)
2 veal kidneys
2 tablespoons unsalted butter
1 teaspoon dry mustard dissolved in 1 teaspoon water
  Coarse salt and freshly ground pepper to taste

1. Peel the orange and cut the peel into julienne. Blanch and drain. Set aside.

2. Separate the orange into segments, removing the pith. Squeeze the juice from the lemons and reserve.

3. In a small saucepan, bring the port to a boil with 1 tablespoon of the sugar. Add the cranberries and cook for 1 minute.

4. Meanwhile, bring the vinegar to a boil with the remaining tablespoon of sugar. (Watch constantly because it can burn in seconds.) When it caramelizes, add the lemon juice, orange segments, and stock. Simmer over low heat for 15 minutes, or until thickened and syrupy. Keep warm.

5. Meanwhile, remove the membrane and fat from the kidneys; then slice them. Sauté the kidneys in 1 tablespoon of the butter over high heat so that they are browned on the outside but still pink on the inside. Remove the kidneys from the pan and keep them warm (but not so warm as to overcook them).

6. Pour off any fat in the pan and deglaze with the port from the cranberries poured through a sieve. Add the lemon-vinegar sauce

and bring to a boil. Stir in the cranberries and then the mustard. Season with salt and pepper to taste and return the kidneys to the pan. Swirl in the remaining butter.

7. Pour into a serving dish, sprinkle with the reserved orange peel, and serve at once.

Yield: 2 servings.

CALVES' LIVER WITH MADEIRA SAUCE

Serve with mashed potatoes. Be careful not to overcook the liver when you return it to the pan with the sauce.

1¼ pounds thinly sliced calves' liver
  2 tablespoons unsalted butter
  2 medium-sized onions, sliced
  ½ cup Madeira
  1 fresh sage leaf, snipped
    Coarse salt and freshly ground pepper to taste

1. Pat the liver dry with paper towels. Melt 1 tablespoon of the butter in a heavy skillet and quickly brown the liver on both sides. Remove to a plate and keep warm.

2. Add the onions to the skillet and cook until they are golden, stirring frequently. Add the Madeira and sage and bring to a boil.

3. Pour in any juices that have accumulated in the plate holding the liver. Correct the seasoning and return the liver to the sauce. Add the remaining butter, working it in over medium heat. Serve immediately.

Yield: 4 servings.

CALVES' LIVER WITH ORANGE JUICE

Be careful not to overcook the liver. It should be pink in the middle.
The amount of vinegar used in the sauce depends on the sweetness of
the orange juice. Serve this dish with braised onions and Potatoes
with Sage or Rosemary, page 222. If making the potato dish, omit
the sage or rosemary from the recipe. These are powerful herbs and
too much can overwhelm the delicate taste of the liver.

1¼ pounds sliced calves' liver
    Flour for dredging
  1 tablespoon peanut or vegetable oil
  2 tablespoons unsalted butter
  4 shallots, minced
  2 fresh sage leaves or 2 sprigs rosemary, chopped
  ½ cup freshly squeezed orange juice
  1 to 3 tablespoons red wine vinegar (more or less according to
      taste)
    Coarse salt and freshly ground pepper to taste

1. Trim any gristle from the liver. Dredge the pieces lightly in flour.

2. In a large frying pan, heat the oil and butter. Gently sauté the
shallots with the sage or rosemary until soft.

3. Raise the heat, add the liver, 2 or 3 pieces at a time, and brown
on both sides. Remove to a heated dish and keep warm.

4. Add the orange juice, bring to a boil, and add a tablespoon of
vinegar. Taste for sweetness and add more vinegar, if necessary. If
the sauce is too dry, moisten it with a little water or dry red wine. If
it is too liquid, reduce it over high heat. Season the sauce with salt
and pepper and pour over the liver. Serve immediately.

Yield: 4 servings.

SEVEN

Soups, Stews, and Curries

Soups and stews are convenient dishes for people with little space in their kitchens, because they can be made ahead of time.

Summer soups, light and delicate, revive appetites dulled by hot weather. There are many to choose from: gazpacho, iced consommé, jellied soups served with slices of lemon, or light vegetables purées, enriched with cream and sprinkled with summer herbs.

In the winter, soups are substantial enough to serve as the main course of a meal, followed with cheese and salad. Legumes, such as dried beans, peas, and lentils, make warming and filling meals that are especially good on cold days.

Stews—hearty, comforting, old-fashioned food—are rather romantic, conjuring up visions of rustic simplicity, farmhouses with a cast-iron pot perpetually simmering gently in the hearth and giving off aromas of thyme, rosemary, wine, and spices. They are also immensely practical. They can be made in one pot, often cooked a day or more in advance, and they are economical, using second-grade cuts of meat, elderly birds, and the coarser, cheaper kinds of fish.

When it comes to meat stews, every country has its own version: New England boiled dinner, Scottish cock-a-leekie, or Moroccan *tagin*. Then there are the beef stews of Italy, made with Chianti and served with slices of toasted polenta, or delicate veal stews seasoned with sage and white wine. One of my favorite beef stews when I was growing up in England was baked in a slow oven until its gravy was thick and mahogany colored, to be soaked up with potatoes boiled in their skins. It was made with Guinness.

But nowhere are stews held in as much esteem as in France where *daubes, cassoulets,* and *pots au feu* are on a par with the most expensive roast or a grill (and in fact have more snob appeal, along with other bistro food such as pig's feet, *tête de veau,* rabbit stew, and *andouillettes*). As Alexandre Dumas said, "Ragoût is the glory of French cuisine."

The other glory of French cooking is in the fish stews from the Mediterranean, made quite simply with fresh fish cooked in a stock with saffron and tomatoes and often eaten with aïoli, a golden garlic mayonnaise, or rouille, a hot pepper and garlic sauce.

The Italians make a delicious winter stew with baccalà (salt cod), cooked with tomatoes and plenty of garlic. The poet Shelley, even though he lived in Italy long enough to broaden his English appetite, would not have approved. "There are two Italies," he wrote. "The one is the most sublime and lovely contemplation that can be conceived by the imagination of man; the other is the most degraded, disgusting and odious. What do you think? Young women of rank actually eat—you will never guess what—garlic!"

The Mediterreanean influence is also felt in Morocco where a familiar sight is the *tagin,* a stew in a shallow earthenware pot with a conical lid, bubbling on the back of the stove. *Tagins* are scented with dried fruits, cumin, coriander, and saffron—even Spanish fly which is said to be an aphrodisiac. Particularly good are the chicken *tagins* made with the most fragrant and unusual combinations of ingredients, such as cracked green olives and preserved lemons, apricots and honey, prunes, pears, or quinces. The chickens have usually been allowed to roam around the farmyard, and the meat is tougher and has more taste than our factory farmed chickens. Marinating a chicken overnight in spices and herbs before it is stewed helps the flavors to penetrate.

Stews should never be boiled or the meat will be stringy. A high temperature will not make them cook any faster. They should, as the French say, *mijoter,* just barely bubble.

It is a waste of money to use expensive cuts of meat for stews. The older, muscular cuts have the most flavor and any gristle dissolves during long cooking to give a syrupy texture to the sauce. A calf's or pig's foot or a piece of pork rind will also enrich and thicken the sauce. Before cooking the meat, trim away as much fat as possible. To further cut down on the fat, skim the stew after it has cooked. If you refrigerate the stew overnight, you can easily lift the fat off in pieces the following day.

When properly made, a stew can be one of the most magnificent of dishes. The stews at my English boarding school, however, did not, alas, live up to the glowing descriptions given by French writers of those of their childhood. Ours reminded us of a limerick by Edward Lear about an incident that was said to have taken place in a Dorset town not far from where we were.

> *A gentleman dining at Crewe*
> *Found a rather large mouse in his stew,*
> *said the waiter. "Don't shout and wave it about*
> *Or the rest will be wanting one too."*

CAULIFLOWER SOUP

This soup is light and delicate, a pale golden color, and can be served hot or cold.

2 tablespoons unsalted butter
1 medium-sized onion, chopped
2 leeks, washed well and chopped
2 celery stalks, chopped
1 large potato, peeled and diced
1 large head cauliflower
½ teaspoon turmeric
    Bouquet garni (thyme and parsley sprigs and bay leaf tied in a cheesecloth bag)
2 cups chicken stock (page 285)
2 cups milk
    Coarse salt and freshly ground pepper to taste
    Chopped fresh chives for garnish
    Crème fraîche (page 282) or heavy cream for garnish

1. Melt the butter in a heavy soup kettle and sauté the onion, leeks, and celery until they are soft. Add the potato and the cauliflower, broken into flowerets. Sauté for 5 minutes. Add the turmeric and mix in thoroughly. Cook for another 2 minutes.

2. Add the bouquet garni, stock, and milk. Cover and simmer for 30 minutes.

3. Strain the liquid and reserve it. Place the vegetables in a food processor and blend until thick and smooth. Return to the soup kettle with the liquid. Stir thoroughly and correct the seasoning.

4. Serve hot or cold, garnishing each serving with chives and a spoonful of crème fraîche or heavy cream.

Yield: 4 servings.

CUCUMBER GAZPACHO

The following is an especially refreshing summer soup, an interesting variation of the traditional Spanish gazpacho which is normally made with ripe tomatoes. Instead, small Kirby cucumbers are used. These have the most flavor and, because they are not normally waxed, they can be used with their skins. For the soup they are puréed with onions, peppers, and basil and mixed with homemade chicken stock. The soup is chilled overnight and served cold, garnished with basil leaves and croutons.

FOR THE SOUP

1 egg
2 slices white bread, crusts removed
3½ cups chicken stock, preferably homemade (page 285)
½ cup extra virgin olive oil
2 garlic cloves, peeled
1 small onion, quartered
4 Kirby cucumbers, cut into chunks
1 sweet green pepper, seeded and coarsely chopped
1 cup whole fresh basil leaves
¼ teaspoon sugar
3 to 4 tablespoons red wine vinegar
   Coarse salt and freshly ground pepper to taste

FOR THE GARNISH

6 slices white bread, crusts removed
3 tablespoons unsalted butter, clarified, if possible (page 283)
1 clove garlic, peeled and crushed
1 small onion
1 sweet green pepper, seeded
1 Kirby cucumber, unpeeled
   Basil leaves for garnish

1. Crack the egg into a blender. Whip until lemon-colored. Meanwhile, soak the bread in ½ cup of the chicken stock.

2. Turn on the motor of the blender and gradually add the olive oil. Add the bread, garlic, onion, cucumber, pepper, and basil leaves, a little at a time. If necessary, moisten with some of the chicken stock. Add the sugar, vinegar, salt, and pepper. Blend in a cup of the chicken stock.

3. Add the remaining stock and blend. (If the blender is too full, mix it in a bowl, making sure that it is thoroughly blended.) Correct the seasoning, cover, and refrigerate overnight.

4. Make the croutons. Cut the bread into small cubes. Melt the butter over low heat and add the garlic. Gently fry the croutons, taking care not to burn them, until they are golden on all sides. Cool on paper towels.

5. Dice the onion, pepper, and cucumber. Arrange in a serving bowl. Serve the croutons in another bowl. Decorate each bowl of soup with basil leaves and pass the remaining garnishes separately.

Yield: 4 to 6 servings.

ORANGE-TOMATO SOUP WITH MASCARPONE CHEESE

An unusual and refreshing variant of chilled tomato soup, this contains orange rind, mascarpone cheese, and fresh mint leaves. Crème fraîche can be substituted for the mascarpone and fresh basil leaves used instead of the mint.

> 5 large tomatoes
> 1 large onion, finely chopped
> 2 tablespoons unsalted butter
> 1 bunch watercress
> 2 cups chicken stock (page 285)
> ½ cup finely grated orange rind
>   Coarse salt and freshly ground pepper to taste
>   Mascarpone cheese for garnish
>   Basil or mint leaves for garnish

1. Peel the tomatoes by dropping them briefly into boiling water. Drain them and slip off the skins. Then seed and chop the tomatoes.

2. In a large saucepan, gently cook the onion in the butter until the onion is soft. Add the tomatoes.

3. Wash the watercress and add it with the stalks. Add the chicken stock, cover, and simmer for about 30 mintues, stirring occasionally.

4. Purée the soup in a food processor. Transfer to a bowl, cover, and chill overnight.

5. Simmer the grated orange rind in water to cover for 5 minutes. Drain and stir it into the soup. Correct the seasoning.

6. To serve the soup, pour it into soup bowls and garnish each with a dollop of mascarpone cheese and basil leaves.

Yield: 4 servings.

BLACK BEAN SOUP

1 pound black beans
  Water to cover
1 large peeled onion stuck with 2 whole cloves
2 carrots, sliced
3 celery stalks, chopped
  Bouquet garni (thyme and parsley sprigs and bay leaf tied in a
    cheesecloth bag)
4 whole allspice
¼ teaspoon ground mace
2 garlic cloves, chopped
1 fresh chili pepper, seeded and chopped
  Coarse salt and freshly ground pepper to taste
½ cup dark rum
  Sour cream for garnish
  Lemon slices for garnish

1. Soak the beans overnight in cold water to cover in a large saucepan. When ready to cook, add the vegetables, bouquet garni, allspice, garlic, chili, salt, and pepper. Simmer gently for about 2½ to
3 hours, adding additional water so there is always plenty of liquid.
Remove the bouquet garni.

2. Purée the soup in a blender. Bring to a boil, correct the seasoning, and serve hot.

3. Pour the soup into heated individual bowls, garnishing each one
with a teaspoon of rum, a dollop of cream, and a lemon slice.

Yield: 6 to 8 servings.

DUTCH SPLIT PEA SOUP (ERWTENSOEP)

Holland's favorite soup, the sort skaters in a Brueghel painting must have consumed by the bank of frozen canals to warm themselves up. It is often served with buttered black bread spread with slices of smoked pork.

1 pound green split peas
1 fresh pig's foot
6 ounces smoked pork, diced
2 leeks, well washed and chopped
1 onion, peeled and chopped
4 celery stalks, chopped
1 small celery root, peeled and chopped
1 bay leaf
    Coarse salt and freshly ground pepper to taste
1 smoked ring sausage, sliced
    Chopped fresh parsley leaves for garnish

1. Put the split peas in 2½ quarts water.

2. Add the remaining ingredients, except the sausage, and simmer for about 2 hours, skimming off any foam that rises to the surface.

3. Remove the pig's foot, scrape any meat from it, and return the meat to the pot. Slice the sausage and add it to the soup. Cook for 10 minutes.

4. Serve the soup hot and garnish each serving with parsley.

Yield: 6 servings.

LENTIL SOUP

Ham or lamb bones can be used to flavor this warm and filling soup.

1½ pounds ripe tomatoes, or 1 1-pound can tomatoes
 1 medium-sized onion, chopped
 2 garlic cloves, minced
 2 celery stalks, including leaves, chopped
 2 slices bacon, chopped
 1 pound brown lentils
 2 tablespoons chopped fresh mint leaves
    Coarse salt and freshly ground pepper to taste

1. Peel the tomatoes by pouring boiling water over them and removing their skins while they are still hot.

2. Sauté the onion, garlic, and celery in a large pot with the bacon, until the onion is soft. Add the lentils and fry for a few minutes, stirring. Pour in 6 cups of boiling water.

3. Stir, add the mint and simmer for about 1 hour, adding more water if necessary. Correct the seasoning and ladle into heated bowls or cups, garnishing each serving with a sprig of mint.

Yield: 6 servings.

BOURRIDE

This famous French fish stew takes a short time to cook. The aïoli (garlic mayonnaise) should be made first. The bread can be toasted or fried in olive oil and rubbed with garlic if you like.

Use a combination of firm white-fleshed fish, such as monkfish and turbot. Squid can also be used. Potatoes can also be served with this, either separately or in the soup. Ask your fishmonger to give you the fish heads. They often will do so free.

- 2 fish heads
- 4 cups water
- 1 lemon, sliced
  Bouquet garni (thyme and parsley sprigs and bay leaf tied in a cheesecloth bag)
- 2 onions
- 4 ripe tomatoes
- 2 sweet red peppers
  Coarse salt and freshly ground pepper to taste
  Pinch of saffron threads
- 3 pounds firm white-fleshed fish fillets
  Fresh parsley or chives to garnish
  Boiled potatoes
  Slices of fried French bread

FOR THE AÏOLI

- 4 garlic cloves
- 1 egg yolk
- 1 cup extra virgin olive oil
  Coarse salt and freshly ground pepper to taste

1. Simmer the fish heads (and any fish bones) in the water with the sliced lemon, bouquet garni, and 1 onion, quartered, for 20 minutes. Meanwhile make the aïoli.

168

2. Peel the garlic and pulverize it with a little salt with a mortar and pestle. Add the egg yolk and mix thoroughly. Add the olive oil, as though for a mayonnaise, drop by drop at first, so that the mixture doesn't curdle. Increase as you go, until you have a thick sauce. If it curdles, add another yolk to the mixture and proceed with the oil. Season with salt and pepper and set aside.

3. Peel the tomatoes and slice the remaining onion. Slice the peppers. Strain the fish stock. Place the tomatoes, onion, and peppers into the pot and return the strained fish stock. Season with salt and pepper and add the saffron. Bring to a boil and add the fish. Cook gently, simmering, for 10 minutes. Remove the fish to a serving plate and keep it warm.

4. Boil the liquid down until you have about 2 cups. Put the aïoli into a large bowl and strain on the fish soup carefully, mixing it well. Return to a clean pan and heat gently until the mixture thickens slightly. Pour over the fish fillets, which you have placed in individual soup bowls, sprinkle with chives, and serve with boiled potatoes and slices of fried bread.

Yield: 4 servings.

MIXED SEAFOOD STEW WITH AÏOLI

Another version of a Mediterranean fish stew, this includes halibut or cod, shrimp, and scallops.

    2 pounds cod or halibut steaks
       Fish heads and bones
    ½ pound medium-sized shrimp
    ½ pound scallops
    ¼ teaspoon saffron threads
    1 small bunch parsley
    1 celery stalk with leaves, if possible
    1 medium-sized onion, chopped
    2 cups dry white wine
       Coarse salt and freshly ground pepper to taste
    2 tablespoons unsalted butter
    1 tablespoon extra virgin olive oil
    1 garlic clove, minced
    2 leeks, chopped
    1 carrot, sliced
    1 loaf French or Italian bread

FOR THE AÏOLI

    1 egg yolk
    1 garlic clove, crushed
       Approximately 1 cup extra virgin olive oil
       Juice of ½ lemon
       Coarse salt and freshly ground pepper to taste

1. Trim the bones from the cod or halibut steaks. Place in a saucepan with the fish heads and bones. Peel the shrimp and add the shells. Place the shrimp in a bowl with the fish, trimmed into 1½-inch pieces, and the scallops, cut in half if they are large. Sprinkle with the saffron, toss, and set aside.

2. To the bones and shells add the parsley stalks (reserve the leaves), celery leaves (reserve the stalk), and a quarter of the onion.

Add 2 cups of water, 2 cups wine, and the salt and pepper. Simmer, covered, for 20 minutes.

3. Meanwhile, heat the butter with the oil in a heavy casserole. Fry the remaining onion, garlic, leeks, carrot, and chopped celery stalk until soft and golden.

4. While the vegetables are cooking, make the mayonnaise. In a small bowl, beat the egg yolk until it is thick and sticky. Add the crushed garlic. Little by little, add the oil, beating constantly until you have a smooth emulsion. If you add too much oil too fast, the aïoli will curdle. If this happens, beat another egg yolk and add it. Add the lemon juice, salt, and pepper. Transfer to a small serving bowl and set aside.

5. Toast the slices of bread in the oven.

6. Strain the fish stock, correct the seasoning, and add it to the vegetables. You should have about 3 cups. Bring to a boil, lower the heat, and simmer for 10 minutes. Add the fish and the scallops. Cook for 3 to 4 minutes; then add the shrimp. Cook for 2 minutes. Remove from the heat and serve the stew in heated bowls, passing the bread and mayonnaise separately.

Yield: 4 servings.

BACCALÀ WITH ONIONS AND TOMATOES

Baccalà, also known as dried salt cod, is an extremely useful and delicious food. But in order to be palatable it must be soaked overnight in several changes of water and rinsed several times, otherwise it will be too salty. It goes with boiled or mashed potatoes.

3 tablespoons extra virgin olive oil
1 large onion, diced
2 garlic cloves, minced
1½ pounds salt cod, soaked and rinsed thoroughly
Bouquet garni (thyme and parsley sprigs and bay leaf tied in a cheesecloth bag)
1 tablespoon tomato purée
2 cups canned plum tomatoes
1 cup dry white wine
Freshly ground pepper to taste
½ cup bread crumbs
2 tablespoons unsalted butter

1. Heat the oil in a heavy, shallow casserole. Sauté the onion and the garlic in the oil.

2. Arrange the pieces of salt cod on top and add the bouquet garni, tomato purée, tomatoes, and wine. Season with pepper, cover, and simmer gently for 1 hour.

3. Meanwhile, preheat the oven to 375 degrees. Sprinkle the casserole with bread crumbs and butter and brown in the oven.

Yield: 4 servings.

CHICKEN TAGIN WITH CHICK-PEAS

The Moroccan tagin *is a spicy stew that is cooked in an earthenware pot with a conical lid that is also called a* tagin. *An earthenware-covered casserole or cast-iron casserole that can be heated on top of the stove will also do the job. This kind of stew is extremely easy to make and can be served in the pot in which it is cooked. In this recipe, pieces of chicken are cooked with chick-peas and raisins and served in a sauce that is spiced with turmeric and saffron. It cooks to a deep golden orange. I use canned chick-peas here, because I really don't think the dried ones are worth all the effort. But if you use dried chick-peas, soak them overnight and cook them separately until nearly done; then drain and add them to the casserole.*

Quick Couscous, page 256, or rice goes with this dish. Serve a fairly robust red wine or a chilled Beaujolais.

1 3- to 4-pound chicken, cut up
2 tablespoons olive oil
2 garlic cloves, minced
1 medium-sized onion, thinly sliced
1 teaspoon ground turmeric
1 cinnamon stick
   Pinch of saffron threads
   Coarse salt and freshly ground pepper to taste
½ cup seedless raisins
¼ cup chopped fresh coriander leaves
1 20-ounce can chick-peas, drained

1. Pat the chicken pieces dry with paper towels and brown them in the oil. Add the garlic, onion, turmeric, cinnamon stick, saffron, salt, and pepper. Cover and simmer gently over low heat, stirring occasionally to prevent the chicken pieces from sticking to the bottom of the pan. Cook for 20 minutes.

2. Add the raisins, coriander, and chick-peas. Mix well, cover, and continue cooking for 20 to 25 minutes, or until the chicken is tender. Correct the seasoning and serve.

Yield: 4 servings.

CHICKEN TAGIN WITH ITALIAN PEPPERS

Serve with Quick Couscous, page 256, or rice.

1 3- to 4-pound chicken, cut up
1 tablespoon extra virgin olive oil
6 Italian frying peppers, seeded and cut into quarters
8 whole unpeeled garlic cloves
1 onion, sliced
1 teaspoon ground cumin
2 tablespoons Hungarian paprika
   Coarse salt and freshly ground pepper to taste

1. Pat the chicken pieces dry with paper towels. Heat the oil in a heavy casserole or *tagin*. Add the chicken pieces and brown gently, a few at a time. Arrange the remaining ingredients around and over the chicken.

2. Cover and cook for 45 minutes, or until tender.

Yield: 4 servings.

OXTAIL STEW DA SILVANO

This recipe comes from Da Silvano's Italian restaurant in New York City. It is simple to make and improves upon being cooked the night before it is eaten. Serve it with boiled potatoes.

2   tablespoons vegetable oil
2   oxtails, cut into 1-inch pieces by the butcher, with fat
        trimmed off
2   tablespoons all-purpose flour for dredging (more if needed)
1   large red onion, sliced
6   celery stalks, chopped
2   carrots, sliced
     Coarse salt and freshly ground pepper to taste
1   teaspoon dried rosemary leaves
3   cups dry red wine
1   1-pound can peeled Italian plum tomatoes

1. Preheat the oven to 350 degrees. Heat the oil in a wide, heavy casserole. Dredge the oxtail pieces in the flour and brown them without burning. Remove the browned pieces of meat and drain them on paper towels.

2. Brown the onion, celery, and carrots. Return the meat to the casserole and season it with salt, pepper, and rosemary. Add the red wine and bring to a simmer. Simmer, uncovered, for 15 minutes, stirring occasionally to prevent sticking.

3. Add the tomatoes with their juice and mix them in. Braise in the oven for 2½ hours, or until the meat comes away from the bones.

Yield: 4 servings.

BASQUE STEW

In Spain, Italy, France, and Mexico, unsweetened chocolate is often used as a thickening agent in stews and sauces, producing a thick, dark gravy without a chocolate taste. This is a good dish for a dinner party. It can be cooked a day ahead and reheated. Serve it with boiled potatoes and French bread.

1½ pounds stewing beef
1½ pounds boneless pork
 1 chicken (about 2 to 3 pounds)
 2 tablespoons olive oil
 1 large onion, chopped
 2 garlic cloves, minced
 1 pound carrots, sliced
 2 teaspoons all-purpose flour
 3 cups dry red wine
 1 square unsweetened baking chocolate
 1 teaspoon sugar
   Bouquet garni (thyme and parsley sprigs and bay leaf tied in a cheesecloth bag)
 3 tablespoons chopped parsley leaves
   Coarse salt and freshly ground pepper to taste

1. Trim the fat from the beef and pork and cut the meat into 1-inch cubes. Cut the chicken into serving portions. Wipe the meat dry with paper towels.

2. In a large heavy casserole, heat the oil and sauté the onion, garlic, and carrots until they are golden. Remove with a slotted spoon and set aside.

3. Brown the meat in the casserole, a few pieces at a time. Pour off the fat.

4. Sprinkle the flour into the casserole and cook for 1 minute. Return the vegetables and meat (not the chicken) to the casserole and add the wine, chocolate, sugar, bouquet garni, and 1 tablespoon of the parsley and season with salt and pepper. Simmer for 1 hour covered, over low heat.

5. Add the chicken and simmer for 45 minutes, or until all the meat is tender. Serve from the casserole, sprinkling the remaining parsley on top.

Yield: 8 servings.

BEEF STEW

The orange peel gives this stew a distinctive flavor. Serve with mashed or boiled potatoes.

  1 tablespoon olive oil
  1 slice bacon, cut into ½-inch pieces
1½ pounds lean stewing beef, cut into 1½-inch pieces
  1 onion, chopped
  1 tablespoon all-purpose flour
  1 garlic clove, minced
  1 to 1½ cups chicken or meat stock (page 285)
  ½ cup beer
  1 tablespoon tomato paste
    Bouquet garni (thyme and parsley sprigs and bay leaf tied in a cheesecloth bag)
  4 strips orange peel
    Coarse salt and freshly ground pepper to taste

1. Heat the oil in a heavy casserole and add the bacon. Dry the cubes of beef with paper towels and brown them a few at a time. Remove and add the onion. Brown lightly. Stir in the flour and cook for 2 to 3 minutes without burning.

2. Return the beef with its juices to the casserole. Add the garlic, stock, beer, tomato paste, bouquet garni, orange peel, salt, and pepper. Bring to a boil, lower the heat, and simmer gently for 1½ hours, stirring occasionally.

3. Correct the seasoning and serve.

Yield: 3 to 4 servings.

GUINNESS STEW

Serve with mashed or boiled potatoes.

  1 tablespoon vegetable oil
  1 slice bacon, cut into ½-inch pieces
  2 pounds lean stewing beef, cut into 1½-inch pieces
  1 large onion, chopped
  2 tablespoons all-purpose flour
  2 carrots, sliced
12 small white onions, peeled
1½ cups meat stock (page 285)
  1 bottle Guinness (6½ fluid ounces)
  2 tablespoons dark brown sugar
  2 tablespoons red wine vinegar
     Bouquet garni (thyme and parsley sprigs and bay leaf tied in a cheesecloth bag)
     Coarse salt and freshly ground pepper to taste

1. Preheat the oven to 350 degrees. Heat the oil in a heavy casserole that will go both on top of and inside the stove. Add the bacon and fry until the bacon is browned. Remove the bacon and drain it on paper towels.

2. Dry the cubes of beef with paper towels and brown them in the casserole a few at a time. Remove and add the chopped onion. Brown the onion lightly. Stir in the flour and cook for 2 to 3 minutes without burning.

3. Return the beef with its juices and the bacon to the casserole. Add the carrots, white onions, stock, beer, sugar, vinegar, bouquet garni, salt, and pepper. Bring to a boil, cover, and bake for 1½ to 2 hours, stirring occasionally.

4. Correct the seasoning and serve.

Yield: 4 servings.

MEATBALLS WITH EGGPLANT

This goes with Quick Couscous, page 256.

- 2 eggplants
- 1 pound ground beef
- 1 onion, sliced
- 3 carrots, sliced
- 4 small red potatoes, halved
- ½ teaspoon ground cumin
- 1 teaspoon ground coriander
- ½ teaspoon ground allspice
- ½ teaspoon Hungarian paprika
  Coarse salt and freshly ground pepper to taste
- 1 1-pound can Italian tomatoes

1. Peel the eggplants and chop them into cubes. Sprinkle with salt and let them drain in a colander for 1 hour.

2. Form the beef into walnut-sized balls. Arrange them, tightly packed, in a shallow, heavy skillet (cast-iron, if possible) or a casserole with a wide bottom. Rinse the eggplant, pat it dry with paper towels and add it to the skillet. Arrange the onion slices, carrots, and potatoes over the top. Sprinkle with the spices, salt, and pepper. Pour on the tomatoes and 1 cup water.

3. Cover and bring to a simmer. Simmer for 1½ hours, removing the lid if the stew seems too liquid.

Yield: 3 to 4 servings.

STEWED LAMB SHANKS WITH WHITE BEANS

Lamb shanks are an inexpensive and underused cut. They are delicious when cooked and baked with beans, and come out tender, with the meat almost falling off the bone.

      4 lamb shanks
      4 garlic cloves, cut into slivers
      1 teaspoon dried rosemary
      3 tablespoons extra virgin olive oil
    ½ pound Great Northern beans
         Water to cover
      3 medium-sized onions, peeled
         Bouquet garni (thyme and parsley sprigs and bay leaf tied in a
           cheesecloth bag)
         Coarse salt and freshly ground pepper to taste
      3 carrots, sliced
      1 cup dry white or red wine
  1½ cups chicken or meat stock (page 285)
    ⅓ cup diced salt pork
    ¾ cup fresh bread crumbs
      2 tablespoons butter
      2 tablespoons chopped parsley leaves

1. Make small incisions in the lamb shanks and stud them with the garlic. Sprinkle with the rosemary. Coat the shanks with 2 tablespoons of the olive oil, cover, and marinate overnight in the refrigerator. Soak the beans overnight in cold water to cover.

2. Rinse the beans, put them in a large saucepan, and cover with fresh water. Add 1 onion, coarsely chopped, bouquet garni, salt, and pepper. Simmer for about 1 hour, or until the beans are tender.

3. Heat 1 tablespoon of the olive oil in a large pan and brown the lamb shanks on all sides. Remove the shanks and pour off the fat.

4. Chop the remaining onions and add them to the pan. Cook gently until the onions are soft. Add the carrots, wine, lamb shanks, and stock. Bring to a boil, lower the heat, and simmer for 1 hour.

180

5. Preheat the oven to 350 degrees.

6. Drain the beans, reserving the cooking liquid. In a large casserole, place a layer of beans, a layer of salt pork, vegetables, and juices from the lamb shanks and then the shanks. Add the remaining beans and juices. If the stew is too dry, add some of the liquid from the beans. Bake for 1 hour.

7. Sprinkle with bread crumbs and butter and bake, uncovered, for 30 minutes longer. Sprinkle with the parsley and serve.

Yield: 4 servings.

VEAL STEW WITH TOMATOES AND RED PEPPERS

    1 onion, chopped
    1 garlic clove, minced
    2 tablespoons peanut or vegetable oil
    2 pounds stewing veal (with extra bones, if possible)
    1 teaspoon all-purpose flour
    2 teaspoons fresh rosemary leaves, or 1 teaspoon dried
        rosemary
    5 ripe tomatoes, peeled, or 2 cups canned tomatoes
    4 sweet red peppers, peeled and sliced
    2 cups dry white wine
    1 cup water
      Coarse salt and freshly ground pepper to taste

1. In a heavy casserole, sauté the onion and the garlic in the oil until they are soft. Remove the onion and garlic and brown the meat a few pieces at a time.

2. Return the onion, garlic, and browned meat to the casserole. Add the flour and cook for 1 minute, stirring so that it does not burn. Add the remaining ingredients, bring to a boil, lower the heat, and simmer for 1½ to 2 hours. If the stew is too dry, add water. If it is too liquid, remove the lid and let it reduce.

Yield: 4 servings.

VEAL WITH LEMON AND ARTICHOKE HEARTS

1½ pounds stewing veal
    Flour for dredging
 1 tablespoon peanut or safflower oil
 1 tablespoon unsalted butter
 1 medium-sized onion, sliced
 2 garlic cloves
 ½ teaspoon dried thyme
 ½ to 1 cup chicken stock (page 285)
 1 cup canned Italian tomatoes with their juice
 1 cup dry white wine
    Coarse salt and freshly ground pepper to taste
 1 pound baby carrots, scraped
 6 artichoke bottoms, quartered, preferably fresh
 ¼ pound mushrooms, sliced
 1 egg yolk
    Juice of 1 lemon
    Chopped fresh parsley leaves

1. Cut the veal into 1½-inch cubes. Dredge lightly with the flour.

2. Heat the oil and butter in a large casserole. Brown the veal pieces a few at a time. Add the onion and 1 garlic clove, minced. Add the thyme, ½ cup of the chicken stock, the tomatoes, and white wine. Season with salt and pepper, cover and simmer for 45 minutes.

3. Add the carrots, artichoke bottoms, and mushrooms. If necessary at this point, add more stock. Cook the vegetables until they are almost tender.

4. In a small bowl, beat the egg yolk. Crush the remaining clove of garlic with a pestle and mortar, adding a little salt. Add the egg yolk and beat with a fork. Pour in the lemon juice and mix thoroughly. Ladle a spoonful of the cooking juices from the casserole into the egg mixture. Mix well. Add the mixture to the casserole and cook over very low heat for 1 minute, stirring. Do not overheat or the mixture will curdle.

5. Remove from the heat, sprinkle with the parsley, and serve.

Yield: 4 servings.

VEAL STEW WITH HERBS AND WHITE TURNIPS

Ask your butcher for some veal bones with marrow. They add a delicious flavor to this stew. Serve the stew with noodles. It is especially good when fresh herbs are in season.

1½ pounds stewing veal
    Juice of 1 lemon
    Coarse salt and freshly ground pepper to taste
1 tablespoon vegetable oil
2 tablespoons unsalted butter
2 shallots, minced
    Veal bones with marrow
    Flour for dredging
2 tablespoons dried sage leaves, or 3 tablespoons fresh sage
    leaves
½ tablespoon dried marjoram, or 1 tablespoon fresh marjoram
1 cup dry white wine
3 white turnips

1. Dry the pieces of veal with paper towels and put them in a bowl. Squeeze on the lemon juice and season with salt and pepper. Set aside (they may be left to marinate overnight).

2. Heat the oil and butter in a heavy casserole. Gently sauté the shallots without browning them. Remove with a slotted spoon.

3. Dredge the veal and veal bones lightly with the flour, shaking off all excess. Brown lightly, a few at a time.

4. Return the shallots and all the meat to the pan and add the herbs and wine. Bring to a boil, scraping up any bits that have stuck to the bottom of the pan. Cover and simmer for 1 hour.

5. Meanwhile, peel the turnips, quarter them, and round off the edges with a sharp knife, so that they are shaped like walnuts. Add them to the stew. Cook for 30 minutes longer, or until the veal is tender and the turnips are cooked.

Yield: 4 servings.

CURRIES

The curry lunch is not an institution familiar to many Americans. It is an Anglo-Indian tradition that became immensely popular among the British, especially those posted abroad. It was the favorite way to entertain on Sundays. The afternoon began with drinks, gin and tonic or a concoction called Pimms No. 1. There are few buffet spreads I remember being as colorful as this one.

The curries, both mild and hot, were made the day before. There was usually a choice among meat, fish, and chicken curries, plus lentils, rice and rice pilaf, two or three vegetable dishes, pickles, chutneys, and relishes. Dry curries would balance moist ones, bland dishes the fiery ones. The table would be set with all kinds of condiments, arranged in bright little bowls. These included sliced bananas with lemon juice squeezed on them, diced mango, raisins, grated coconut, and peanuts, tomatoes, onions, cucumbers, parsley, chives, scallions, and hard-boiled eggs, all chopped. Indian breads were also set out in baskets or on plates, covered with napkins to keep the breads warm. It was indeed an enticing display.

But even with only one or two curries and a small selection of condiments, the cook with a small kitchen can produce a festive meal for lunch or dinner. The rich color and the appetizing smell of the slow cooking that produces the pungent sauces, all tempt people to try curries for themselves. Plus, they are not expensive or hard to make. It is the careful use of aromatics that produces the best sauces. The word curry comes from the Indian word "kari" meaning sauce. In India, this sauce is made from a mixture of spices prepared by the cook. It is not made with an all-purpose commercial powder. The latter is often made from the cheapest ingredients and has a harsh, flat taste, making all curries seem alike.

A good curry is made with fresh home-ground spices.

These should be stored in a cool place away from the light. The basic curry powder is known as masala. The proportions and balance of this masala are tremendously important. After trying a few combinations, most cooks settle on a mixture that suits their taste. And it is not so much which spices you use as how you use them that makes the difference. Some spices are fried in ghee (see Clarified Butter, page 283) and added at the beginning. Others are added at the end.

The following masala is an aromatic powder that can be used as a basis for curries or for marinating meat. It can also be sprinkled over roast chicken just before serving. To make a hot powder, add two dried red chili peppers. Serve the curried dishes with rice.

GARAM MASALA

4 ounces peeled cardamom seeds
2 tablespoons ground cinnamon
2 ounces ground cloves
4 tablespoons ground mace
4 tablespoons coriander seed
2 ounces whole black peppercorns
3 tablespoons black cumin seeds (if not available, use regular cumin seeds)

1. Preheat the oven to 200 degrees. Roast the cardamom seeds for ½ hour without browning them.

2. Remove the pods and combine the seeds in a blender or spice grinder with the remaining ingredients. Grind very fine. Store in a tightly closed jar away from the light.

SIMPLE CHICKEN CURRY

1 3- to 4-pound chicken, cut up
2 tablespoons ghee or clarified butter (page 283)
2 medium-sized onions, chopped
2 garlic cloves, minced
2 teaspoons garam masala (see preceding recipe)
   Water or chicken stock (page 285) to cover
   Coarse salt and freshly ground pepper to taste

1. Dry the chicken pieces with paper towels. Heat the ghee or clarified butter in a heavy-bottomed casserole and fry the chicken until it is golden. Remove and set aside.

2. Soften the onions and the garlic in the ghee. Add the masala and cook, stirring for 2 minutes, taking care to prevent burning.

3. Add the stock or water, season with salt and pepper, and return the chicken to the casserole. Simmer gently until the chicken is done, about 30 to 45 minutes.

Yield: 4 servings.

CHICKEN KORMA

- 1 3- to 4-pound chicken, cut up
- 8 ounces plain yogurt
- 2 garlic cloves, minced
- 2 teaspoons finely chopped fresh ginger
   Coarse salt and freshly ground pepper to taste
- 2 tablespoons clarified butter or ghee (page 283)
- 1 medium-sized onion, chopped
- 1 teaspoon ground coriander
- ½ teaspoon cayenne pepper, or to taste
- 1 teaspoon ground cumin
- 4 cardamom seeds, peeled
- 1 teaspoon ground turmeric
- ¼ cup water
- 2 tablespoons chopped fresh mint leaves

1. Place the chicken in a bowl and marinate for a couple of hours or overnight in the yogurt, 1 clove of the garlic, the ginger, salt, and pepper. Remove the chicken pieces from the marinade and dry them with paper towels. Reserve the marinade.

2. Melt the clarified butter in a large heavy pan and fry the chicken pieces until they are golden. Remove and add the onion and remaining garlic. Cook until softened. Add the coriander, cayenne, cumin, cardamom seeds, and turmeric. Fry for 2 to 3 minutes.

3. Return the chicken pieces to the pan with the water and the marinade. Add the mint and simmer, covered, over low heat for about 30 minutes, or until the chicken is tender.

Yield: 4 servings.

BEEF VINDALOO

1 medium-sized onion, coarsely chopped
2 garlic cloves, peeled
1 tablespoon turmeric
1 tablespoon coriander seeds
2 teaspoons chili powder (or according to taste)
½ teaspoon light mustard seeds
½ teaspoon fenugreek
1 teaspoon ground ginger
1 teaspoon cumin seeds
¼ cup vinegar to make a paste
2 pounds boneless stewing beef, cut into 1-inch cubes
3 tablespoons clarified butter or ghee (page 283) or vegetable
   oil
4 cups water
   Coarse salt to taste

1. Put the onion and the garlic in the jar of an electric blender. Grind the spices in a spice grinder and combine with the onion mixture. Blend, adding enough vinegar to make a thick, stiff paste.

2. Pat the beef cubes dry with paper towels. Put the meat in a large bowl and coat thoroughly with the paste. Allow to marinate for 4 hours or overnight.

3. Melt the clarified butter in a heavy casserole. Brown the beef carefully without burning and add the water. Cover and cook over low heat until tender, about 1½ to 2 hours. If there is too much liquid, remove the cover and turn up the heat. If the curry is too dry, add more water.

Yield: 4 servings.

LAMB KEEMA CURRY

 1 tablespoon clarified butter or ghee (page 283)
 1 medium-sized onion, chopped
 2 garlic cloves, minced
 2 tablespoons chopped fresh coriander or parsley leaves
 2 pounds ground lamb
 1 teaspoon turmeric
 ½ teaspoon chili powder, or to taste
 1 pound ripe tomatoes, peeled, seeded, and chopped
    Coarse salt to taste
 1 tablespoon garam masala (page 185)
 ½ pound fresh peas, shelled

1. Heat the clarified butter and fry the onion with the garlic until it is golden. Add the coriander, lamb, turmeric, and chili powder. Bring to a simmer, add the tomatoes and salt and cook over very low heat for 30 minutes.

2. Add the garam masala and the peas. Cook for another 15 to 20 minutes.

Yield: 4 servings.

EIGHT

Vegetables

In the last few years the choice and quality of vegetables available at my local markets have improved so much that I can again take pleasure in cooking them. I like to serve at least one, if not two, vegetables with most meals. Many of the dishes in this chapter are good for serving with plain roasted or grilled fish, poultry, or meat. Others can be served as a course on their own.

ARTICHOKES

Artichokes, perhaps the most elegant of vegetables, are merely edible thistles. But, during the Renaissance, they enjoyed a reputation for being an aphrodisiac. According to the late Waverley Root, Catherine de Medici, who is said to have introduced them to France, ate so many that a contemporary chronicler recorded that "she liked to burst." A shocked elderly woman of the period wrote: "If one of us had eaten artichokes we would have been pointed at in the street. To-day young women are more forward than pages at court."

Large artichokes can be steamed or boiled and drained upside down in a colander. Then they can be served with hollandaise sauce or a vinaigrette dressing, or simply with melted butter or lemon juice. They can also be three-quarters cooked and a mixture of cooked bacon or prosciutto, bread crumbs, garlic, and parsley stuffed between the leaves. Place them in a baking dish in a preheated 350-degree oven with an inch of dry white wine to prevent them from sticking to the bottom of the pan, and cover them with aluminum foil. Bake for 20 minutes, or until tender.

When artichokes are very young and small the fuzzy choke that lies under the leaves can be eaten. When the artichoke matures, the choke becomes too bristly and should be discarded.

To prepare baby artichokes for cooking, use a sharp knife and cut off the tops of the artichoke leaves horizontally, about an inch or so down, so that you are left with about an inch and a half of leaf on the bottom half. Trim the stalk and remove any tough or discolored outer leaves. (Occasionally you may come across baby artichokes that have black patches on them. Cut the patches away.) Once cooked, the entire artichoke should be tender enough to eat.

Frozen artichoke hearts can be used in place of fresh small artichokes. They require less cooking time and they do not have the flavor or texture of fresh ones. Canned artichokes tend to be rather insipid.

The following recipes for baby artichokes can be made with frozen artichoke hearts or partially cooked artichoke bottoms. If using either of these, cook the sauce for 15 to 20 minutes *before* you add the artichokes. Cook them for about 10 minutes, or until they are tender.

BABY ARTICHOKES WITH ANCHOVIES

20 baby artichokes, fresh or frozen, thawed
1½ lemons
½ cup extra virgin olive oil
1 small onion, minced
2 garlic cloves, minced
4 tablespoons chopped parsley leaves
1 2-ounce can anchovies, drained and minced
½ cup dry white wine
    Coarse salt and freshly ground pepper to taste

1. Trim the outer leaves from the fresh artichokes and cut off the stalks and the tops, two-thirds down horizontally. Cut a lemon in half and squeeze half the juice into a bowl of cold water. Put the lemon half in the bowl and add the artichokes as you trim them. The lemon and water will stop them from turning dark brown.

2. Heat the oil in a large frying pan big enough to hold the artichokes in one layer. Gently sauté the onion and the garlic until they are soft. Add the parsley, anchovies, and wine. Mix thoroughly and simmer for 3 minutes.

3. Add the fresh artichokes, cover, and cook for 20 to 30 minutes, or until they are tender. If using frozen artichokes, cook the sauce for 15 minutes before adding them. Season with salt and pepper. Serve garnished with the remaining lemon cut into quarters. Spoon the sauce over the top of the artichokes.

Yield: 4 servings.

Note: This dish can be served hot or cold.

Vegetables

BRAISED BABY ARTICHOKES WITH ONIONS AND CAPERS

Serve this as a first course or luncheon dish. Use the smallest white onions you can find.

16 baby artichokes, fresh or frozen, thawed
 1 lemon
 4 tablespoons extra virgin olive oil
24 small white onions, peeled
 1 teaspoon sugar
 1 garlic clove, minced
   Coarse salt and freshly ground pepper to taste
1½ tablespoons red wine vinegar
 2 tablespoons tomato purée
 1 cup dry white wine
 2 tablespoons drained capers
 ½ cup oil-cured black olives, preferably pitted
   Chopped fresh parsley leaves for garnish

1. Trim the outer leaves from the fresh artichokes and cut off the stalks and the tops, two-thirds down horizontally. Cut the lemon in half and squeeze half the juice into a bowl of cold water. Put the lemon half in the bowl and add the artichokes, as you trim them. The lemon and water will stop them turning dark brown.

2. Heat the oil in a large frying pan and brown the artichokes (if using frozen ones, pat them dry with paper towels before browning). Remove, and brown the onions. Sprinkle the onions with the sugar. Add the garlic and return the fresh artichokes to the pan (if using frozen, do not add until the sauce has cooked for 15 minutes). Season and cook the fresh artichokes for 5 minutes, stirring frequently.

3. Add the vinegar, tomato purée, wine, capers, and olives. Cover and simmer, stirring frequently, until the sauce has thickened (after 15 minutes, add the frozen artichokes) and the artichokes are

193

cooked, about 30 minutes. If the sauce is too thick, add a little water. If it is too thin, uncover and reduce. Sprinkle with lemon juice and parsley and serve.

Yield: 4 servings.

ARTICHOKES BARIGOULE

Artichokes Barigoule is a well known recipe from Provence. There are many variations—sometimes mushrooms are added to the stuffing and the whole artichokes are wrapped in thin strips of pork fat and tied with string. The following version is lighter and can be served as a lunch dish or first course. The artichokes should fit comfortably in one layer in the frying pan.

4   large or 12 baby artichokes
2   tablespoons unsalted butter
2   medium-sized onions, chopped
1   garlic clove, minced
2   slices bacon, chopped
4   tablespoons dry bread crumbs
3   tablespoons chopped parsley leaves
    Coarse salt and freshly ground pepper to taste
2   carrots, chopped
1   cup dry white wine
1   cup chicken stock (page 285)

1. Trim the artichokes and blanch them in boiling water for 5 minutes. Refresh under cold running water and drain. Using a sharp knife, remove the choke.

2. Melt the butter in a frying pan and soften 1 onion and the garlic. Add the bacon and cook until lightly browned. Mix with the bread

194

crumbs, 2 tablespoons of the parsley, and season with salt and pepper. Stuff the mixture into the center of the artichokes.

3. Put the remaining onion into the skillet with the chopped carrots. Add the artichokes and pour in the wine and stock. The liquid should come about two-thirds the way up the artichokes. If necessary, add a little more.

4. Cover and simmer for about 1¼ hours, or until the artichokes are tender. (Baby artichokes will take about 30 minutes.) Baste frequently. When the artichokes are done, remove them to a serving dish. Strain the cooking liquid and reduce it slightly if necessary. Pour into a bowl and sprinkle with remaining parsley. Serve separately.

Yield: 4 servings.

ROMAN-STYLE ARTICHOKES

If possible, use medium-sized artichokes for this dish. It is based on a recipe given by Marcella Hazan in The Classic Italian Cookbook. *Serve at room temperature.*

    4 artichokes
    1 lemon
    1 garlic clove, minced
    1 tablespoon chopped fresh mint leaves
    2 tablespoon chopped parsley leaves
       Coarse salt and freshly ground pepper to taste
  ½ cup extra virgin olive oil

1. Leaving the stalks on the artichokes, trim the ends. Using a sharp knife, scrape the outer layer of skin off the stalk. Pull away the outer leaves of the artichokes, leaving the bottom part of the leaves still clinging to the chokes. Do this by holding the bottom part of the leaf against the choke and snapping off the top.

2. Scrape away the fuzzy choke. As each artichoke is prepared, place it in a bowl of cold water with the lemon, cut in half and squeezed into the water. Place the lemon halves in the water, too. They will prevent the artichokes from turning dark brown.

3. Combine the garlic, mint, and parsley. Season with salt and pepper. Stuff some of the mixture into the center of each artichoke.

4. Place the artichoke upside down in a heavy saucepan. Add the oil, an inch of water, and the remaining mint-parsley mixture. Place two thicknesses of paper towels, soaked in water, over the top and cover with a lid. This will allow the artichokes to steam.

5. Cook until tender, cool, and serve.

Yield: 2 servings.

FAVA BEANS WITH SUMMER SAVORY

Fava beans are a great favorite in England where they are known as broad beans and in Italy where they are eaten both fresh and dried. On May 1, Romans take to the countryside and eat the beans raw with Pecorino cheese grated on top. With this they drink Frascati, the local white wine.

Americans, however, have been slow to discover the pleasure of these large tender green beans with their big furry pods. The pods should be removed unless the beans are very young indeed—and this is unlikely unless you are picking them from your own garden. If the beans are very large or at all tough, the outer skin of each one should be removed. Then they can be simmered or steamed, and served with ham, bacon, or roasted meats. They have a special affinity for lamb (the Greeks often stew lamb with fava beans).

  2 pounds fava beans
  1 tablespoon unsalted butter
  2 tablespoons fresh summer savory or tarragon leaves
     Coarse salt and freshly ground pepper to taste

1. Remove the pods from the beans. Bring 2 inches of water to a rolling boil. Add the beans, lower the heat, and simmer until the beans are tender, about 10 minutes.

2. Drain, dot with butter, and sprinkle with the herbs, salt, and pepper.

Yield: 2 to 3 servings.

STEWED STRING BEANS

American string beans are picked when too mature to be much good steamed or boiled briefly and served with butter. Sometimes thin haricots verts imported from Africa or France are available. They are expensive but they are much more tender than our string beans.

The answer for American string beans is to spice them up. They are good sautéed with other vegetables. Bacon or new potatoes can be added to this recipe, and olive oil may be used in place of the butter. Sauté a minced clove of garlic with the onion if you wish.

- 1   medium-sized onion, chopped
- 2   tablespoons unsalted butter
- 2   ripe tomatoes, peeled, seeded, and chopped, or 1 cup
       canned tomatoes
- 1   teaspoon tomato purée
- ½   teaspoon dried oregano
- 1   pound string beans, ends trimmed
       Coarse salt and freshly ground pepper to taste

1. Sauté the onion in the butter until it is soft. Add the tomatoes, tomato purée, and oregano. Cover and simmer gently for 10 minutes, adding a little water if too dry.

2. Meanwhile, blanch the beans. Drain and add them to the tomatoes. Cook for 15 minutes, or until the beans are tender.

Yield: 4 servings.

SPICED STRING BEANS WITH COCONUT

*A good side dish to serve with a spicy stew or curry. Use unsweet-
ened grated coconut.*

1   pound string beans
1   tablespoon peanut or sesame oil
1   small fresh green chili, seeded and minced
1   tablespoon minced fresh ginger
1   garlic clove, minced
½   teaspoon turmeric
1½ tablespoons grated unsweetened coconut
    Coarse salt and freshly ground pepper to taste

1. Trim and wash the beans. Heat the oil in a wok or large frying
pan and gently sauté the chili, ginger, and garlic until golden.

2. Add the beans and the turmeric and sauté for 1 minute, coating
with the oil. Add 1 cup water, stir, and simmer for 5 minutes,
covered.

3. Add the coconut and simmer, covered, for 10 minutes, or until
the beans are tender. Season, add more water if necessary, and stir
frequently.

Yield: 3 to 4 servings.

STRING BEANS WITH WASABI AND TAMARI DIP

This recipe comes from John Cage. He serves these string beans al dente with a dip made from soy sauce mixed with wasabi powder, a green horseradish which tastes rather like Colman's mustard. It is sold in Oriental and health food stores.

These beans go with chicken roasted with garlic and served hot or cold or with steamed fish.

 1 pound string beans
 1 tablespoon wasabi paste
 ¼ cup tamari soy sauce

1. Trim the string beans and steam for 7 minutes.

2. Cool for 10 minutes in the freezer.

3. Moisten the wasabi with a few drops of water to form a pale green ball; then mix with the tamari. Put in a small bowl to serve as a dip for the beans.

Yield: 4 servings.

BEETS IN ORANGE BUTTER

Use young beets. Either boil them in their skins (leaving an inch of stem on) or roast them—in their skins—in the oven until they are tender. Slip off the skins, slice the beets, and toss them in the orange butter. The beets may also be chopped in the food processor, using the sharp blade.

 12 small cooked beets
  3 tablespoons unsalted butter
 ¼ cup freshly squeezed orange juice
  1 tablespoon grated orange rind
     Coarse salt and freshly ground pepper to taste
  2 tablespoons chopped fresh tarragon (parsley can be used if
     tarragon is out of season)

1. While the beets are cooking, prepare the butter. Melt the butter, add the orange juice, rind, salt, pepper, and tarragon. Mix thoroughly.

2. Slice the cooked beets or chop them in the food processor. Pour on the butter sauce and serve.

Yield: 4 servings.

BEET GREENS WITH SESAME

The best way to buy beets is with their greens intact. Many people throw these away. A pity, since they are delicious. They can be mixed with spinach or turnip greens and stir-fried. The following recipe is a good side dish in a meal that has Oriental overtones. It goes with rice or fish dishes. Use dark Chinese sesame oil, which has more flavor than most health food sesame oils.

1 bunch beet greens
2 tablespoons sesame oil
1 tablespoon tamari soy sauce
2 tablespoons toasted sesame seeds

1. Trim the beet greens and wash them thoroughly. Simmer in boiling water for about 5 to 10 minutes. Refresh under cold water and squeeze dry.

2. Sprinkle the beet greens with sesame oil, soy sauce, and toasted sesame seeds and serve.

Yield: 2 servings.

SPICED BROCCOLI RABE

Broccoli rabe, broccoli, mustard greens, or spinach make a delicious purée when cooked with onions, garlic, and green chilies thickened with a little cornmeal. The purée is quite delicate and goes with grilled fish or chicken.

The following has been adapted from a Punjabi recipe given in Madhur Jaffrey's World-of-the-East Vegetarian Cooking.

1½ pounds broccoli rabe
 1 ½-inch piece fresh ginger
 1 fresh green chili, seeded
    Coarse salt to taste
 2 tablespoons peanut or vegetable oil
 3 tablespoons unsalted butter
 3 tablespoons cornmeal
    Chopped fresh coriander or parsley leaves for garnish.

1. Chop the stalks and leaves of the broccoli rabe into 1½-inch pieces. Simmer in 1 cup of water until they are barely tender. Drain, reserving the cooking liquid.

2. Combine the broccoli rabe in a blender with the ginger and chili. Purée until smooth, adding a little of the cooking liquid if necessary. Season with salt to taste.

3. Heat the oil and butter in a frying pan. Add the cornmeal and fry, stirring, for 2 to 3 minutes. Moisten with ¼ cup broccoli rabe cooking liquid. Stir thoroughly. Add the broccoli rabe and cook gently over medium heat for 10 minutes. Garnish with coriander or parsley and serve.

Yield: 4 servings.

STEWED CABBAGE

A spicy dish, this goes with Chicken Tagin with Italian Peppers, page 174, Marinated Pork Ribs with Orange and Rosemary, page 145, or curry.

- 1 small cabbage (about 1 pound)
- 2 tablespoons clarified butter (page 283)
- 1 teaspoon ground cumin
- ¼ teaspoon turmeric
- 1 teaspoon finely chopped fresh ginger
- 1 garlic clove, peeled and minced
- 2 fresh green chilies, minced
  Coarse salt and freshly ground black pepper to taste
- 2 tablespoons chopped fresh coriander leaves

1. Core and shred the cabbage. Melt the butter in a frying pan and add the cumin, turmeric, ginger, garlic, and chilies. Cook, stirring, for 2 to 3 minutes.

2. Add the cabbage, cover, and cook over low heat for 10 minutes more, or until the cabbage is tender. Season with salt and pepper. Sprinkle with the coriander and serve.

Yield: 4 servings.

STIR-FRIED CABBAGE WITH
SHIITAKE MUSHROOMS

Shiitake mushrooms are available dried in health food and specialty stores. They are also sometimes available fresh, in which case they need not be soaked before being cooked. They are a rich and meaty mushroom. This dish goes with chicken or could be served as a vegetarian meal, with rice.

  5 shiitake mushrooms
1¼ pounds green cabbage
  2 tablespoons peanut or vegetable oil
  1 garlic clove, minced
  1 teaspoon minced fresh ginger
  1 fresh green chili, seeded and minced
  4 scallions, chopped
     Coarse salt and freshly ground pepper to taste

1. Soak the mushrooms, if dried, in warm water to cover for 20 minutes. Drain, reserving the liquid, and slice the mushrooms.

2. Slice the cabbage against the grain. Heat the oil in a wok or large frying pan and gently sauté the garlic, ginger, chili, and scallions for 2 to 3 minutes, stirring.

3. Add the mushrooms and the tougher parts of the cabbage. Stir-fry for 3 to 4 minutes. Add the leafy parts of the cabbage and the mushroom soaking liquid. Stir-fry until the cabbage is tender. Season to taste and serve.

Yield: 4 servings.

BABY CARROTS WITH FENNEL

Serve this spring vegetable dish with grilled or roast chicken or fish.

1 pound baby carrots, scraped
1 large or 2 small heads fennel
2 tablespoons unsalted butter
1 tablespoon extra virgin olive oil
   Coarse salt and freshly ground pepper to taste
   Freshly grated nutmeg
   Freshly grated Parmesan cheese
   Fresh tarragon leaves for garnish

1. Trim the carrots and cut the fennel into quarters if large, in halves if using 2 small heads.

2. Bring 2 inches of water to boil in a saucepan and cook the vegetables until tender but *al dente*.

3. Heat the butter and oil in a heavy skillet. Toss the vegetables in the butter and cook for 2 to 3 minutes. Sprinkle with salt, pepper, and a little nutmeg.

4. Place in a heated serving dish and sprinkle with Parmesan cheese and tarragon leaves. Serve immediately.

Yield: 4 servings.

PURÉED CARROT TOP CONDIMENT

The composer John Cage serves this as a condiment for rice. Use it with brown or white rice. It compliments fish or chicken.

    Tops from 1 bunch fresh young carrots
1 tablespoon sesame oil
2 tablespoons tamari soy sauce

1. Purée the carrot leaves in a food processor, using a little water if needed to make it smooth.

2. Heat the oil in a heavy frying pan. Sauté the purée until it begins to dry (about 5 minutes). Stir in the soy sauce and remove from the heat. Serve in a small bowl.

Yield: 4 servings.

CAULIFLOWER PURÉE

For this simple purée, cauliflower is gently steamed in a little milk, then puréed. A beurre noisette, butter that has been cooked until it is golden-brown and has a nutty flavor, *is stirred in just before the purée is served. It goes with roast duck or chicken, chops or broiled meats.*

1 small head cauliflower
    Approximately ½ cup milk
    Coarse salt and freshly ground pepper to taste
2 tablespoons unsalted butter

1. Trim the cauliflower of leaves. Place it whole in a saucepan with the milk and cook, covered, until tender. Check to make sure the milk does not rise up over the sides of the saucepan.

2. Meanwhile, melt the butter over a medium heat in a small pan until it turns golden-brown. Do not burn.

3. Put the cauliflower in a food processor with enough of its cooking liquid to allow it to turn into a smooth purée. Pour into a heated serving dish and stir in the melted butter.

Yield: 3 to 4 servings.

BAKED CELERY WITH LEEKS

Serve this with chicken, lamb, veal, or pork.

    1 head celery in one piece
    1 teaspoon sesame oil
       Juice of ½ lemon
    2 large leeks

1. Preheat the oven to 350 degrees.

2. Trim the stem and carefully wash the celery, pulling back the stalks to remove the grit without breaking them off at the stem. Put the sesame oil into a casserole or Römertopf. Add the celery and squeeze the lemon juice over it. Cover and bake for 30 minutes.

3. Meanwhile, carefully wash the leeks, slicing the green leaves off to 1½ inches and cutting the stalks vertically down the middle. Rinse carefully several times to remove all the grit. Add to the celery.

4. Bake for 30 to 45 minutes, or until the vegetables are tender.

Yield: 4 servings.

CELERIAC AND POTATOES DAUPHINOISE

Celeriac, also called celery root, has never made it to the vegetable top ten. It is ugly and gnarled, so coarse looking that those who have never cooked it are put off doing so by its appearance. But under the skin, this vegetable has an ivory flesh much like a potato, with a delicate hint of celery. It is at its best in late autumn and early winter, and goes particularly well with game and roasts, especially chicken, pork, or turkey. It most often appears on the menus of French restaurants as an hors d'oeuvre—céleri rémoulade—shredded raw and tossed in a mustard-flavored mayonnaise.

But there are many other ways of preparing celery root. It can be cooked and served like potatoes—mashed or boiled and buttered or sliced and baked in the oven. It can also be puréed with equal amounts of potato or diced and sautéed.

Like potatoes, celery root discolors quickly when peeled. It should be put into water with half a lemon when cut.

Serve this with roast duck, turkey, beef, or pork. It can bake in the oven while the meat is roasting.

1 pound potatoes
1 pound celeriac
6 tablespoons unsalted butter
Coarse salt and freshly ground pepper to taste
1 cup heavy cream

1. Preheat the oven to 350 degrees.

2. Slice the potatoes and the celeriac thinly. In a large buttered gratin dish, arrange the slices of potato and celery root, adding a little butter, salt, and pepper to each row as you go. Top with the cream, salt, and pepper and bake until the vegetables are tender (about 45 minutes). If the top has not browned, finish it under the broiler.

Yield: 4 to 6 servings.

EGGPLANT WITH FENNEL AND FENUGREEK

Fenugreek seeds are yellow or reddish-brown and square shaped. They have a slightly bitter taste and a sweet, spicy scent when heated. They are sold in Indian or Asian stores.

The following recipe goes with lamb or chicken. It improves if made the day before and left overnight so that the flavors can develop.

- 2 medium-sized eggplants
  Coarse salt
- 4 tablespoons vegetable oil
- 1 tablespoon fennel seeds
- 1 tablespoon fenugreek seeds
- 1 medium-sized onion, chopped
- 2 tablespoons chopped fresh ginger
- 1 garlic clove, minced
- 1 teaspoon ground coriander
- ⅛ teaspoon cayenne pepper
- ¼ teaspoon ground cumin
- 2 tablespoons tomato purée
- 2 teaspoons fresh lemon juice
  Chopped fresh coriander or parsley leaves for garnish

1. Peel and cube the eggplants. Salt the cubes and let them stand in a colander for 1 hour. Pat dry with paper towels.

2. Heat the vegetable oil in a frying pan and add the fennel and fenugreek seeds. Fry, stirring, for 1 minute. Add the onion, ginger, garlic, and eggplant cubes. Stir, cover, and cook over low heat for 15 to 20 minutes, stirring occasionally. If the eggplant seems a little dry, add a dash of water to prevent it from sticking to the bottom of the pan.

3. Add the coriander, cayenne, cumin, tomato purée, and lemon juice. Add ¾ cup water, cover, and cook for 15 to 20 minutes, or until the eggplant is fully cooked. Correct the seasoning. Garnish with coriander or parsley and serve.

Yield: 4 servings.

BAKED BABY EGGPLANT

The eggplant, one of our most beautiful vegetables, is commercially available in several varieties. In addition to the familiar large, shiny purple eggplant suitable for slicing and frying or for stuffing and baking, there are its smaller cousins, not more than 2 inches wide at the thickest part, with skins that are almost black. In Korean and Chinese markets you can find the long, thin pale mauve eggplants with a sweet flavor and tender skin, and in early summer white eggplant that has an especially delicate taste and no bitterness.

Eggplant is excellent sliced and broiled or baked in the oven, which gives it a smoky taste. Once it has been grilled, chopped anchovy, garlic, and fresh herbs can be sprinkled over it just before it is served.

When buying eggplants choose those with firm, unblemished and unwrinkled skins. The larger ones should be salted and allowed to sit for an hour and then wiped dry before being cooked. This rids them of bitter juices. Salting also prevents them from absorbing too much oil when you cook them.

This recipe calls for baby eggplants but the larger variety can also be used. Simply slice them before cooking.

Serve this dish with chicken or lamb.

8   baby eggplants, or 1 large eggplant
    Coarse salt
¼   cup bread crumbs
2   garlic cloves, minced
½   cup extra virgin olive oil
    Freshly ground pepper
3   tablespoons snipped fresh basil leaves

1. Slice off the green tops and cut the eggplant in half. Score in a criss-cross pattern using a knife. Salt and let the eggplant drain in a colander for 1 hour. Pat dry.

2. Preheat the oven to 375 degrees.

3. Sprinkle the eggplant with bread crumbs and garlic. Place them in an oiled baking pan. Trickle on the olive oil and season with the pepper.

4. Bake the eggplant for 20 to 30 minutes, or until soft and golden. Sprinkle with the basil and serve at room temperature.

Yield: 4 servings.

BAKED ENDIVE

Baked endive is one of my favorite vegetables. When it is cooked this way it comes out rich and buttery, with juices that are almost cara-melized. Endive is also good parboiled and then drained and sautéed in butter or olive oil.

```
6  endives
2  tablespoons unsalted butter
½  cup chicken stock (page 285)
   Coarse salt and freshly ground pepper to taste
```

1. Preheat the oven to 375 degrees. Place the endives in a buttered baking dish and add the butter, chicken stock, salt, and pepper. Cover with wax paper or aluminum foil.

2. Bake for 30 to 40 minutes, or until the endives are tender.

Yield: 2 to 3 servings.

ENDIVE POLONAISE

This dish is good with broiled sausages or bacon.

6 endives
3 tablespoons unsalted butter
3 hard-boiled eggs
3 tablespoons bread crumbs
2 tablespoon chopped parsley
   Coarse salt and freshly ground pepper to taste

1. Blanch the endives until tender and drain. In a flat casserole dish, melt 2 tablespoons of the butter and gently sauté the endives until they are brown.

2. Chop the hard-boiled eggs and crumble them over the endives.

3. In a separate pan, melt the remaining butter and sauté the bread crumbs until they are golden. Add the parsley, mix together, and sprinkle over the endives. Season with salt and pepper and serve.

Yield: 2 to 3 servings.

FENNEL WITH WALNUT OIL AND PARMESAN CHEESE

4 fennel bulbs
4 tablespoons unsalted butter
4 tablespoons walnut oil
   Coarse salt and freshly ground pepper to taste
   Juice of ½ lemon
¼ cup freshly grated Parmesan cheese

1. Cut the fennel into quarters or halves if the bulbs are small. Simmer for 15 to 20 minutes in salted boiling water, until tender but firm. Drain and pat dry with paper towels.

2. Heat the butter and oil in a casserole. Add the fennel and sauté lightly. Sprinkle with salt, pepper, and lemon juice. Cook for about 8 minutes.

3. Add the Parmesan cheese, mix thoroughly, and serve hot.

Yield: 4 servings.

BAKED GARLIC

Whole baked garlic has a sweet creamy delicate flesh, with none of the harshness of raw garlic. It is delicious with roast meats and chicken. Heads broken into unpeeled cloves can be placed around meat or chicken while they are roasting.

Also good baked this way are whole heads of shallots (these go very well with grilled kidneys).

   2 tablespoons extra virgin olive oil
   4 heads garlic
   4 sprigs fresh rosemary or thyme, or 1 teaspoon dried

1. Preheat the oven to 375 degrees.

2. Place the oil in a small pan and put the garlic on top. Sprinkle with the herbs and bake for 1 hour, or until the skin is dry and wrinkled and the garlic soft.

Yield: 4 servings.

KALE WITH RED PEPPER AND CHILI

Serve with broiled chicken or pork chops.

1 pound kale
1 sweet red pepper
1 fresh green chili
1 tablespoon clarified butter (page 283)
3 scallions, minced
   Coarse salt and freshly ground pepper to taste

1. Trim the stems from the kale. Blanch the leaves in boiling water for 3 minutes. Drain.

2. Meanwhile, toast the pepper and chili over a gas flame or under a broiler. Wrap them in paper towels for a minute; then scrape off the charred outer skin. Slice them, removing the seeds and ribs. Set aside.

3. Heat the clarified butter in a large frying pan and add the scallions, pepper, and chili. Stir-fry for 1 minute; then add the kale. Stir-fry for 5 minutes.

Yield: 2 to 3 servings.

LEEK MOUSSE

If you have a food processor, this recipe will take very little time to prepare. A whole leek can be set aside for decoration, sliced vertically and arranged over the mousse in a spoke-like pattern. Serve with roast chicken or steak.

- 3 pounds young leeks
- 3 tablespoons unsalted butter
  Coarse salt and freshly ground pepper to taste
- ¼ cup crème fraîche (page 282) or heavy cream
  Freshly grated nutmeg to taste

1. Trim the ends of the stalks of the leeks and remove any tired leaves. Set 1 leek aside. Rinse the remaining leeks briefly, then chop into ½-inch pieces by hand or with a food processor. Carefully rinse the whole leek after cutting it vertically into four pieces. Set aside.

2. Melt the butter in a casserole. Add the leeks a cup or so at a time—they will reduce as they cook—and sauté until soft. Season with salt and pepper.

3. Purée the leeks in a food processor with the crème fraîche until smooth. Add the nutmeg and correct the seasoning.

4. Meanwhile, cook the remaining leek in the casserole until soft. Set aside for decoration.

5. Place the leek purée in a warm serving bowl. Arrange the long pieces of leek in a spoke-like fashion across the top.

Yield: 4 servings.

LEEKS WITH MUSTARD SAUCE

The leek is an underused vegetable that is becoming more and more available in supermarkets and at grocery stores. The stalks should be young and firm, with fresh bright green leaves and an unblemished stem. Clean leeks very carefully because they contain a great deal of grit. If they are to be cooked sliced, it is better to slice them, rinse them thoroughly and leave them to soak for a short time in cold water so that the dirt can seep out. Then they should be thoroughly washed again. If they are to be left whole, as in the following recipe, they should be slit down the side and soaked, then rinsed several times. Pull back the leaves to make sure the water goes inside.

This recipe is adapted from one for grilled leeks by Alice Waters of Chez Panisse restaurant in Berkeley. She grills the leeks over charcoal for 3 or 4 minutes before coating them with the mustard cream sauce. This dish goes with Marinated Lamb and Pepper Kebabs, page 137.

8 small leeks
3 tablespoons extra virgin olive oil
½ cup heavy cream
4 tablespoons unsalted butter
1 tablespoon Dijon mustard
Coarse salt and freshy ground white pepper to taste
Fresh tarragon leaves for garnish

1. Trim all but 1½ inches of green leaf from the leeks and cut off the roots. With a sharp knife, slit the leeks down the middle and rinse them under cold water. Place them in a bowl of cold water for 5 minutes so that more grit will run out; then rinse again several times under running water, separating the leaves so that you don't miss any gritty parts.

2. Cook the leeks in boiling water until the stalks are tender. Drain and, while hot, coat with olive oil. Set aside until ready to eat.

3. Make the mustard sauce. Bring the cream to a boil over high heat. Add the butter, whisk in off the heat and then add the mustard. Mix thoroughly and return to low heat, stirring until thickened. Season with salt and white pepper. Pour over the leeks and serve, garnished with the tarragon.

Yield: 4 servings.

MUSHROOMS

As everyone knows, interest in American home-grown products has never been greater, so it is hardly surprising that there are now so many varieties of mushrooms to choose from in the markets. Golden-orange chanterelles come in during the fall; there are also buttery oyster mushrooms, thin little enoki mushrooms for salads, meaty shiitake mushrooms from California, and wild oak mushrooms from Virginia. Cèpes, also called funghi porcini, are strong-flavored and succulent, available both fresh and dried, are delicious cooked with garlic, parsley, olive oil, and prosciutto or pancetta (Italian bacon). The dried ones may seem extravagantly priced, but once they have been soaked they expand in volume and their concentrated richness goes a long way.

White cultivated mushrooms, although widely sold in grocery stores and supermarkets, don't have as much flavor as the wild or semi-cultivated but they can be good when imaginatively prepared. All mushrooms are wonderful with fresh herbs, such as tarragon, chives, rosemary, or thyme.

Chanterelles and morels should be thoroughly washed to rid them of dirt and then cooked slowly in butter. They are spectacular mixed with tarragon and crème fraîche and served on pasta (see Fettuccine with Chanterelles, page 36).

OKRA WITH MUSTARD SEEDS AND
TAMARIND PASTE

Spicy vegetable dishes, so much a part of the cuisines of India, the Middle East, and parts of Asia, are generally overlooked in Western cooking. But there are dozens of dishes that go beautifully with roast chicken, a grilled piece of fish, steak, or lamb chops. Tamarind paste has a sour flavor and is used much like lemon in Western cooking. It can be found in Indian or Asian stores.

The following recipe is especially good with chicken or lamb.

1½ pounds okra
3 tablespoons vegetable oil
1 tablespoon light mustard seeds
1 medium-sized onion, chopped
2 garlic cloves, minced
1 teaspoon turmeric
1 teaspoon ground coriander
1 teaspoon ground cumin
1 cup water
1 tablespoon tamarind paste
2 tablespoons fresh lemon juice
1 teaspoon sugar

1. Trim the okra and leave them whole. Heat the oil in a frying pan and add the mustard seeds. Stir and add the onion and garlic and gently fry until the onion has softened. Add the turmeric, coriander, and cumin. Stir and cook for 1 minute.

2. Add 1 cup water. Bring to a boil and add the okra. Lower the heat, cover, and simmer for 10 minutes.

3. Stir in the tamarind paste, lemon juice, and sugar. Bring to a simmer, cover, and cook over low heat until the okra is done, about 5 minutes.

Yield: 4 servings.

SPICY STEWED OKRA

Serve hot or cold. This goes with grilled chicken or lamb.

  2 leeks, well washed and chopped
  1 small onion, chopped
  1 garlic clove, minced
  2 fresh long green chilies minced
  2 tablespoons olive oil
1½ pounds okra, trimmed
    Juice of 1 lemon
  1 pound tomatoes, peeled, seeded, and chopped, or 1½ cups
      canned tomatoes
    Coarse salt and freshly ground pepper to taste
    Fresh basil or parsley leaves for garnish

1. Soften the leeks, onion, garlic, and chilies in the oil in a heavy skillet (cast-iron if available). Add the okra and sauté for 2 to 3 minutes.

2. Add the lemon juice, tomatoes, salt, and pepper. Add a little water to prevent the okra from burning, cover, and simmer for 20 minutes, stirring occasionally. If necessary, add more water.

3. Correct the seasoning and serve hot or cold, garnished with the basil.

Yield: 4 servings.

PEPPERS STUFFED WITH CORN

If possible, use Mexican green peppers for this dish. They have a piquant taste that goes very well with corn. This vegetable goes with summer barbecued meats.

6 fresh chilies *poblano* or sweet red peppers
2 tablespoons unsalted butter
1 medium-sized onion, peeled and finely chopped
1 garlic clove, peeled and minced
   Kernels scraped from 3 ears of fresh corn
   Coarse salt and freshly ground black pepper to taste
½ pound farmer's cheese
1 cup crème fraîche (page 282) or sour cream
½ cup grated Monterey Jack or mild Cheddar cheese

1. Char the peppers over a gas flame or under a broiler, turning them so that they char as evenly as possible. Wrap them in a dish-cloth and leave them for a couple of minutes.

2. Carefully scrape off the charred skin and try to avoid making holes in the peppers. Make a slit down the side of the peppers and remove the seeds. Set the peppers aside.

3. Preheat the oven to 350 degrees.

4. Melt the butter in a frying pan and soften the onion with the garlic. Add the corn, salt, and pepper and cook for 2 minutes.

5. Stuff the peppers with the corn mixture and a spoonful of farmer's cheese.

6. Butter a baking dish large enough to hold the peppers comfortably in one layer. Place them in the dish slit side up. Pour on the crème fraîche. Bake for 10 minutes; then sprinkle with the grated cheese and brown lightly under the broiler.

Yield: 3 servings.

POMMES BOULANGÈRE

These go very well with duck.

2 pounds potatoes
2 tablespoons duck fat or melted unsalted butter
1 teaspoon dried thyme, or 4 sprigs fresh thyme
1 garlic clove, peeled and minced
 Coarse salt and freshly ground pepper to taste

1. Preheat the oven to 400 degrees. Slice the potatoes thinly. Rinse them in cold water and drain.

2. Spread a tablespoon of duck fat or butter over the bottom of a shallow baking dish that will go both inside the oven and on top of the stove. Spread a layer of potatoes over the bottom and sprinkle with thyme, garlic, salt, and pepper.

3. Continue making layers of potatoes, seasoning lightly as you go. Top with the garlic, thyme, salt, and pepper and the remaining tablespoon of duck fat or butter.

4. Place the dish over medium heat. Add enough boiling water to come two thirds of the way up to the top of the potatoes. Bring to a boil and simmer for 5 minutes.

5. Put the potatoes in the oven and bake for 20 to 30 minutes, or until the potatoes are cooked and the top is brown.

Yield: 4 servings.

POTATOES WITH SAGE OR ROSEMARY

Fresh sage is a wonderful accompaniment to potatoes. In this recipe the potatoes are cut into 1-inch cubes and pan-fried in olive oil with garlic and sage leaves. They have a delicious aroma and go wonderfully with broiled meats or chicken. Fresh rosemary may be used in place of the sage. Use a cast-iron pan and cook, uncovered, over low heat. Whole new potatoes can be cooked like this, too. Cover them and shake the pan from time to time to prevent them from sticking.

1½ pounds potatoes
 4 tablespoons extra virgin olive oil
 6 fresh sage leaves
 2 unpeeled garlic cloves
   Coarse salt and freshly ground pepper to taste

1. Peel the potatoes and cut them into 1-inch cubes. Pat dry with a towel.

2. Heat the oil in a large skillet (preferably cast-iron) and add the potatoes, the sage leaves, and the garlic. Sauté for 2 minutes.

3. Cover the pan and cook for about 20 minutes, stirring frequently to prevent the potatoes from sticking and to ensure they become cooked on all sides.

4. Sprinkle with salt and pepper and serve.

Yield: 4 servings.

POTATOES SAUTÉED WITH MUSTARD SEEDS

A cast-iron pan is the best utensil for this dish. The potatoes emerge a golden yellow. Serve them with Roast Chicken with Garlic, page 101, or grilled fish.

1 pound potatoes
2 to 3 tablespoons peanut or vegetable oil
1 teaspoon turmeric
3 tablespoons light mustard seeds
Coarse salt and freshly ground pepper to taste

1. Cut the potatoes into 1-inch cubes. Rinse and pat dry with paper towels.

2. Heat the oil in a skillet. Add the potatoes, turmeric, and mustard seeds. Sauté, stirring frequently to prevent them from sticking, for about 20 minutes, or until cooked. Season with salt and pepper and serve.

Yield: 3 to 4 servings.

BAKED SHALLOTS

Choose large whole shallots. They should not have green stalks sprouting out of the middle and should not be dry and wrinkled.

Whole baked shallots are delicious with grilled kidneys, liver, chicken, and roast meats. They can also be baked in the same pan as a meat that is roasting.

8 shallots
2 tablespoons extra virgin olive oil

Preheat the oven to 375 degrees. Spread the oil in a baking dish and bake the shallots for 40 minutes, or until they are soft.

Yield: 4 servings.

PURÉED SPINACH

One of the nicest ways to cook fresh young spinach, and very easy.

3 pounds young fresh spinach
3 tablespoons unsalted butter
  Coarse salt and freshly ground pepper to taste
¼ cup heavy cream
  Pinch of freshly grated nutmeg

1. Trim the stems from the spinach and wash the leaves in several changes of water.

2. Melt the butter in a large frying pan and sauté the spinach over high heat. Season with salt and pepper.

3. Place the spinach in a food processor and purée. Return to the pan. Press down with the back of a spoon and squeeze out the juice. Discard the juice.

4. In a separate pan, heat the cream. Stir into the spinach and season with nutmeg to taste. Serve hot.

Yield: 2 to 3 servings.

Vegetables

SPINACH WITH RAISINS AND PINE NUTS

¼ cup raisins
2 pounds young fresh spinach
2 tablespoons clarified butter (page 283) or vegetable oil
1 garlic clove, minced
½ cup pine nuts, toasted
 Coarse salt and freshly ground pepper to taste

1. Soak the raisins in hot water to cover for about 10 minutes.

2. Trim the stems from the spinach and wash the leaves. Shake them dry.

3. Melt the butter in a large frying pan. Add the garlic and cook for 2 minutes. Add the spinach and stir-fry until wilted but bright green. Sprinkle with the raisins and pine nuts. Toss, season with salt and pepper, and serve.

Yield: 2 to 3 servings.

BAKED WINTER SQUASH

This goes with pork, game, or turkey.

2 acorn squash
1 teaspoon dark brown sugar
2 teaspoons rum or brandy
2 tablespoons unsalted butter
 Coarse salt and freshly ground pepper to taste

1. Preheat the oven to 350 degrees.

2. Cut the squash in half and place it on aluminum foil. Sprinkle the cavity with sugar, rum or brandy, butter, salt, and pepper. Cover loosely with foil and bake for 30 minutes, or until tender. Remove the foil after 20 minutes.

Yield: 2 servings.

BAKED PLUM TOMATOES WITH ROSEMARY

Use only vine-ripened tomatoes in season. These go well with broiled meats, such as steak or lamb.

8 large ripe plum tomatoes
   Pinch of sugar
2 garlic cloves, peeled
½ teaspoon fresh rosemary leaves, or ¼ teaspoon dried
   rosemary
   Coarse salt and freshly ground pepper to taste
¼ cup extra virgin olive oil
½ cup homemade bread crumbs

1. Preheat the oven to 350 degrees. Slice the tomatoes in half horizontally. Sprinkle each half with a little sugar.

2. Mince the garlic with the rosemary and combine in a small bowl with the salt, pepper, olive oil, and bread crumbs. Mix thoroughly and place about a teaspoon of the mixture on each tomato.

3. Bake for 25 to 30 minutes.

Yield: 4 servings.

ZUCCHINI WITH SUMMER HERBS

1½ pounds tender young zucchini
  2 tablespoons unsalted butter
  1 tablespoon chopped chives
  1 tablespoon chopped tarragon leaves
  2 tablespoons snipped basil leaves
      Coarse salt and freshly ground pepper to taste

1. Trim the zucchini and cut them in half across the middle. Cut into strips about ⅛ inch thick.

2. Steam the zucchini until barely tender. Meanwhile, melt the butter in a saucepan.

3. Put the zucchini in a heated serving dish and pour on the butter. Sprinkle with herbs, salt, and pepper and serve.

Yield: 4 servings.

NINE

Rice, Legumes, and Grains

▨▨▨

This chapter contains mostly one-pot dishes which need nothing to follow except salad. There is a selection of un-complicated rice dishes—rice baked in the oven and served with seafood, spring vegetables, or duck; a true paella; risotto with squid, or alla Milanese, tinted with saffron. Also from Italy there is polenta, an especially delicious evening meal served in winter with sausages or liver.

I have also included some legume dishes that can be made in advance, and cassoulet, a fairly elaborate dinner-party dish that, once made, is very simple to serve. Moroccan couscous, semolina grains steamed over vegetables or meat, is also a festive dinner-party dish, served with a spicy harissa sauce. It is especially good when you are entertaining a large number of guests.

BAKED RICE

So much attention is being paid to pasta these days that rice seems to have gone quite out of fashion. But from Stephen Spector and his chef Ray Dinardo at The Pear Tree restaurant in Rumson, New Jersey, I discovered some excellent rice dishes made from the long-grain Carolina rice that is available in every supermarket. They are based on Italian risotto but they are simpler to prepare and they do not have to be watched over. Instead of being cooked on top of the stove with liquid added little by little, the rice is baked in the oven for 20 minutes. First it is sautéed in butter with saffron and onions until it is opaque. Then it is baked in a mixture of chicken stock and light cream in a hot oven for 20 minutes. Freshly grated Parmesan cheese is stirred in, and the rice is sprinkled with parsley or chives. The saffron turns it a beautiful golden color.

Leftover baked rice is excellent fried. Sauté chopped shallots in vegetable oil and add the rice. Beat an egg and add; cook, stirring frequently, until firm.

2 cups chicken stock (page 285)
1 cup milk
½ cup heavy cream
  Bouquet garni (thyme and parsley sprigs and bay leaf tied in a
    cheesecloth bag)
  Coarse salt and freshly ground pepper to taste
1 medium-sized onion, diced
2 tablespoons unsalted butter
1½ cups Carolina rice
  Pinch of saffron threads
2 tablespoons freshly grated Parmesan cheese
2 tablespoons chopped chives

1. Preheat the oven to 400 degrees.

2. In a saucepan, combine the chicken stock, the milk, cream, bouquet garni, salt, and pepper. Simmer, covered, for 20 minutes.

3. Using a large heavy skillet that can go into the oven, soften the onion in the butter. Add the rice and saffron and cook, stirring frequently, until the grains are opaque.

4. Add the chicken stock mixture and stir thoroughly. Cover and bake for 20 minutes. Remove and test for doneness. If the rice is underdone, cover, and let steam at room temperature until it is done.

5. Stir in the cheese and chives and serve.

Yield: 4 servings.

BAKED RICE PRIMAVERA

Serve this with Broiled Duck Legs, page 120, or roast chicken, steak, or chops.

    Baked rice (page 229)
2 tablespoons unsalted butter
¼ head red cabbage, thinly sliced
1 small red onion, sliced
1 carrot, cut in julienne
2 small zucchini, cut in julienne
1 small bunch broccoli, divided into flowerets
4 mushrooms, sliced
    Coarse salt and freshly ground pepper to taste
1 cup heavy cream
2 egg yolks
2 tablespoons Parmesan cheese (omit from baked rice recipe)
    Fresh tarragon or chives to garnish (omit from baked rice
      recipe)

1. Prepare the baked rice and while it is cooking in the oven, cook the vegetables. Melt the butter in a large saucepan and add the vegetables. Coat them thoroughly with the butter and cook for 2 minutes over moderate heat. Season with salt and pepper.

2. Add the cream and cook for 8 minutes. Remove the vegetables from the heat and stir in the egg yolks briskly. Return over gentle heat until the sauce has thickened. Do not overcook or the sauce will curdle.

3. Remove the baked rice from the oven. Either place the vegetable mixture in a hollow in the center of the rice or arrange the vegetables around a mound of rice in the middle. Sprinkle with the cheese and herbs.

Yield: 4 servings.

BAKED RICE WITH SEAFOOD

Baked rice (page 229)
2 teaspoons minced shallots
1 tablespoon unsalted butter
¾ pound shrimp, peeled
¾ pound scallops
1 cup heavy cream
1 tablespoon tomato purée
2 tablespoons brandy
1 egg yolk
Coarse salt and freshly ground pepper to taste
2 tablespoons chopped chives

1. Soften the shallots in the butter. Add the shrimp and scallops and cook for 2 minutes.

2. Add the cream, tomato purée, and brandy. Bring to a simmer, stir, and cook until reduced slightly and the shrimp are pink. Do not overcook.

3. Off the heat, add the egg yolk and stir thoroughly. Cook over low heat, just long enough to thicken the sauce. Season with salt and pepper.

4. Arrange the mixture either around a mound of baked rice or in a well in the center of the rice. Sprinkle with chives and serve.

Yield: 4 servings.

Note: When simmering the chicken stock for the baked rice, the shrimp shells may be added for flavor. Strain the stock before adding the rice.

RICE WITH SQUID

This recipe is based on Penelope Casas' Arroz Negro from her excellent book The Foods and Wines of Spain. *The result is a superb, rich black risotto. Use only Italian short-grain rice; otherwise the dish will not work: The rice will be mushy.*

1½ pounds squid with tentacles
4 tablespoons olive oil
1 large onion, chopped
1 pimiento, chopped
1 tomato, peeled, seeded, and chopped
2 garlic cloves, minced
1 tablespoon minced parsley
   Coarse salt and freshly ground pepper to taste
   Large pinch of saffron threads
½ pod chili pepper, seeds removed, crumbled
¼ to ½ cup dry red wine
2 cups short-grain rice
3 to 4 cups fish broth or clam juice, heated to a boil
1 pimiento, cut into strips

GARLIC SAUCE

3 garlic cloves, crushed
½ cup extra virgin olive oil

1. Clean the squid, reserving their ink sacs and the tentacles. Cut the squid into ½-inch-wide rings or into pieces. Chop the tentacles.

2. In a wide, shallow casserole, preferably earthenware and about 12 inches across, heat the oil and sauté the onion until it is wilted. Add the squid rings and tentacles and sauté for 5 minutes; then add the chopped pimiento, tomato, garlic, parsley, salt, pepper, saffron, and chili pepper. Cover and simmer for 30 minutes.

3. Break the ink sacs into a cup and mix with the wine. Pass this mixture through a sieve several times until most of the ink is ex-

tracted. Reserve. Add the rice and boiling hot broth to the casserole and stir in the ink mixture. Season with salt and pepper. Bring to a boil and cook over medium-high heat, uncovered, and stirring occasionally, for 10 minutes, or until the rice is no longer soupy but some liquid remains. Decorate with the pimiento strips and transfer to a 325-degree oven. Bake for 15 minutes, uncovered, until the liquid is absorbed but the rice is not quite done. Remove from the oven, cover lightly with foil and let sit for 10 minutes.

4. While the rice is resting, make the garlic sauce. Place the crushed garlic in a processor or blender. Very gradually, with the motor running, pour in the oil. Blend until smooth. Serve separately.

Yield: 4 to 6 servings.

Note: Serve this dish with a salad and a dry white wine.

RISOTTO ALLA MILANESE

Classic risotto is made with rice cooked in white wine and chicken broth flavored with saffron; butter and grated Parmesan cheese are stirred in at the end of cooking. A rich and filling dish, it is served either on its own or as an accompaniment to ossobuco (braised veal shanks).

Risotto alla Milanese is a descendant of the Spanish paella and dates from the Renaissance. When cooked, each saffron-tinted grain of rice looks as though it were made of gold.

The dish is said to date from 1535, when Charles V made his son Philip the Duke of Milan, initiated nearly two centuries of Spanish rule. Saffron from Spain became the craze in Milan. It was so overused by one well-known cook that he was nicknamed Zafferino. When he married in 1574, friends put saffron into every dish at the wedding banquet—in those days quite a feat considering the number of courses that must have been served.

234

Saffron, the dried stigma of the crocus, has a penetrating aroma and a pungent taste. The orange and brick-red threads look like pipe tobacco. After they have been added to the rice the hue begins to deepen and develop like a print in a photographer's lab.

Because the threads have to be harvested by hand, saffron is very expensive. Luckily, a little goes a long way. Powdered saffron is sometimes adulterated.

Rice was introduced into Lombardy in the fifteenth century and was soon to the northern provinces of Italy what pasta was to the South. Italy is Europe's largest producer of rice, and the best kind to use in risotto is Italian Arborio rice, which has short, stubby grains and is available in specialty stores.

"I wish I knew who was the genius who first grasped the fact that Piedmontese rice was ideally suited to slow cooking and that its particular qualities would be best appreciated in what has become the famous Milanese risotto," says Elizabeth David in Italian Food. *"The fact that this rice can be cooked contrary to all rules, slowly, in a small amount of liquid, and emerges in a perfect state of creaminess with a very slight resistant core in each grain gives the risotto its particular character."*

The trick is to keep stirring until the grains are just to the point of softness but still retain their shape. The rice should not stick to the bottom of the pan—and the best pan to use is one with a copper bottom.

4 tablespoons unsalted butter
1 tablespoon finely chopped onion
1 tablespoon beef marrow
2 cups Arborio rice
1 cup dry white wine
1 generous pinch of saffron threads
   Approximately 1½ quarts hot chicken stock (page 285)
   Coarse salt and freshly ground pepper to taste
4 tablespoons freshly grated Parmesan cheese

235

1. Over medium heat, melt 2 tablespoons of the butter and soften the onion with the bone marrow.

2. Pour in the rice and stir with a wooden spoon to coat the grains with butter. Let the rice cook 3 to 4 minutes, stirring frequently, so that it will absorb the butter and turn opaque.

3. Add the wine, stir, and then add the saffron.

4. Add the hot stock a ladle at a time and cook, stirring. Keep stirring and adding stock for about 20 minutes. The rice will absorb the liquid. Make sure the stock is being absorbed and there is not too much liquid on top. The bottom of the pan should be clean.

5. Test the rice for hardness. The yellow color will deepen as it cooks. Salt the rice. Keep tasting the rice until it is done.

6. Let the rice sit off heat for 3 to 4 minutes. Stir in the remaining butter. Do not return to the heat or the butter will melt without binding. Then add the Parmesan cheese.

7. Spoon the rice onto individual plates and sprinkle with additional cheese and freshly ground pepper.

Yield: 4 servings.

RISOTTO DI FRUTTI DI MARE

½ pound shrimp
½ pound squid
½ pound mussels
2 small onions
1 carrot, sliced
1 celery stalk, sliced
   Bouquet garni (thyme and parsley sprigs and bay leaf tied in a
     cheesecloth bag)
   Coarse salt and freshly ground pepper to taste
4 tablespoons unsalted butter
2 cups Arborio rice
1 cup dry white wine
4 tablespoons freshly grated Parmesan cheese

1. Peel the shrimp. Place the shells in a large pot. Slice the shrimp
and squid into ¼-inch pieces. Set aside. Beard and scrub the mussels well to remove any grit or seaweed.

2. Quarter 1 small onion and add to the shrimp shells with the
carrot, celery, bouquet garni, salt, and pepper. Add 6 cups water,
cover, and simmer gently for 20 minutes.

3. Add the mussels and cook until they open (a few minutes). Remove with a slotted spoon and cool.

4. Chop the remaining onion and cook in a large frying pan in 2
tablespoons butter until soft. Add the rice and cook, stirring, until it
has absorbed all the butter and has turned opaque.

5. Pour in the white wine. Cook, stirring, until it is absorbed. Add
the strained fish broth, 1 cup at a time. Each time the liquid has
been absorbed, add another cup, until the rice is *al dente,* chewy
but firm. Meanwhile, chop the mussels into quarters. Add with the
shrimp and the squid. Cook for a minute or two, until they are
opaque.

6. Stir in the remaining butter and the Parmesan cheese. Season
with salt and pepper and serve.

Yield: 4 servings.

PAELLA

Sangria, gazpacho, and paella are popular Spanish specialties all over the world, and Americans have come to associate them with summers at the beach or holidays in Spain. Paella, a combination of seafood and meats cooked with rice, is especially appropriate for people with small kitchens because it is visually attractive and simple to prepare, besides having a distinctive flavor.

A typical paella may contain such seafood as mussels, clams, shrimp, and lobster and such meats as chicken, pork (chorizo, peppery Spanish sausage), and Spanish ham. Pimiento and peas are also classic ingredients. Saffron is nearly always added to the rice, imparting a rich golden color.

But no two Spaniards are likely to agree on the ingredients, and there are hundreds of different versions of paella. There are those who insist that meat and seafood should never be mixed, or that a real paella contains only rice and snails, or that a paella that has not been cooked over a wood-burning fireplace is not a paella at all.

The dish originated in Valencia on the Mediterranean coast. Peasants working in the rice fields would collect snails and eels from the marshes and cook them with saffron and rice. Since then, endless variations have been developed, some of them very exotic and recherché. There are paellas made with chick-peas, chicken, and pork meatballs, and cooked with a crust of eggs, and paellas seasoned with the flesh of soaked and dried red peppers, cooked with garlic and served with a rich aïoli sauce.

Paellá should be made in flat metal paella pans with handles on both sides. The word paella in fact comes from the Latin patella, meaning a flat, shallow shape. I find that you can make a perfectly good paella using a cast-iron skillet.

Paella should be well scented with saffron, and the rice should be firm, even slightly crispy, never mushy or watery. The broth, fish- or chicken-flavored, should be strong and well seasoned with parsley, bay leaf, pimiento, garlic, and onions. The best pimientos are Spanish and are sold in cans. Valencia rice, or California pearl rice,

Rice, Legumes, and Grains

or Italian Arborio rice should be used, not long-grain rice which turns mushy. Chorizos can be found at Spanish specialty shops. Rioja wines from northern Spain, either red or white, go well with paella. The following recipe is adapted from one made by Penelope Casas, an authority on Spanish food, with whom I spent some weeks searching for the perfect restaurant paella. She also gives a version in her book The Food and Wines of Spain.

> About 2 pints strong homemade chicken stock (page 285)
> ½ teaspoon saffron threads
> 1 2- to 3-pound chicken, cut up
> 2 tablespoons olive oil
> 2 chorizos, sliced
> ¼ pound prosciutto, diced
> 1 medium-sized onion, chopped
> 2 garlic cloves, minced
> 2 pimientos, chopped
> 2 cups uncooked short-grain or Arborio rice
> ½ cup dry white wine
> ¼ pound fresh or frozen peas
> Juice of ½ lemon
> Coarse salt and freshly ground pepper to taste
> 1 pound shrimp, shelled
> 1 dozen small clams, washed well
> 1 dozen small mussels, washed well
> Lemon quarters for garnish
> Chopped fresh parsley leaves for garnish
> Pimiento strips for garnish

1. Simmer the stock with the saffron for 15 minutes. Set aside.

2. Meanwhile, dry the chicken pieces with paper towels and brown them lightly in the olive oil. Remove and set aside. Add the chorizos and the prosciutto and fry for about 8 minutes, stirring. Add the onion, garlic, and pimiento and fry until the onion is soft.

3. Preheat the oven to 325 degrees.

4. Add the rice to the pan and stir thoroughly with a wooden spoon to coat with the oil. Meanwhile, bring the chicken stock to a boil and add it to the rice. Add the wine, lemon juice, salt, and pepper and cook over high heat for 10 minutes.

5. Bury the chicken in the rice and bake for 15 minutes. Add the peas, shrimp, clams, and mussels and continue baking until all the liquid is absorbed from the rice, about 20 minutes. It is best to remove the paella from the oven before it is completely cooked and let it sit on top of the stove, covered with foil, until done, about 10 minutes more. Decorate the paella with the parsley and pimiento strips and serve.

Yield: 4 to 6 servings.

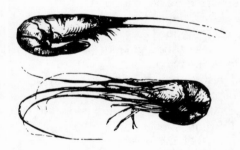

BROWN RICE WITH CARROTS AND CELERY

Brown rice goes well with roast chicken or a fatty fish, such as mackerel or herring. Cooked with carrots and celery and a tablespoon of miso (a soybean paste that is sold in health food or Oriental stores) it also makes a fine course on its own. This rice is a favorite of health food devotees because it has more vitamins and minerals than white rice. The outer coating of bran supplies fiber and Vitamin B. It takes about 40 to 45 minutes to cook.

1 onion, chopped
1 tablespoon vegetable oil
4 carrots, chopped
2 celery stalks, chopped
1 cup brown rice
3 cups water or chicken stock (page 285)
1 tablespoon miso paste
   Freshly ground pepper

1. In a heavy casserole, soften the onion in the oil. Add the carrots and celery and brown them lightly. Add the rice and mix thoroughly.

2. Pour in the water or stock. Add the miso and the pepper and stir. Cover and simmer gently for 40 to 45 minutes, stirring occasionally. If necessary, add more stock or water. If the rice is too liquid, uncover, raise the heat, and cook until the liquid has evaporated.

Yield: 3 to 4 servings.

NAVY BEANS WITH GARLIC BUTTER

Navy beans are inexpensive and can be served with lamb (see Roast Leg of Lamb with Chinese Mustard, page 135) or ham, or on their own. While they are cooking, salt pork, bacon, tomatoes, or tomato purée can be added for flavor. These beans need some fat or oil at the end because they can become very dry. Olive oil, butter, or beef marrow can be stirred in just before the beans are served.

An excellent dish especially good on its own or with lamb is the following, in which the beans are first stewed and then topped with bread crumbs and browned in the oven after garlic butter has been stirred in. The beans develop a golden brown crust. This dish is particularly useful for dinner parties because it can be prepared the night before.

It is not necessary to soak the beans in water before they are cooked, although you can save some cooking time if you do so. They usually take 1 to 1½ hours. Add salt only toward the end of the cooking time, otherwise the skins of the beans may split and the centers harden.

½ pound navy beans
1 onion, quartered
2 carrots, coarsely chopped
1 celery stalk, with leaves, chopped
   Bouquet garni (thyme and parsley sprigs and bay leaf tied in a cheesecloth bag)
   Coarse salt and freshly ground pepper to taste
½ cup minced Italian parsley leaves
1 garlic clove, minced
4 tablespoons unsalted butter, plus 2 tablespoons chopped butter
½ cup dry bread crumbs

1. Simmer the beans in water to cover with the onion, carrots, celery, and bouquet garni for 1 to 1½ hours, or until tender. Season with salt and pepper.

2. Preheat the oven to 400 degrees. Meanwhile, combine the parsley, garlic, and 4 tablespoons of the butter. Mix thoroughly.

3. Remove the bouquet garni and stir the garlic butter into the cooked beans. Sprinkle the beans with the bread crumbs and the remaining chopped butter. Place in the oven until the top is sizzling and brown.

Yield: 4 servings.

SPICED LENTILS

Lentils come in red, brown, yellow, and green, whole or split. Green ones have the most flavor. Split lentils cook more quickly but can turn into mush if they are not carefully tended.

One of the most pleasant dishes for a late night meal is the following spiced lentils sprinkled with fresh coriander leaves and chopped hard-boiled eggs—and served with a light red wine.

½ pound lentils
   Coarse salt to taste
1 onion, chopped
1 garlic clove, minced
2 tablespoons vegetable oil
½ teaspoon turmeric
1 tablespoon ground coriander
¼ teaspoon chili powder
¼ teaspoon ground cumin
   Freshly ground pepper to taste
2 tablespoons chopped fresh coriander leaves

1. Rinse the lentils carefully and remove any grit. Bring them to a boil in salted water to cover and cook until soft.

2. In a frying pan, soften the onion and the garlic in the oil. Add the spices and fry for 2 to 3 minutes, stirring. Add to the lentils. Correct the seasoning, sprinkle with the coriander leaves, and serve.

Yield: 4 servings.

CASSOULET

The art of cassoulet-making is taken so seriously in France that many cooks treat the dish like a soufflé. Lest a draft ruin their masterpiece, the oven door is not opened until the cassoulet is ready to eat. Hence the cobbler's shop with the notice outside: "Closed against currents of air—cassoulet in oven. Please return tomorrow."

Cassoulet is a rich mixture of goose or duck, meats such as lamb or pork, plus sausage and white beans, flavored with garlic, tomato, and herbs, baked in the oven and usually served under a topping of crisp browned bread crumbs. This delicious French dish is excellent for a Sunday lunch party, after which guests may be dispatched for a brisk, salutary walk.

Because it is so filling, a light young red wine, green salad, and fruit to follow are all you need to serve with cassoulet. For those who want a more elaborate meal, oysters are a good first course.

Cassoulet originated in the region of the Languedoc, and although it is supposed to be a peasant dish it is considered one of the pinnacles of French cuisine. Each region has its own variation on the central theme of beans. Cassoulet Toulousain includes preserved goose *(confit d'oie)*—a way of using geese from the area whose fattened livers have been made into foie gras. Cassoulet from Carcassonne includes lamb; that from the region of Castelnaudary contains pork. There are also versions from Perigord, Alsace, and Gascony.

Cassoulet's most important feature, the beans, should be moist but not mushy, firm but not hard. The slowest possible cooking is necessary, but with the very fresh beans available in shops these days, be careful not to overcook them.

Making a cassoulet is quite a long process, but not difficult, particularly if it is made over a couple of days. The meats and vegetables are cooked separately on top of the stove, then baked together in the oven.

In the old stone farmhouses of southeast France, where the wind often blows disconcertingly cold, sending a draft along the icy flagstone floors, a cassoulet is often left to simmer gently in the oven, which also serves to heat the house. Ford Madox Ford, who spent much time in France, eloquently described the superb cassoulet of Castelnaudary. "The beans," he said, "are stewed in mutton broth until just tender, then a piece of goose, a piece of mutton, some truffled liver–sausage in slices, a small quantity of tomato juice, fine herbes, and garlic to taste are added. Then the cassoulet in its earthern casserole is put on the corner of the stove to simmer for hours and hours, 24 if you like or longer. An hour or so before serving, it is gratinéd—sprinkled with bread crumbs and grated cheese with little lumps of butter and put into the oven. In the famous inn of Castelnaudary there is a stove that has never been out since the fourteenth century and ever without a cassoulet on it."

CASSOULET TOULOUSAIN LA CÔTE BASQUE

1½ pounds navy beans
5 quarts water
2 4-pound ducks
Coarse salt to taste
1 onion, chopped
1 onion studded with cloves
2 whole carrots
Bouquet garni (thyme and parsley sprigs and bay leaf tied in a
  cheesecloth bag)
2 pounds boneless pork loin
½ pound fresh pork rind
2 pounds lamb shoulder, cut into 1½-inch pieces
1 cup beef, pork, or chicken stock
3 cups dry vermouth or white wine
1 tablespoon tomato purée
8 smoked sausage links
Approximately 1 pound garlic sausage in one piece
½ pound salt pork, coarsely chopped
6 garlic cloves, peeled
4 shallots, peeled

1. Soak the beans overnight in cold water to cover.

2. Cut each duck into 10 pieces (legs, thighs, breasts cut in half).
Salt and leave overnight in the refrigerator.

3. Drain the beans and put them in a large casserole or kettle. Add
water to cover. Simmer for 2 minutes, drain, and add fresh water to
cover. Add the onions, carrots, and bouquet garni. Bring to a boil,
lower the heat, and simmer gently over low heat for 1½ hours.

4. In a preheated 325-degree oven, roast the pork loin for 1½ to 2
hours, or until it has reached an internal temperature of 175 to 180
degrees.

5. Simmer the pork rind in water to cover for 2 minutes and cut into
½-inch strips and then again into small triangles. Simmer in fresh
cold water to cover for 30 minutes. Drain and set aside.

6. In a large frying pan, fry the pieces of duck skin side down until the skin is golden. Reserve the fat for frying potatoes on another occasion.

7. Brown the lamb pieces in the frying pan in which you have browned the duck (they will not need extra fat). Put the lamb in a casserole, add the stock, vermouth, and tomato purée and cook slowly in a preheated 325-degree oven for 1½ hours.

8. Prick the sausages all over with a fork and fry until browned. Drain on paper towels.

9. Boil the garlic sausage for 30 minutes in water to cover and drain.

10. In a food processor, combine the salt pork, garlic, and shallots and blend until smooth.

11. With a slotted spoon, remove the carrots from the beans. Raise the heat under the beans, bringing them to a boil. Stir in the salt pork mixture and immediately turn off the heat. Set aside until final assembly.

12. When the lamb is cooked, remove it from the oven and mix the juices from the pan into the beans. Slice the roast pork.

13. Arrange a layer of beans in a large casserole. Put pieces of lamb, duck, pork, rind, and sausages on top. Add alternating layers of beans and meat, finishing with beans. Bake in a preheated 375-degree oven for 30 minutes.

Yield: 8 to 10 servings.

QUESADILLAS (CHEESE-STUFFED TORTILLAS)

Tortillas stuffed with cheese and served with a spicy relish are a popular Mexican snack. In San Cristobal de las Casas, the little mountain town where I once lived, the smell of these would waft down the street at dusk. On the corner a woman would stand huddled over a comal *(a charcoal brazier) and fry the quesadillas over the coals. People from the neighborhood would start to line up, and from a few doors down we could hear the sound of a marimba band getting ready for the evening's rehearsals which would begin in earnest once they'd had their quesadillas and copious amounts of a dark beer called León Negro.*

The following recipe is a good dish to serve late at night or for lunch.

  3 fresh green chilies, seeded and minced
  1 large onion, finely chopped
  2 ripe tomatoes, peeled, seeded, and chopped
  1 bunch fresh coriander, chopped
  1 pound Monterey Jack cheese
16 tortillas
     About ¾ cup light olive or peanut oil

1. Put the chilies, onion, tomatoes, and coriander in a small serving bowl and mix thoroughly. Set aside.

2. Slice the cheese into 2-inch-long pieces. Pour the oil into a flat pan or shallow pan big enough to dip a tortilla into it.

3. Heat a heavy cast-iron skillet. Dip each tortilla into the oil, coating it lightly, and fold it over a slice of cheese. Place it in the skillet taking care not to break the tortilla in half. If necessary, hold the upper side down with a fork for a few seconds so that the tortilla doesn't open out flat. Fry for 1 or 2 minutes on either side, or until golden.

4. Serve at once, spooning a little relish on top of each quesadilla as it is served.

Yield: 8 servings.

QUESADILLAS WITH CHORIZO

Chorizo is a dry, spicy sausage that is sold in Spanish markets.
Serve this with Mexican Green Tomato Sauce, page 280.

1 small onion, finely chopped
1 garlic clove, minced
4 tablespoons vegetable oil
2 chorizos, chopped
2 ripe tomatoes, charred, peeled, and seeded
1 fresh green chili, charred, peeled, and seeded
6 tortillas
¾ cup grated Monterey Jack or Cheddar cheese

1. Cook the onion and garlic in 1 tablespoon of the vegetable oil in a small frying pan until soft. Add the chorizo, tomatoes, and chili. If necessary moisten with a little water. Cook for 10 minutes.

2. Heat the remaining oil in a large frying pan. Place a tortilla in the oil and put a couple of spoonfuls of the chorizo mixture in the center of the tortilla. When the tortilla has softened, fold the other side over to make an envelope. Fry for a minute; then remove to a serving dish. Two tortillas can be cooked at once.

3. Sprinkle the quesadillas with cheese and serve.

Yield: 2 servings.

RED ENCHILADAS

Epazote is a dried herb that can be found in Spanish markets. If you cannot get it, leave it out. Guacamole is a good salad to be served with or following these enchiladas.

- 4 dried *ancho* chilies
- ½ pound ripe tomatoes
- 1 medium-sized onion, finely chopped
- 1 garlic clove, minced
- ½ teaspoon sugar
- 1 teaspoon epazote
- 5 to 6 tablespoons lard or peanut oil
- 2 eggs, lightly beaten
- ½ cup heavy cream
  Coarse salt and freshly ground pepper to taste
- ½ pound ground beef
- 8 tortillas
- ¼ pound freshly grated Cheddar or Monterey Jack cheese

1. Soak the chilies in boiling water to cover for 30 minutes. Drain and remove the tops and seeds. Chop coarsely.

2. Peel the tomatoes by dropping them into boiling water or charring them under a broiler or over a gas flame and slipping off the skins while the tomatoes are still warm.

3. Combine the chilies, tomatoes, half the onion, garlic, sugar, and epazote in a blender and purée.

4. Heat 2 tablespoons of the oil in a heavy skillet and add the purée. Cook for 5 minutes. Add the eggs and cream. Stir, season with salt and pepper and remove from the heat.

5. Fry the beef in 1 tablespoon of the oil in another heavy skillet and remove with a slotted spoon. Drain. Mix in with about half the sauce. Pour the fat from the skillet.

6. Add the remaining oil to the skillet and gently fry the tortillas one by one just enough so they go limp. If they are fried too long they become hard.

7. Put a little of the beef mixture in each tortilla and roll it up, as for a crêpe. Place the enchiladas side by side in an ovenproof baking dish.

8. Sprinkle with the cheese and the remaining chopped onion and pour on the remaining sauce. Bake in a 400-degree oven for 15 minutes.

Yield: 4 servings.

POLENTA

Polenta is finely ground cornmeal. It is served plain or cut in slices, sometimes toasted, sometimes served with a cheese or tomato sauce. Italians eat slices of polenta with fried calves' liver. It is very inexpensive and simple to cook, although you do have to keep stirring to make sure that it does to develop lumps. The cornmeal must be added in a gradual thin stream to boiling water. If it is dumped in all at once, it will get lumpy.

To toast polenta, let it cool, slice it and place the slices under a hot broiler.

  2 quarts water
     Salt
  1 pound yellow cornmeal

1. Bring the water and salt to a boil. Add the cornmeal in a thin stream, very slowly, stirring as you go to prevent lumps from forming. Stir and simmer for 30 minutes. Stir as frequently as possible.

2. Turn the heat off and let the polenta stand for 2 to 3 minutes. Reverse onto a wooden board and cool. It will set. To cut, slide a long piece of string under the polenta and pull through. (You can also use a sharp knife.) Slices can now be toasted under a broiler or placed on individual plates.

Yield: 4 servings.

COUSCOUS

It is every cook's dream to produce a meal that is at once spectacular, easy to make, and different. Such is couscous, the classic Berber dish of fine golden semolina grains steamed over meat and vegetables.

The couscous is arranged on a large platter with pieces of meat—lamb or chicken, perhaps—which have been simmered with vegetables such as chick-peas, onions, zucchini, or carrots. The broth is flavored with spices redolent of North Africa, such as saffron, turmeric, ginger, and cinnamon. The variations are endless and the dish can be prepared in advance. A relish called "harissa," made from dried red chili peppers ground with garlic and spices and thinned with a little water, is served with it.

Couscous is made in a couscousière, a perforated colander set over a pot in which the stew is cooked. (I use mine as a vegetable steamer, too.) The vapors from the stew swell the grains of couscous. A strip of damp cheesecloth sprinkled with flour is wrapped around the rim of the bottom couscousière so that no steam will escape through the sides when the perforated top is placed over it. It can also be made in an ordinary colander placed over a pot holding the simmering broth.

While making couscous is a fairly simple operation, eating in the correct manner, with the right hand, is another story. In *Pillars of Hercules,* a book published in 1848, David Urquhart instructs: "With the point of the fingers of the right hand a portion of the grains is drawn towards the side of the dish. It is fingered as the keys of a pianoforte till it gathers together; it is then taken up into the hand, shaken, pressed until it adheres, molded till it becomes a ball; tossed up and worked until it is perfect, and then shot by the thumb, like a marble, into the mouth."

Rice, Legumes, and Grains

CHICKEN COUSCOUS

4 quarts water
1 3-pound chicken, cut up
Coarse salt to taste
4 teaspoons freshly ground pepper
3 pounds onions, sliced
½ teaspoon saffron threads
¼ teaspoon ground turmeric
2 teaspoons ground cinnamon
2 pounds couscous
1 pound raisins
2 cups rinsed and drained canned chick-peas
3 tablespoons chopped fresh coriander leaves
4 tablespoons unsalted butter at room temperature

1. In the lower part of the steamer, put the water, chicken, salt to taste, pepper, onions, saffron, turmeric, and cinnamon. Bring to a boil and simmer, covered, for 30 minutes.

2. Meanwhile, put the couscous in a large bowl and add cold water to cover it. Work the water into the grains with your hands for a minute or two. Drain. Transfer the grains to a large foil baking pan or similar container and spread them out with your hands. Let the grains swell for 10 to 15 minutes.

3. Using wet fingers, break up any lumps that may have formed in the grains and work through so that all the grains are separate.

4. Take a piece of cheesecloth long enough to go around the circumference of the steamer. Dampen it with water and dust it with flour. Remove the lid from the stew and add the top of the steamer, wrapping the piece of cheesecloth around the rim of the bottom part. Secure and make sure no steam is escaping from the sides.

5. Add a quarter of the couscous. When the steam comes through, add the remaining grains and steam, uncovered, for 20 minutes.

6. Remove the steamer from the stew and cover the stew with a lid.

7. Transfer the couscous to the foil baking pan. With a metal spoon, stir through the grains and spread them out. Sprinkle them with salt to taste and pour on 1 cup of cold water. Let stand for 30 minutes. (The couscous can be made in advance up to this point and left covered with a damp cloth.)

8. Add the raisins, chick-peas, and coriander to the stew. Return the couscous to the steamer and replace it over the stew. Steam, uncovered, for 30 minutes longer.

9. Put pieces of the butter over the couscous and stir through. Arrange the couscous on a large round serving platter. Make a well in the middle and arrange the chicken with its broth in a mound in the center. Spoon the cooking liquid and vegetables onto the chicken and the couscous. Serve any extra broth and stew on the side.

Yield: 8 to 10 servings.

LAMB COUSCOUS

    4 quarts water
    3 pounds lamb shoulder, cut into pieces, including bone
    2 pounds onions, sliced
      Coarse salt to taste
    4 tablespoons freshly ground pepper
    ½ teaspoon saffron threads
    3 pounds couscous
    2 pounds white turnips, peeled and cut into 2-inch pieces
    2 pounds carrots, peeled and cut into 2-inch pieces
    2 pounds zucchini, cut to 2-inch pieces
    4 tablespoons chopped fresh coriander leaves
    4 tablespoons unsalted butter at room temperature

1. In the lower part of the steamer put the water, lamb, onions, salt, pepper, and saffron. Bring to boil and simmer, covered, for 45 minutes.

2. Meanwhile, put the couscous in a large bowl and add cold water to cover. Work the water into the grains with your hands for a

minute or two. Drain. Transfer the grains to a large foil baking pan or similar container and spread them out with your hands. Let the grains swell for 10 to 15 minutes.

3. Using wet fingers, break up any lumps that may have formed in the grains and work through so that all the grains are separate.

4. Take a piece of cheesecloth long enough to go around the circumference of the steamer. Dampen it with water and dust it with flour. Remove the lid from the stew and add the top of the steamer, wrapping the piece of cheesecloth around the rim of the bottom part. Secure and make sure that no steam is escaping from the sides.

5. Add a quarter of the couscous. When the steam comes through, add the remaining grains and steam, uncovered, for 20 minutes.

6. Remove the steamer from the stew and cover the stew with a lid.

7. Transfer the couscous grains to the foil baking pan. With a metal spoon, stir through the grains and spread them out. Sprinkle with salt to taste and pour on 1 cup of cold water. Let stand for 30 mintues. (The couscous may be made in advance up to this point and left covered with a damp cloth.)

8. Add the turnips, carrots, and coriander to the stew. Return the couscous to the steamer and replace it over the stew. Steam, uncovered, for 15 minutes. Add the zucchini to the stew and continue cooking for 15 minutes longer.

9. Put pieces of the butter over the couscous and stir through. Arrange the couscous on a large serving platter. Make a well in the middle and arrange the lamb and vegetables in it. Spoon the cooking liquid onto the lamb and couscous. Serve any extra stew and broth on the side.

Yield: 10 servings.

Note: If you are preparing these recipes in advance and your stew is fully cooked, finish cooking the couscous over boiling water, otherwise the stew will be overdone.

QUICK COUSCOUS

As an accompaniment to certain dishes, such as tagins *or a fish that has been baked Moroccan-style, stuffed with spices, instant couscous can be delicious. I use a strong homemade chicken stock, which I bring to a boil and pour onto the couscous grains, which I have placed in a skillet or large saucepan. Then I cover the pan with a cloth and let the grains sit for about 5 minutes, or until they have swollen and absorbed the stock. A little butter, salt, and pepper is stirred in and the couscous is ready.*

TEN

Desserts

T he last thing someone with a small kitchen feels like doing is making elaborate desserts. The tendency is to finish a meal with cheese and fruit, or with something bought at the local bakery. But there are times when a homemade dessert is appropriate.

Pastry making creates a mess in a small kitchen, but if you do it ahead of time and refrigerate the dough, then you can roll it out quite easily when you need it. I like to make pies such as blueberry pie or tarte tatin in a cast-iron pan, or make a blind pastry case that can be filled just before being brought to the table.

The fruit we buy is not always at its best when eaten raw because it has been picked before it has had time to ripen properly. It improves enormously, however, upon being poached and served at room temperature with crème fraîche or whipped cream.

If there is a day-old loaf of French or Italian bread on hand, it can be used for making an excellent and easy dessert with any pitted fruit. Slices of the bread are dipped in melted butter and fruit, such as peach, apricot or plum halves, placed skin down on the slices and sprinkled with sugar. When baked in a hot oven, the bread becomes crisp and golden, the fruit sticky and caramelized.

A spectacular-looking but easy dessert can be made with poached apricots or peaches or fresh figs placed on a crimson pool of puréed raspberries and decorated with a sprig of mint. Another good way to serve peaches is skinned and sliced into large wineglasses. Just before sitting down to the meal, sprinkle the peaches with a little sugar, place them in wineglasses and fill up the glasses with red wine. Champagne can also be used, with the addition of a strawberry or two.

To drink with desserts I love a good chilled sweet wine such as Sauternes or Beaumes de Venise.

APPLE CRUMBLE

When you don't have the time or the inclination to make pastry, this topping does the job without the work. Serve the crumble with crème fraîche, page 282, or heavy cream—or plain.

8 McIntosh apples
¼ cup cold butter, plus 2 tablespoons butter
½ teaspoon ground cinnamon
½ cup dark brown sugar
⅔ cup all-purpose flour
½ teaspoon peeled cardamom seeds

1. Preheat the oven to 400 degrees. Peel the apples, cut them into quarters, and core them. Butter a flat 8-inch baking dish with the 2 tablespoons butter. Arrange the apples in the dish and sprinkle them with the cinnamon.

2. Cut the remaining cold butter into pieces. In a mixing bowl, combine the sugar, flour, and butter and work together with your fingers until the mixture resembles bread crumbs. Add the cardamom seeds to the apples. Sprinkle with crumble mixture.

3. Place the apples in the oven and bake for 10 minutes. Lower the oven temperature to 375 and bake for 30 minutes longer, or until the topping is golden brown and the apples are tender.

Yield: 4 servings.

ELIZABETH DAVID'S CHOCOLATE MOUSSE

1 ounce semisweet chocolate per person
1 tablespoon rum per person
1 tablespoon water or black coffee
1 egg per person

1. Separate the whites from the yolks. Whip the whites and beat the yolks.

2. Meanwhile, melt the chocolate in a heavy pan over low heat with the rum and water or coffee.

3. Add the chocolate to the yolks and mix. Fold in the egg whites and mix gently until thoroughly blended.

4. Pour into individual bowls and refrigerate until set.

PASTRY DOUGH

When making pastry it is important to keep everything as cool as you can. Handle the dough as little as possible (for this reason, the food processor is a help in blending the butter and flour). Use a cold surface—preferably of marble—for rolling out the pastry. If the pastry is tough, you have overworked it or used too much water. If it is too soft and tears easily, you have used too little water or too much butter.

For a sweet shortcut pastry, mix in 1 tablespoon of granulated sugar with the flour and salt.

1½ cups all-purpose flour
 ½ teaspoon salt
12 tablespoons unsalted butter
 3 to 4 tablespoons ice water

1. To make the pastry by hand, sieve the flour and the salt into a large bowl. Cut the butter into small pieces and work it into the flour with two knives, crossing the blades and pulling them away from each other rapidly, using a light touch, until the mixture resembles coarse bread crumbs.

2. Sprinkle on 2 tablespoons of ice water. Gather the dough into a ball and knead gently with the heel of your palm to bind. Shape into a ball and dust with flour. Place in a plastic bag and refrigerate for 1 hour.

3. To make the pastry in a food processor, place the flour, salt, and butter, cut into pieces, into the bowl of the machine fitted with the steel blade. Buzz stop 15 times (each time long enough to count to three). Add 2 tablespoons water and repeat 10 times. The dough should look like sticky coarse bread crumbs. It should not be allowed to form a ball in the machine or it will become difficult to roll out and the crust will be tough.

4. Turn the dough onto a floured surface and knead with the heel of your palm. Shape into a ball. Dust with flour, place in a plastic bag and refrigerate for 1 hour.

5. To roll out the dough, dust a working surface and rolling pin with flour. Place the ball of dough in the center and give it a few smacks with the rolling pin to flatten it. Then roll the dough away from you in quick, short strokes, clockwise. Roll out into a 15-inch circle, always working clockwise and in the same direction. Do not roll back and forth.

6. Place the dough into the center of a tart tin and fit the pastry inside the tin. Using the prongs of a fork or the blade of a blunt knife, press the dough down over the edges of the pie tin. Cut away any overhanging flaps. They can be saved and used for individual tarts. Refrigerate the tart tin.

7. Preheat the oven to 400 degrees. When the oven is ready, remove the pastry from the refrigerator and prick the bottom of the dough all over with a fork. Line the pastry with aluminum foil or parchment paper and crimp around the edges. Pour some dried beans into the foil to weight it down. Bake for 15 minutes.

8. Remove the foil and beans and bake for 5 minutes if you intend fill the pieshell and bake it again. If you want a completely cooked pieshell, bake for 10 minutes more.

Yield: 1 10- to 11-inch pieshell.

APRICOT TART

One of the most delicious summer desserts is unquestionably an apricot tart; the fruit, burnished and gleaming, arranged in concentric patterns in a pastry shell (the filling might also be peach, plum, or pitted cherries). The French always seem to produce such tarts perfectly, without the sogginess that one often encounters elsewhere. To reduce sogginess, brush the pastry with lightly beaten egg white before it is baked. Alternatively, when rubbing the butter into the flour, set aside some of the rubbed-in mixture and scatter it over the bottom of the tart before it is baked.

Pastry dough (page 260), made with 1 tablespoon sugar

FOR THE FILLING

2 pounds apricots, pitted
¾ cup apricot jam
Juice of ½ lemon

1. Make the pastry according to the directions.

2. Preheat the oven to 425 degrees. When the oven is ready, remove the pastry from the refrigerator. Cut the fruit into halves or quarters and place skin side down on the pastry in concentric circles. Bake for about 20 minutes, or until the edges of the fruits are lightly browned.

3. Melt the jam with ½ cup water in a heavy pan, removing any lumps. Add the lemon juice.

4. Remove the tart from the oven and coat with the apricot mixture.

Yield: 1 9- to 10-inch pie.

BLUEBERRY PIE IN A CAST-IRON PAN

This is an ideal way to cook blueberries. First they are simmered on top of the stove so that you can boil down some of the inordinate amount of juice that the berries yield as they cook. Then, when they have cooked, the pan is covered with pastry and baked. For two or three people, I have found that half the pastry dough recipe works perfectly for a 6-inch cast-iron or enameled iron skillet. Use 1 pint of blueberries.

    Pastry dough (page 260), made with 1 tablespoon sugar
2 pints blueberries
    Juice of ½ lemon
1 tablespoon sugar
    Milk or egg yolk for glazing the pastry

1. Make the pastry dough and chill it. Preheat the oven to 350 degrees. Meanwhile, place the blueberries in a pan over medium heat with the lemon juice and sugar. Cook until soft, tasting for sweetness. If there is too much juice, pour some off and save it to make a fruit sauce later.

2. Roll out the pastry dough into a circle an inch larger than a 9-inch cast-iron or enameled cast-iron skillet. Place the circle on top of the pan and press down the edges with the blade of a butter knife. Brush with milk or egg yolk and bake for 20 to 30 minutes, or until the pastry is golden brown.

Yield: 6 servings.

LEMON TART

*This involves making a lemon custard and baking it in a tart shell.
The custard and the pastry can be made a day in advance.*

> Fully cooked 9-inch pieshell (see pastry dough, page 260),
> made with 1 tablespoon sugar
>
> 3 lemons
> 3 eggs
> 2 egg yolks
> ¾ cup sugar
> ¼ pound unsalted butter

1. Make the pieshell.

2. Meanwhile, make the custard. Grate the rind of 2 of the lemons
and put it in a heavy saucepan. Squeeze the juice from all 3 lemons
and add it with the eggs, egg yolks, sugar, and butter. Place over
low heat and cook slowly, whisking continuously, until the mixture
has thickened to a custard. When the mixture begins to thicken,
you can raise the heat a little, but be careful not to turn it too high or
the mixture will curdle. It should take 15 to 20 minutes to make the
custard. Set aside.

3. Pour the custard into the pieshell a few hours before serving. Do
not refrigerate.

Yield: 8 servings.

POIRE TARTE TATIN

This can also be made with apples—the more traditional fruit for this tart.

  Pastry dough (page 260), made with 1 tablespoon sugar
4 pounds Comice or Bosc pears
½ cup unsalted butter, melted
¼ cup sugar
  Milk or egg yolk for glazing the pastry

1. Make the pastry dough and chill it.

2. Preheat the oven to 400 degrees. Peel, core, and slice the pears thinly.

3. Pour half the butter into a 9-inch cast-iron skillet. Sprinkle with the sugar. Arrange the pears in circles on top and pour on the remaining butter.

4. Roll out the pastry dough to a circle big enough to leave an inch overhanging the pan. Place over the pears, turning the extra dough under. Using the point of a sharp knife, make several slits in the dough so that steam can escape while the tart is baking. Brush the pastry with milk or egg yolk and bake for 25 to 30 minutes, or until the crust is golden brown.

5. Remove the pan from the oven and, using a bulb baster, remove most of the liquid from the tart through the holes in the pastry. Cook the tart on top of the stove over high heat for 10 to 15 minutes, or until it caramelizes. Cool for 20 minutes and unmold, inverting a serving plate on top and turning the tart over. Serve at room temperature with crème fraîche (page 282).

Yield: 8 servings.

APRICOTS BAKED IN WHITE WINE

How often do we get the chance to taste an apricot that is warm from the sun and bursting with flavor, or a peach so juicy you almost need to wear a bathing suit to eat it? We get our peaches, plums, nectarines, or apricots from the supermarket or fruit stand. These usually look perfect. But their looks deceive. All show, it turns out, for when it comes to eating, very often they fall into two categories: hard or woolen.

What to do with such fruits? The answer is to cook them. Even the hardest peach is transformed when poached or baked; the flesh becomes tender and the juices form a syrupy glaze. Apricots, too, become soft and juicy when baked with a little sugar (flavored with vanilla, perhaps) and a splash of kirsch or white wine. Cardamom seeds, taken out of their pods and wrapped in cheesecloth, can be added for flavor. Plums can be baked in a similar way, with sugar and port.

Serve with crème fraîche, page 282, or heavy cream.

2 pounds apricots
1 cup dry white wine
6 cardamom seeds, peeled and tied in cheesecloth
   Sugar to taste

1. Preheat the oven to 300 degrees. Rinse the apricots and place them in a baking dish.

2. Add the remaining ingredients and bake for 40 minutes to 1 hour. Serve at room temperature.

Yield: 6 servings.

APRICOT MOUSSE

The concentrated sweetness of the dried fruits makes no sugar necessary in this recipe. Dried peaches or prunes may be used here instead of apricots.

½ pound dried apricots
    Water to cover
2 eggs
¼ teaspoon vanilla extract
1 cup milk
    Juice of ½ lemon (or to taste)
½ cup slivered almonds, toasted

1. Put the apricots into a saucepan and add water to cover. Simmer for ½ hour.

2. Meanwhile, beat the eggs in another saucepan until thick and sticky. Add the vanilla extract and the milk. Mix thoroughly and thicken over low heat, stirring frequently until the mixture is as thick as heavy cream. Be careful not to overcook or the custard will curdle.

3. Combine the lemon juice, apricots, and the custard in the jar of an electric blender and purée until smooth. Pour into a serving bowl or individual bowls and refrigerate for an hour or two before serving.

4. Just before serving, sprinkle with the almonds.

Yield: 4 servings.

FIGS WITH RASPBERRY SAUCE

When fresh figs are in season this is a beautiful and easy dessert. Fresh or frozen raspberries or cooked red currants are puréed in a blender to make a red sauce. The sauce is poured onto a serving dish and the figs are cut in quarters and placed on the sauce. The plate is decorated with fresh mint leaves.

1 pint raspberries, or 1 12-ounce package frozen raspberries
   Sugar to taste
8 fresh black figs
   Fresh mint leaves to garnish
   Crème fraîche (page 282) or whipped cream

1. Put the raspberries in a blender and purée until smooth. Add sugar to taste, if necessary. Pour the sauce onto a serving dish.

2. Cut the figs in quarters, starting from the pointed end, but do not cut all the way through. Place the figs in an attractive pattern on top of the sauce. Arrange the mint leaves around the borders of the serving dish. Pass the crème fraîche or heavy cream separately.

Yield: 4 servings.

BAKED PEACHES EN CROÛTE

This is very easy and it is a useful dessert when you have a leftover loaf of French or Italian bread. Slice the bread and trim the crusts. Skin the peaches by dropping them first into boiling water and then slipping off their skins. Cut them in half and remove the pits.

Dip the bread slices into melted butter and place the slices on an oiled piece of aluminum foil in a baking pan. Place a peach half on each piece of toast. Sprinkle with sugar.

Bake in a preheated 400-degree oven for about 40 minutes. The peaches will come out with a caramelized syrup and the bread will be crisp on the sides. Serve with heavy cream or crème fraîche, page 282.

PEACH MOUSSE

Serve with amaretti cookies or sprinkle with toasted almonds.

    1 pound ripe peaches
       Juice of ½ lemon
    ¼ pint heavy cream
    2 large egg whites at room temperature
       Pinch of cream of tartar
    ¼ cup sugar

1. Peel the peaches by putting them in boiling water for 2 minutes, draining them, and slipping off their skins. Quarter, remove the pits, and place the peaches in a food processor. Add the lemon juice and purée until smooth.

2. In a bowl, beat the cream until it stands up in stiff peaks. In a separate bowl, beat the egg whites with the cream of tartar, until they form stiff peaks. Gradually add the sugar and beat until stiff and glossy.

3. Combine the peach purée and the cream. Gradually fold in the egg whites. Pour the mixture into six glasses and refrigerate for 3 to 4 hours before serving.

Yield: 6 servings.

PEACHES WITH RASPBERRY SAUCE

This is an extremely pretty dessert. The peaches sit like golden mounds on a pool of crimson raspberry purée and are decorated with sprigs of fresh mint. Apricots or nectarines can be used in place of the peaches.

- 6 ripe peaches
- 2 teaspoons sugar
- ½ cup white wine, dry vermouth, or champagne
- 1 cup fresh raspberries, or 1 10-ounce package frozen raspberries
- 2 tablespoons fresh lemon juice
  Fresh mint leaves for garnish

1. Bring enough water to cover the peaches in one layer to boil in a large saucepan. Drop the peaches in and simmer for 2 to 3 minutes. Remove, drain and slip off the skins.

2. With a sharp knife, cut the peaches in half along the indentation mark. Remove the pits.

3. Place the peach halves in a saucepan with the sugar and wine. Simmer for about 5 minutes, depending on how ripe the peaches are. Remove the peaches from the juices with a slotted spoon and place them in a bowl. Thicken the syrup over high heat and pour it over the peaches. Set aside but do not refrigerate.

4. Put the raspberries in a blender with the lemon juice and purée. Strain the purée through a sieve.

5. To assemble, pour a pool of purée on each serving dish. Arrange 2 peach halves on top. Sprinkle with mint leaves and serve.

Yield: 4 servings.

STEWED PEARS WITH CARAMEL

It is not easy to find good eating pears because the fruit is usually picked well before it has ripened. But if you cook them, pears can make a delicious dessert.

4 pears
2 cups water
¼ cup sugar
1 orange

CARAMEL

⅓ cup superfine sugar

1. Peel, core, and quarter the pears. Simmer, uncovered, in the water with the ¼ cup sugar until tender, about 30 to 40 minutes.

2. Peel the orange and simmer the peel in water for 5 minutes. Drain and chop finely.

3. Put the ⅓ cup sugar in a small saucepan and simmer until golden brown (be careful not to burn it). Have an oiled piece of aluminum foil ready and, when the sugar is golden, pour it onto the foil. Spread it out so that it makes a thin pool. Cool and break it into small chips.

4. Place the pears in a bowl and cool. Sprinkle with orange peel and caramel chips.

Yield: 4 servings.

Note: This is good with crème fraîche, page 282, or whipped cream.

PEAR SORBET

Serve the sorbet in glasses, garnished with a sprig of mint, and accompany with thin cookies.

2	pounds pears
1	pint water
1½	cups sugar
	Juice of ½ lemon
2	tablespoons pear liqueur

1. Peel, core, and halve the pears. Put them in a heavy saucepan with the water and sugar. Poach for 20 minutes.

2. Purée the pears with their syrup in a food processor. Combine with the lemon juice and pear liqueur. Pour the mixture into an ice tray and freeze until firm. The freezer should be on its coldest setting. Stir once before it is fully set to prevent ice crystals from forming.

Yield: 8 servings.

272

PLUM UPSIDE-DOWN CAKE

If you have a food processor, this cake will take almost no time at all to prepare and uses only one pan. The fruit can be sliced in the machine, then the batter is mixed, poured over the fruit and the cake is baked. For people without a food processor, the cake is still very easy. Peaches or nectarines can be used with the plums.

3 plums
7 tablespoons unsalted butter
¾ cup sugar
1 large egg
1 cup all-purpose flour
¼ teaspoon salt
1 teaspoon double-acting baking powder
1 teaspoon vanilla extract
3 tablespoons brandy
⅓ cup milk

1. Pit the plums; then quarter and slice them thinly.

2. Using a round 9-inch nonstick baking pan, melt 1 tablespoon of the butter with ¼ cup sugar on top of the stove. Remove from the heat and arrange the plums in an attractive pattern on the bottom. Return to the heat and cook gently for about 5 minutes.

3. Preheat the oven to 350 degrees.

4. Make the batter. Cream the remaining butter with the remaining sugar by hand or in a food processor. Beat in the egg. Add the flour, salt, and baking powder. Add the vanilla, brandy, and milk and beat until smooth.

5. Pour the batter onto the plums and spoon it evenly over the fruit. Bake in the middle of the oven for 30 minutes, or until a knife inserted in the middle comes out clean. Cool on a rack and serve, fruit side up. Whipped cream or crème fraîche, page 282, can be served with the cake.

Yield: 6 servings.

PLUMS WITH PORT

These plums can be served at room temperature with crème fraîche, page 282, or they can be made into a tart, using the pastry recipe on page 260. They also make a delicious ice cream, pitted and blended with a custard (see Raspberry Ice Cream, page 276).

1½ pounds plums
½ cup port
   Sugar to taste

1. Preheat the oven to 375 degrees. Wash the plums and place them in an ovenproof dish. Add the port and sprinkle each plum with a little sugar.

2. Bake for about 30 minutes, or until the plums are soft.

Yield: 4 servings.

PRUNES IN RED WINE

With the advent of health food stores, dried fruits regained their popularity—somewhat. But they still remain much overlooked, eaten once in a while with breakfast cereal or munched on as a snack. Perhaps too many people never recovered from the stewed prunes of their childhood. But the dreaded prune, when properly cooked, can be spectacular in soufflés, mousses, or stewed in red wine with orange and lemon peel. The best prunes, in the following recipe, come out dark, silky, and rich, tasting almost as though they were chocolate. Serve with crème fraîche, page 282.

1 pound prunes, pitted
1½ to 2 cups dry red wine, or more to cover
   Peel of 1 lemon
   Peel of 1 orange
2 tablespoons sugar

1. If possible, marinate the prunes in the red wine overnight.

2. Add the lemon and orange peels and the sugar. Cover and simmer for 30 minutes, or until the prunes are tender.

3. Cool and serve at room temperature.

Yield: 4 to 6 servings.

BAKED QUINCES

    4 quinces
      Unsalted butter
 ½ cup sugar
    2 tablespoons orange liqueur
 ½ cup water

Peel, core, and slice the quinces. Place in a buttered baking dish with the remaining ingredients. Bake at 350 degrees for 1 hour.

Yield: 4 servings.

RASPBERRIES WITH ZABAGLIONE

Pour this Italian sauce over fresh raspberries in individual glasses. It can be made in advance and served cold, or served hot, cooked at the last minute.

6 egg yolks
3 tablespoons sugar
⅔ cup Marsala
2 pints raspberries

1. Heat the egg yolks in the top of a double boiler with the sugar until thick and creamy.

2. Add the Marsala and beat with a whisk until creamy and tripled in size. Pour over the raspberries and serve.

Yield: 4 servings.

RASPBERRY ICE CREAM

This is for people who don't own an ice-cream maker. Cover the ice cream in an ordinary ice tray with foil and freeze it at a low temperature. Stir it a couple of times as it freezes to prevent ice crystals from forming. Before serving let the ice cream thaw slightly. It goes well with blueberries.

1 pint raspberries, or 1 10-ounce package frozen raspberries, thawed
3 egg yolks
¾ cup sugar
⅔ cup milk
⅔ cup heavy cream

1. Rinse the raspberries, if fresh, and drain them. Set them aside.

276

2. Put the egg yolks and sugar in a blender. Beat until light and pale.

3. Combine the milk and cream in a saucepan. Heat until just below boiling. Add to the egg mixture in the blender in a thin stream, beating as you add. Return the mixture to the saucepan and heat over a very low heat, stirring occasionally, until you have thick custard that coats the back of a spoon. Cool.

4. Put the raspberries in a blender and purée. Add the custard and blend until smooth. Taste for sweetness. The mixture should be fairly sweet since ice cream will taste less sweet after it is frozen. Transfer the mixture to an ice-cream maker or freezer tray. (If putting in a freezer tray, cover with aluminum foil.) Stir once before fully frozen to prevent ice crystals from forming.

Yield: 4 servings.

STRAWBERRY ICE CREAM

2 pints ripe strawberries
Juice of 1 lemon
¾ cup sugar
¾ cup water
½ cup heavy cream, whipped

1. Purée the strawberries in a blender. Add the lemon juice and mix thoroughly.

2. Boil the sugar and water in a small saucepan for 10 to 15 minutes or until a thin syrup forms. Cool.

3. Mix the syrup into the strawberry pulp. Add the cream and mix well. Pour the mixture into two ice cube trays. Freeze overnight.

Yield: About 8 servings.

ELEVEN

Basic Sauces and Stocks

It is sauces and stocks that divide the good cook from the merely passable. Sauces made from cans or stock cubes taste alike. But by making your own stocks and freezing them, you will always have the basis for a good sauce. If you make your own hollandaise or béarnaise, you will have a delicious sauce to go with grilled steak, lamb, chicken, or fish. If, during the summer, you take time to put up fresh tomatoes, you'll have a ready sauce for pasta during the winter.

BÉARNAISE SAUCE

Serve this with steak or lamb chops, chicken or fish. Instead of the tarragon, you can use a tablespoon of tomato purée for grilled meat or fish, or a tablespoon of fresh mint for lamb or duck.

3 tablespoons dry white wine
3 tablespoons tarragon vinegar
2 shallots, minced
   Coarse salt and freshly ground pepper to taste
1 tablespoon chopped fresh tarragon leaves
   Hollandaise sauce (see recipe)

1. Combine all the ingredients except the hollandaise sauce and tarragon in a small saucepan. Bring to a boil and simmer until you have about 2 tablespoons. Strain and cool.

2. Meanwhile, make the hollandaise sauce. Add the strained juices to the hollandaise and mix well. Add the tarragon and serve.

Yield: Approximately 1 cup.

HOLLANDAISE SAUCE

Serve with broiled fish, poached eggs, artichokes, or asparagus.

2 egg yolks
2 tablespoons water
8 tablespoons unsalted butter at room temperature
   Coarse salt to taste
   Cayenne pepper to taste
   Juice of ½ lemon

1. Whisk the egg yolks and the water in a double boiler over moderate heat until the mixture is creamy, about 5 minutes. If the mixture gets too hot, take the saucepan off the heat and continue whisking. Return to the heat when it has cooled off.

2. Whisk in some of the butter, a little at a time. If you add too much the mixture will curdle. Continue whisking in the butter until the sauce is thick and creamy. Add the salt, pepper, and lemon juice to taste.

Yield: 1 cup.

MEXICAN GREEN TOMATO SAUCE

Mexican green tomatoes are not tomatoes at all, but a cousin of the Cape gooseberry.

Use this sauce with sausages, grilled pork chops, chicken, rice, eggs, or tacos. It also goes with Quesadillas, page 248. It keeps for a month in a tightly closed jar in the refrigerator.

1 pound green tomatoes
2 fresh green chilies chopped
2 tablespoons chopped onion
  Coarse salt to taste
2 tablespoons chopped coriander leaves

1. Put the tomatoes in a saucepan with water to cover. Cook for about 20 minutes, just below simmering point. Turn the tomatoes occasionally.

2. Remove with a slotted spoon and place in a blender.

3. Add the remaining ingredients to the blender and purée briefly. If necessary, moisten with a little cooking water.

Yield: 1 to 1½ cups.

TOMATO SAUCE

In the summer when there is a glut of deep red juicy tomatoes and they are low-priced, it is the time to freeze them. Winter will see the return of those plastic-wrapped "slicing" tomatoes, hard as a rock or mushy as paper towels and unfit for any use in the kitchen. To freeze tomatoes for use in sauces and stews, put them briefly in boiling water and slip off their skins. Then pack them in freezer containers.

The following tomato sauce will last for several weeks in the refrigerator, provided it is sealed with an inch of olive oil. It can also be frozen. It makes a fine last-minute sauce for pasta.

3 pounds ripe tomatoes
2 large onions, chopped
2 garlic cloves, minced
3 tablespoons extra virgin olive oil
2 tablespoons snipped fresh basil leaves
1 tablespoon chopped fresh oregano, or ½ tablespoon dried
    oregano
    Coarse salt and freshly ground pepper to taste

1. Peel the tomatoes by dropping them into boiling water and slipping off their skins.

2. In a large saucepan, gently soften the onion and the garlic in the oil. Add the tomatoes, basil, oregano, salt, and pepper and stew for 20 to 30 minutes, or until you have a thick sauce. Cover if the sauce is getting too dry.

3. When the sauce has cooled, pour it into plastic containers and cover tightly. Freeze until needed.

Yield: About 6 cups.

Note: It is more useful to pack the sauce into 1- or 2-cup containers so that you can unfreeze the amount you need at a given time.

TOMATO MAYONNAISE

This recipe comes from chef Michel Fitoussi. Serve it with seafood mousse or pâté, poached salmon, or white-fleshed fish. Use only juicy red tomatoes ripened on the vine.

1 egg yolk
1 tablespoon Dijon mustard
1 tablespoon sherry vinegar
1 cup French extra virgin olive oil
1 large ripe tomato (enough for ¼ cup juice)
  Coarse salt and freshly ground pepper to taste

1. Beat the egg yolk until thick and sticky.

2. Add the mustard and vinegar and beat some more.

3. Carefully add the olive oil a few drops at a time. If you add too much at once the mayonnaise will curdle. The mayonnaise should be extremely thick.

4. Peel the tomato by dropping it briefly into boiling water and slipping off the skin. Pass the juice and pulp through a fine sieve until you have ¼ cup juice.

5. Put mayonnaise into a bowl. Slowly beat the tomato juice into the mayonnaise. The sauce should be smooth and velvety.

Yield: 1 cup mayonnaise.

CRÈME FRAÎCHE

Many recipes in this book call for crème fraîche. It is made from heavy cream and has a very pleasant tart flavor. It doesn't curdle, which makes it especially useful for sauces. You can also use it instead of butter to seal in the juices when broiling fish, chicken, or liver. I also love it with fresh fruit.

Many specialty shops sell crème fraîche but it is expensive. You can make it at home with buttermilk or with Solait freeze-dried crème fraîche starter. This is available from Crayon Yard Corporation, 75 Daggett Street, New Haven, Connecticut 06519. The telephone number is (203) 624-7094. The following recipe using buttermilk is very simple to make.

   1 pint heavy cream at room temperature
   2 tablespoons buttermilk

1. Combine the heavy cream with the buttermilk. Pour into a clean, warmed Thermos or glass jar and close tightly. Keep in a warm place for 6 to 8 hours.

2. When the mixture has thickened, refrigerate it. It will thicken further in the refrigerator. This amount will keep for about 10 days. To make more crème fraîche, add 2 tablespoons from the last batch to a cup of heavy cream. You can keep making more this way, but after about six months a slightly fermented taste may develop; in which case, kill the batch and start another.

Yield: 2 cups.

CLARIFIED BUTTER

Once the milk solids have been removed from butter fat, the butter burns at a far higher temperature and does not go rancid so easily. The butter is simmered, the milk solids strained off, and the clear fat that is left can be stored for up to three months. It gives an interesting nutty flavor to the food it is cooked in.

1. Melt 1 pound of unsalted butter over medium heat, stirring frequently with a wooden spoon. Do not let it brown.

2. Raise the heat and simmer the butter gently, turning it down to low when the butter has begun to simmer. Simmer for 45 minutes,

skimming off the foam which rises to the surface. The butter should be clear and the milk solids a golden brown.

3. Strain the liquid through a triple thickness of cheesecloth or a linen teacloth. If there are any impurities, strain again. Store the clarified butter in a tightly closed jar in the refrigerator or in a cool place.

Yield: About 1½ cups.

FISH STOCK

For flavoring sauces and fish stews it is useful to have a stock on hand. I get heads and bones from the fishmonger (don't use those from an oily fish) and when I have made the stock I put it in small plastic containers and freeze. (Don't use large containers to freeze or you will have to thaw the whole lot out even if you only need a little.) To flavor this stock you can add fennel (plus the leaves), dill, celery root, and white wine.

2 pounds fish bones and heads (from white-fleshed fish)
1 medium-sized onion, thinly sliced
    Bouquet garni (thyme and parsley sprigs and bay leaf tied in a cheesecloth bag)
    Juice of ½ lemon
    Coarse salt and freshly ground pepper to taste
    About 4 pints water

Put the fish bones and heads in a large pot. Add the onion, bouquet garni, lemon juice, salt, pepper, and water. Bring to boil, skim, lower the heat, and simmer for 20 minutes. Strain and cool.

Yield: About 4 pints.

CHICKEN OR MEAT STOCK

White and brown stocks are extremely useful for sauces and stews. White stocks can be made with chicken or veal, brown stocks from these two plus beef. For a brown stock, the bones are browned first, either by being sautéed on top of the stove or roasted in the oven. Mushroom trimmings, onion skins, and tomatoes can be added.

For a white stock, the bones are simmered on top of the stove with the vegetables. The following is a basic white stock.

Chicken carcass or veal bones
1 onion, quartered
2 carrots, sliced in chunks
2 celery stalks with leaves, sliced
1 leek, well washed and sliced
Bouquet garni (thyme and parsley sprigs and bay leaf tied in a cheesecloth bag)
Coarse salt and freshly ground pepper to taste
4 pints water

Place everything in a large pot and cover with cold water. Bring to a boil, lower the heat, and simmer for 1 to 1½ hours. Strain and cool. Refrigerate in tightly sealed containers. The stock may be frozen.

Yield: About 4 pints.

BIBLIOGRAPHY

Beard, James. *The New James Beard*. New York: Knopf, 1981.

Bettoja, Jo, and Anna Maria Cornetto. *Italian Cooking in the Grand Tradition*. New York: Dial, 1982.

Bugialli, Giuliano. *The Fine Art of Italian Cooking*. New York: Times Books, 1977.

Child, Julia, Louisette Bertholle, and Simone Beck. *Mastering the Art of French Cooking*, Volume I. New York: Knopf, 1961.

Child, Julia, and Simone Beck. *Mastering the Art of French Cooking*, Volume II. New York: Knopf, 1970.

Conran, Terence, and Caroline Conran. *The Cook Book*. New York: Crown, 1980.

David, Elizabeth. *Mediterranean Food*. London: Penguin, 1964.

————. *French Country Cooking*. London: Penguin, 1964.

————. *Summer Cooking*. London: Penguin, 1965.

————. *French Provincial Cooking*. London: Penguin, 1960.

————. *Italian Food*. London: Penguin, 1976.

————. *Spices, Salt and Aromatics in the English Kitchen*. London: Penguin, 1970.

Davidson, Alan. *Mediterranean Seafood*. New York: Penguin, 1980.

————. *North Atlantic Seafood*. New York: Viking, 1980.

Dumas, Alexandre. *Dictionary of Cuisine*. New York: Simon & Schuster, 1958.

Field, Michael. *All Manner of Food*. New York: The Ecco Press, 1982.

Grigson, Jane. *Fish Cookery*. London: Penguin, 1973.

————. *Food with the Famous*. London: Penguin, 1981.

————. *Good Things*. London: Penguin, 1973.

————. *Jane Grigson's Vegetable Book*. London: Penguin, 1981.

————. *The Fruit Book*. New York: Atheneum, 1982.

Hazan, Marcella. *The Classic Italian Cookbook*. New York: Knopf, 1976.

————. *More Classic Italian Cooking*. New York: Knopf, 1978.

Johnston, Mireille. *Cuisine of the Sun*. New York: Random House, 1976.

Bibliography

Kennedy, Diana. *The Cuisines of Mexico*. New York: Harper & Row, 1972.

———. *Recipes from the Regional Cooks of Mexico*. New York: Harper & Row, 1978.

Marshall, Lydie. *Cooking with Lydie Marshall*. New York: Knopf, 1982.

Mosimann, Anton. *Cuisine à la Carte*. London: Northwood Books, 1981.

Olney, Richard. *Simple French Food*. New York: Atheneum, 1974.

Ortiz, Elizabeth Lambert. *Cooking with the Young Chefs of France*. New York: Evans, 1981.

Roden, Claudia. *A Book of Middle Eastern Food*. New York: Vintage, 1974.

Root, Waverley. *Food*. New York: Simon & Schuster, 1980.

Roux, Michel, and Albert Roux. *New Classic Cuisine*. London: Macdonald, 1983.

Troisgros, Jean, and Pierre Troisgros. *The Nouvelle Cuisine*. London: Papermac, 1982.

Wolfert, Paula. *Couscous and Other Good Food from Morocco*. New York: Harper & Row, 1973.

———. *Mediterranean Cooking*. New York: Times Books, 1977.

Index

Aillade toulousaine (garlic
    mayonnaise), 10, 12
Aïoli (garlic mayonnaise), 10, 11, 168,
    170
Antipasti, 10
Apple crumble, 258
Apricot(s)
    baked in white wine, 266
    and cracked wheat stuffing for roast
        chicken, 102
    mousse, 267
    tart, 262
Artichokes
    about, 190–91
    baby with anchovies, 192
    barigoule, 194
    braised baby with onions and capers,
        193
    and fava beans, linguine with, 38
    Roman style, 196
Asparagus
    and almonds, chicken with, 103
    fettuccine with, 33
Avocado salad with red currant
    vinaigrette, 10

Baccalà with onions and tomatoes, 172
Barbecue sauce, marinated pork chops
    with, 144
Basque stew, 176
Bass, striped
    baked whole with oranges and
        lemons, 60
    with coriander, 61
Bean(s)
    cassoulet toulousain la côte Basque,
        246
    fava beans
        Niçoise, 13
        with summer savory, 197
    navy beans with garlic butter, 242
    salad
        aux haricots verts, 12
        white bean, 14
    soup, black bean, 165
    string beans
        spiced with coconut, 199
        stewed, 198
        with tamari and wasabi dip, 200

white beans, stewed lamb shanks
    with, 180
Béarnaise sauce, 279
Beef
    braised in milk, 130
    cold with tarragon vinaigrette, 23
    ground, kofta kebabs in yogurt and
        dill sauce, 129
    meatballs with eggplant, 179
    oxtail stew da Silvano, 175
    and pork stew (Basque), 176
    steak aux deux poivres, 128
    stew, 177
        Guinness, 178
    vindaloo (Indian stew), 188
Beet(s)
    greens with sesame, 201
    salad mimosa, 15
    in orange butter, 200
Beurre blanc for swordfish, 78
Birds, small, 113
    about, 111
Black bean soup, 165
Blueberry pie in a cast-iron pan, 263
Bourride, 168
Broccoli
    and chicken, fettuccine with, 35
    and porcini mushrooms, fettuccine
        with, 34
    broccoli rabe, spiced, 202
Bulgur. See Cracked wheat
Butter
    beurre blanc for swordfish, 78
    clarified, 283
    ginger-lime for halibut, 63
    herb-garlic for rack of lamb, 138
    herb for grilled salmon steaks, 67

Cabbage
    stewed, 203
    stir-fried with shiitake mushrooms,
        204
Cake, plum upside-down, 273
Calamari. See Squid
Calves' liver
    with Madeira sauce, 156
    with orange juice, 157
Carrots
    baby, with fennel, 205
    and celery, brown rice with, 241

Carrot top condiment, puréed, 206
Cassoulet
  about, 244–45
  toulousain la côte Basque, 246
Cauliflower
  purée, 206
  soup, 161
Celeraic
  about, 208
  with mushrooms and Parmesan, 16
  and potatoes dauphinoise, 208
  vinaigrette, 16
Celery
  and apple rings, pheasant with, 113
  with leeks, baked, 207
Chanterelles, fettuccine with, 36
Cheese
  ham and rice salad, 26
  soufflé, goat, 58
  -stuffed tortillas (quesadillas), 248
Chicken
  asparagus and almonds with, 103
  braised with prosciutto and porcini,
    109
  breasts, steamed with fennel, 110
  and broccoli, fettuccine with, 35
  broiled, in lemon-garlic marinade,
    107
  chili and walnut sauce with, 106
  couscous, 253
  curry, simple, 186
  korma, 187
  paella, 239
  Provençal, 104
  roast
    with garlic, 101
    stuffed with apricots and cracked
      wheat, 102
  salad with walnut vinaigrette, 22
  stock, 285
  tagin (stew)
    with chick-peas, 173
    with Italian peppers, 174
  tandoori marinated, 108
  tarragon with crème fraîche, 111
  in white wine with parsnips, 105
Chili and walnut sauce, chicken
  with, 106
Chilies poblanos (peppers) stuffed
  with corn, 220
Chocolate mousse, Elizabeth David's,
  259
Chorizo, quesadillas with, 249
Clam chowder, 84

Clarified butter, 283
Cod, dried salt stew (baccalà), 172
Composed salad, 7–8
  dressing for, 8–9
Conchiglie with eggplant and zucchini,
  32
Condiment, puréed carrot top, 206
Cornish (game) hens
  apricot and cracked wheat stuffing
    for, 102
  baked in a salt crust, 116
  with rosemary and turnips, 112
Couscous
  about, 252
  chicken, 253
  lamb, 254
  pigeon stuffed with, 114
  quick, 256
Crabs, soft shell with lime sauce, 85
Cracked wheat (bulgur)
  and apricot stuffing for roast
    chicken, 102
  tabbouleh with feta, 18
Cranberry sauce for veal kidneys, 155
Crème fraîche, 282
Cucumber gazpacho, 162
Curry(ies)
  about, 184–85
  beef vindaloo, 188
  chicken korma, 187
  chicken, simple, 186
  chicken, tandoori marinated, 108
  garam masala, spice mix for, 185
  lamb kheema, 189

Desserts
  about, 257–58
  apple crumble, 258
  apricot(s)
    mousse, 267
    tart, 262
    baked in white wine, 266
  blueberry pie in a cast-iron pan, 263
  chocolate mousse, Elizabeth David's,
    259
  figs with raspberry sauce, 268
  lemon tart, 264
  pastry dough for, 260
  peach(es)
    mousse, 269
    baked en croûte, 268
    with raspberry sauce, 270
  pear(s)
    tarte tatin, 265

sorbet, 272
stewed, with caramel, 271
plum(s)
upside-down cake, 273
with port, 274
prunes in red wine, 274
quinces, baked, 275
raspberry(ies)
ice cream, 276
with zabaglione, 276
strawberry ice cream, 277
Duck
about, 118–19
breast with green peppercorns, 119
legs, broiled, 120
roast with juniper berries, 122
with sauce piquante, 120

Eggplant
about, 210
baked baby, 210
fennel and fenugreek with, 209
and lamb kebabs with yogurt-basil
sauce, 136
meatballs with, 179
and mozzarella, pizza with, 52
sauce, tagliatelle with, 44
and tongue, rice salad with, 24
and zucchini, conchiglie with, 32
Egg(s)
frittata, 56
goat cheese soufflé, 58
omelets, how to make, 53
piperade, 55
scrambled, 54
sorrel omelet, 57
Enchiladas, red, 250
Endive
baked, 211
polonaise, 212
Equipment for small kitchen, 3

Fava beans
and artichokes, linguine with, 38
Niçoise, 13
with summer savory, 197
Fennel
baby carrots with, 205
baked trout with, 80
chicken breasts steamed with, 110
with walnut oil and Parmesan
cheese, 212
Feta cheese
and salami salad, 20

tabbouleh with, 18
Fettuccine ·
asparagus with, 33
broccoli
and chicken with, 35
and porcini mushrooms with, 34
chanterelles with, 36
white truffles with, 37
Figs with raspberry sauce, 268
First courses (or hors d'oeuvres)
antipasti, 10
artichokes barigoule, 194
artichokes, braised baby with capers,
193
celeriac with mushrooms and
Parmesan, 16
celeriac vinaigrette, 16
peppers, red or yellow, charred, 17
scallop seviche, 28
smoked salmon terrine, 27
See also Salad(s)
Fish
fillets steamed with seaweed, 73
grilled Yucatán style, 72
stew
French bourride, 168
baccalà with onions and tomatoes,
172
stock, 284
See also Individual names of fish
Frittata (Italian omelet), 56
Fruit desserts. *See* Desserts, Individual
names of fruit

Game birds, about, 111, 113
Game hens. *See* Cornish game hens
Garam masala, spice mix for curry, 185
Garlic
baked, 213
butter (herb), 138
mayonnaise, 11, 12, 168, 170
sauce for rice with squid, 233
Gazpacho, cucumber, 162
Goat cheese
soufflé, 58
and sun-dried tomato pizza, 51
Gooseberry sauce, mackerel with, 64
Green bean salad (haricots verts), 12
Green beans. *See* Beans, string
Green peppers. *See* Peppers
Green tomato sauce, Mexican, 280
Ground beef, kofta kebabs in yogurt
and dill sauce, 129
Guinness (beef), stew, 178

Halibut
   broiled with ginger-lime butter, 63
   steaks, braised with oranges and
      green peppercorns, 62
Ham, cheese, and rice salad, 26
Haricots verts salade, 12
Herb butter. *See* Butter
Hollandaise sauce, 279
Hors d'oeuvres. *See* First courses

Ice cream
   raspberry, 276
   strawberry, 277

Kale with red pepper and chili, 214
Kidneys
   veal with cranberry sauce, 155
   veal in mustard sauce, 154
Kofta kebabs with yogurt and dill
   sauce, 129

Lamb
   chops, fried breaded, 134
   chops with sorrel and mint sauce,
      132
   chops with tomato-basil sauce, 133
   couscous, 254
   kebabs and eggplant with yogurt-
      basil sauce, 136
   keema curry, 189
   leg of, roast with Chinese mustard,
      135
   and pepper kebabs, marinated, 137
   rack with herb-garlic butter, 138
   shanks with white beans, 180
Lapin (rabbit) à la moutarde, 126
Leek(s)
   about, 216
   celery with, baked, 207
   mousse, 215
   with mustard sauce, 216
Lemon tart, 264
Lentil(s)
   soup, 167
   spiced, 243
Lime sauce for soft shell crabs, 85
Linguine with fava beans and baby
   artichokes, 38
Liver. *See* Calves' liver

Mackerel with sorrel or gooseberry
   sauce, 64

Madeira sauce, calves' liver with, 156
Marinade
   dill for broiled shrimp, 95
   lemon-garlic for broiled chicken, 107
   See also Vinaigrette
Mayonnaise
   garlic (aillade, aïoli), 11, 12, 168, 170
   tomato, 282
Meat (or chicken) stock, 285
Meatballs with eggplant, 179
Mexican green tomato sauce, 280
Monkfish with saffron sauce, 66
Monkfish tails, broiled, herbes de
   Provençe, 65
Moules. *See* Mussels
Mousse
   apricot, 267
   peach, 269
Mushrooms
   about, 217
   salad, raw, 21
   tomatoes, and rosemary, spaghetti
      with, 42
   See also Chanterelles, Porcini,
      Shiitake mushrooms
Mussels
   about, 86
   moules Marinière, 86
Mustard sauce
   leeks with, 216
   veal kidneys in, 154

Okra
   with mustard seeds and tamarind
      paste, 218
   spicy stewed, 219
Omelet(s)
   Italian, frittata, 56
   how to make, 53
   sorrel, 57
One-pot dishes
   cassoulet toulousain la côte Basque,
      246
   chicken couscous, 253
   enchiladas, red, 250
   lamb couscous, 254
   paella, 239
   quesadillas (cheese-stuffed tortillas),
      248
   with chorizo, 249
   rice
      baked primavera, 230
      baked with seafood, 232
      with squid, 233